Reveal Your Destiny Years
Steven Culbert

W. Foulsham & Co. Ltd.
London • New York • Toronto • Cape Town • Sydney

W. Foulsham & Company Limited
Yeovil Road, Slough, Berkshire, SL1 4JH

ISBN 0–572–01476–7

Printed and bound in Great Britain by
Cox & Wyman Ltd, Reading

Contents

Page

Introduction 6

How to find your solar degree 7

How to find your Angelic Ruler 10

Other active degrees in your chart 12

How to find your Destiny Year 13

Working from a horoscope chart 16

Chart example 17

Degree interpretation 19

360 Degrees of Wisdom

Degrees in a chart
May all seem the same
Unless you take time
To know each by name.

For each rules a day
Of your calendar year
And armed with their knowledge
Your life can be clear.

Free from restrictions
The unknown we fear
So study this wheel
For your Destiny Year.

For then you'll have all
That any soul needs
To give and relate
With others in deeds.

So step forth with wisdom
Your insight is sharp
For the wheel keeps on turning
In lightness and dark.

S.J. Culbert
The Fortune Teller

Introduction

The astrological horoscope is a map of the planets and the Signs of the Zodiac as seen from the place and time of birth of the individual. The horoscope chart, in the form of a circle, is divided into 12 Signs of the Zodiac. As a circle consists of 360 degrees, each of the 12 Signs therefore consists of 30 degrees.

The interpretation of a horoscope depends on the position of the Sun, Moon and planets and a great deal has been written about the horoscope chart and the effects of the Sun and planets in the Signs. However, in current astrological literature, the effects of the Sun and planets on the individual when in any specific degree of the horoscope chart have been largely ignored. This book has been written to rectify this situation. Interpretations are given for each of the 360 degrees position.

The next section shows you how easy it is to find your solar degree — the exact position of the Sun at your time of birth. Your own solar degree can then be related to the appropriate interpretation.

The 360 degrees which make up the horoscope can be divided into five regions, each of which is ruled by an elemental or magical force which I have chosen to call the Angelic Ruler. You will be able to judge how this force alters the very essence of your life.

This book will also show you how to find your Destiny Year. The knowledge of when it occurs and how to use it can help you plan for the future — remember, many a brilliant scheme fails because it is hatched at the wrong time.

The numerological value of each degree is given, so that you may ascertain which degrees in the horoscope wheel have compatibility with each other and you will thus be able to judge your inherent compatibility with your friends and loved ones.

The system described in this book has been tried and tested with thousands of clients who have visited my centre over the years. It should therefore help you to understand yourself better and also understand and what makes your friends and loved ones tick. But be warned, your Angelic Ruler watches you. Anyone who uses others for their own self-gratification must pay a heavy penalty.

How to find your solar degree

A year has 365 days (366 in a Leap Year), while the horoscope wheel has only 360 degrees. The Sun moves on average 0.983606557 degrees every 24 hours, i.e. approximately 1 degree in a day. Ignoring for the moment the fact that the Sun does not move *exactly* 1 degree a day, one can say that each degree counts a day. Taking 0° Aries as the starting point, each degree of each Sign of the Zodiac could then be slotted into a specific date for each year.

But because the Sun's movement is slightly irregular, it is impossible to determine exactly when it will enter or leave a Sign each year. It does so normally around the 20th/23rd days of each month, except February, when it does so around the 19th (see the Table of Signs on page 8).

So how can you be certain which degree the Sun was in at your birth?

The answer is that it is necessary to read my degree interpretation on either side of your calculated one, should that seem inappropriate. One of them will be correct. To be *absolutely* certain about which degree the Sun was in at your birth, you should obtain a properly calculated horoscope chart for yourself (see page 12).

The rule of thumb method of calculation, however, is to take the starting day of each Sign as being the first degree of that Sign. If, say, you were born on the 28th day from the beginning of any particular Sign, simply add one degree for each of those 28 days. But remember to add on 30 degrees for each birth Sign between yours and that of Aries which is the start of our horoscope wheel. (See the Table of Signs on page 8 for the order in which the Zodiac Signs run.)

Example 1

Born 31st January = Aquarius (11th Sign).
Ten complete Signs before yours = 300 degrees.
Aquarius start date is 20th January.
Days to 31st January = 11; add 11 degrees to 300 = 311.
In this example the solar degree is the 311th degree of the Wheel of Destiny.

(The reading from *Raphael's Ephemeris*, which is for mid-day, was in this instance 11° 22′ Aquarius.)

Table of Signs
It should be noted that these dates are approximate only, since owing to Leap Year the Sun does not always enter a Sign on exactly the same day every year.

Sign	Dates	Planetary ruler
1. ARIES	March 21st — April 19th	Mars
2. TAURUS	April 20th — May 20th	Venus
3. GEMINI	May 21st — June 20th	Mercury
4. CANCER	June 21st — July 22nd	Moon
5. LEO	July 23rd — August 22nd	Sun
6. VIRGO	August 23rd — September 22nd	Mercury
7. LIBRA	September 23rd — October 22nd	Venus
8. SCORPIO	October 23rd — November 21st	Mars/Pluto

Sign	Dates	Planetary ruler
9. SAGITTARIUS	November 22nd — December 21st	Jupiter
		_____
10. CAPRICORN	December 22nd — January 19th	Saturn
		_____
11. AQUARIUS	January 20th — February 18th	Saturn/ Uranus
		_____
12. PISCES	February 19th — March 20th	Jupiter/ Neptune
		_____

Example 2

Born 3rd May = Taurus (2nd Sign).
One complete Sign before yours = 30 degrees.
Taurus start date is 20th April.
Days to the 3rd May = 13; add 13 degrees to 30 = 43.
In this example the solar degree is the 43rd degree of the Wheel of Destiny.
(The reading from *Raphael's Ephemeris*, which is for mid-day, was in this instance 12° 47′ Taurus, which is 13° Taurus to the nearest degree.)

Example 3

Born 22nd December = Capricorn (10th Sign).
Nine complete signs before yours = 270 degrees.
The 22nd December is the start date for this Sign, so add no days.
In this example the solar degree is the 270th degree of the Wheel of Destiny.
(The reading from *Raphael's Ephemeris*, which is for mid-day, was in this instance 0° 23′ Capricorn.)

Example 4

Born 21st March = Aries (1st Sign).
This is the start date for the Sign of Aries. Read the degree interpretation for the 360th degree of the Wheel of Destiny. But you may find the reading for the 1st degree seems appropriate.

Example 5

Born 22nd March = Aries (1st Sign).
No complete Signs before yours.
Aries start date is 21st March.
One day to 22nd March; add 1 day to 0 = 1.
In this example the solar degree is the 1st degree of the Wheel of Destiny.

How to find your Angelic Ruler

Astrology divides humanity into four basic groups corresponding to the Elements of Nature: Air, Water, Fire and Earth. Each of these groups is linked with three Zodiac Signs —

GEMINI		CANCER	
LIBRA	AIR	SCORPIO	WATER
AQUARIUS		PISCES	
ARIES		TAURUS	
LEO	FIRE	VIRGO	EARTH
SAGITTARIUS		CAPRICORN	

Also, it should be noted, people are divided into another three categories, according to their behavioural type. These are the Qualities: Cardinal (Aries, Cancer, Libra, Capricorn), Fixed (Taurus, Leo, Scorpio, Aquarius) and Mutable (Gemini, Virgo, Sagittarius, Pisces).

The Elements aboved are ruled by angelic forces —

Raphael is the ruler of Air and sylphs.

Michael is the ruler of Fire and salamanders.

Gabriel is the ruler of Water and undines.

Auriel is the ruler of Earth and gnomes.

So, if you were born when the Sun was in a Fire Sign, your Angelic Ruler is Michael and his helpers are the elemental beings called salamanders.

The angelic forces govern many important things in our lives —

Air: general health, sickness, healers, arbitrators, arguments, quarrels.
Water: social activities, entertainment, fertility, marriage, good luck.
Fire: leadership, authority, power, prestige, energy, expansion, dominion.
Earth: land and property, business, money, employment, practical matters.

The above will give you a general idea about what you should endeavour to base your career upon and how to direct your life if you want to be successful. This does not mean to say that all Air types should come nurses, doctors or healers, or that all Earth types should become farmers or businessmen. But these do indicate how we may best express our talents.

There are other factors within the chart, namely the eight planetary forces, which may by their placement show a certain amount of influence from other Angelic Rulers. The solar energy is, however, one of the major indicators of your conscious self and how you would have others see you.

Other active degrees in your chart

The degree in which the Sun is placed is not the only one in the natal chart which can determine our characteristics or the events that we must experience. The various planets have their influence too.

If you have a horoscope drawn up (and for this you need to know the place and time of your birth as well as the date) it will give you the exact positions of the Sun and the planets. It is possible to look up the positions of the planets on the day of your birth in *Raphael's Ephemeris* for the year in question. However, as the faster moving planets, i.e. the Moon, Mercury and Venus, move from Sign to Sign rather quickly this is not a satisfactory method, and is likely to give incorrect degrees more often than not.

If you do not already have your horoscope, Old Moore's Easy Guide to Astrology *(W. Foulsham, 1986) tells you how to do it. But if you wish to take a short cut, send you birth details together with a stamped addressed envelope to W. Foulsham, Yeovil Road, Slough, SL1 4JH with a remittance of £2.00, who will send a horoscope chart to you.*

Summary of the aspects of human life affected by the Sun and planets

Sun	the conscious self, vitality, leadership, urge to achieve
Moon	the emotional self, the subconscious mind, instinct, sensitivity, domestic life
Mercury	mental ability, adaptability
Venus	creativity and pleasure, affection
Mars	energy to accomplish, courage, assertiveness
Jupiter	money sense, higher mind, expansiveness, wisdom

Uranus	inspiration, inventive powers
Saturn	maturity, old age, self-discipline, endurance
Neptune	psychic faculties, idealism, intuition
Pluto	sexuality, death

Each of the above planets will occupy a particular degree of our horoscope wheel, and the Angelic Ruler of the Sign that that degree falls in will have an effect upon the energy at play.

For example, the Moon is the ruler of Cancer which is one of the Water Signs. The Moon has an affinity for Water, the Element which represents the emotions, and so is well placed in this Sign. However, should the Moon be placed in a Fire Sign, it would tend to inflame the emotions, causing reckless actions. In an Earth Sign, it would give more stability to the emotions. You should be able to work out for yourself the effects of the different planets in the Zodiac Signs.

How to find your Destiny Year

The last and perhaps most important degree you must seek is your Destiny or Karmic Degree, which reveals your Destiny Year. First of all, place the positions of your Sun and planets onto the blank master wheel on page 15. There is a pentagram overlaid upon this wheel and it is the points of this pentagram which are of major significance. If at birth you were lucky enough to have the Sun or a planet on one of these degrees, it will play a major part in your life.

You calculate your Destiny Year by adding one degree to the position of the Sun at birth for each year of your life, and it is when the Sun passes over one of the points of the pentagram that your Destiny Year is revealed. This is a year when your ambitions are likely to be fulfilled and your dreams realised, or it might present an opportunity to put right that which is not as it should be in your life.

In fact the Destiny Year can be looked upon as a pinnacle of achievement, because the five years prior to it and the five years following it are also under the same magical influence though to a lesser degree.

The points on the pentagram are 72 degrees apart, so depending on where the Sun was at your birth your Destiny Year could arrive very early in your life; some must wait until old age to achieve their heart's desire.

It must be pointed out again, however, that the Sun's movement is slightly irregular although on average it moves about a degree in a day. For the older folk among you, over several decades there may be a discrepancy of up to one whole degree less than the calculated degree, so you should bear this in mind.

As a reminder —

The 54th degree is point 2
The 126th degree is point 3
The 198th degree is point 4
The 270th degree is point 5
The 342nd degree is point 1

Example 1

Born on 3rd May; Sun is in the 43rd degree of the Wheel of Destiny.
Age is 25, so add 25 degrees to the position of the Sun = 68th degree.
Nearest point on the pentagram is point 2, the 54th degree.
Destiny Year occurred at age 54 – 43 = 11, i.e. 14 years ago.

Example 2

Born on 31st January; Sun is in the 311th degree of the Wheel of Destiny.
Age is 20, so add 20 degrees to the position of the Sun = 331st degree.
Nearest point on the pentagram is point 1, the 342nd degree.
Destiny year will occur at age 342 – 311 = 31, i.e. 11 years to go.

If your Destiny Year is far away, do not despair. One of the planets may be nearing one of the points of the pentagram, bringing benefits or opportunities.

We have seen that the Sun moves approximately 1 degree a day and that a day represents a year of the life in this form of

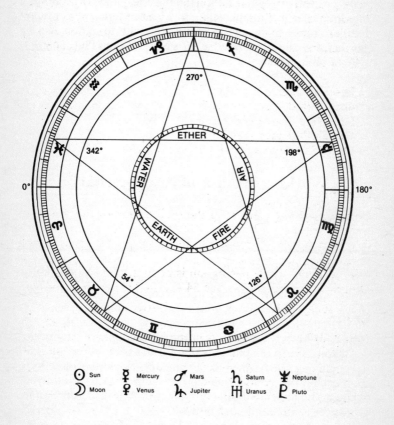

☉ Sun	☿ Mercury	♂ Mars	♄ Saturn	♆ Neptune
☽ Moon	♀ Venus	♃ Jupiter	♅ Uranus	♇ Pluto

Place your Sun and planets on this blank chart and see if you were born with any magically active degrees. If your Sun falls on points 2 or 3, you will work quietly behind the scenes. If your Sun falls on points 1 or 4, you will seek a more public path. Point 5 does not concern material matters but is orientated towards spiritual aspirations.

astrological progression. Let us suppose you are 30 years of age. The position of the Sun 30 days after your birth is representative of this current year of your life. You now buy the little booklet, *Raphael's Ephemeris*, for the year of your birth, and you see that in this period of 30 days the planets as well as the Sun are moving forwards. By the 30th day several of them will have changed their position considerably. Each of the various planets, of course, moves at a different speed (only the Sun moves a degree per day), and without the ephemeris there would be no easy way of ascertaining the planets' positions. Only the faster moving planets, i.e. Moon, Mercury, Venus or Mars, are likely to change in position enough to matter much. The very slow, outer planets, such as Neptune and Pluto, hardly move at all in 30 days.

Working from a horoscope chart

When you first receive your horoscope chart, you may be somewhat confused by it. The exact positions of the Sun and planets will be shown and/or listed, according to the Sign of the Zodiac that they were in at your birth. As you know, each Sign consists of 30 degrees, so the Sun may be put down as 16° 47′ Cancer, or Mars 8° 18′ Leo, just to give a couple of examples.

All you have to remember is that for our purposes we start at the beginning of Aries and, in an anti-clockwise direction, count each little notch as one degree, all the way round till you end up at the tail end of Pisces, 360° (= 0° Aries). So the Sun in 17° Cancer is three full signs plus $17° = 90° + 17° = 107°$, i.e. in the 117th degree of the Wheel of Destiny.

We are only concerned with the position of the Sun and planets, so you may ignore any other points or symbols that appear on your horoscope. These include the Ascendant, MC, Node and Part of Fortune and do not come into our scheme.

Chart Example

To help you, I have set out my own horoscope chart and a list of the planetary positions to show how the respective degrees are arrived at.

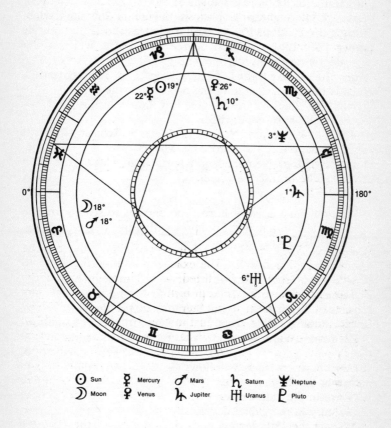

Example birth chart

D.O.B. 9/1/57 at 5.58 a.m. Place of birth, Coventry, England.

Listing of planetary positions —
Sun 18°52′ Capricorn. Nearest degree is 19° Capricorn, which is the 289th degree of the horoscope wheel.
Moon 18°10′ Aries. Nearest degree is 18° Aries, which is the 18th degree of the horoscope wheel.
Mercury 21°38′ Capricorn. Nearest degree is 22° Capricorn, which is the 292nd degree of the horoscope wheel.
Mars 18°15′ Aries. Nearest degree is 18° Aries, which is the 18th degree of the horoscope wheel.
Venus 25°34′ Sagittarius. Nearest degree is 26° Sagittarius, which is the 266th degree of the horoscope wheel.
Jupiter 1°23′ Libra. Nearest degree is 1° Libra, which is the 181st degree of the horoscope wheel.
Saturn 10°15′ Sagittarius. Nearest degree is 10° Sagittarius, which is the 250th degree of the horoscope wheel.
Uranus 6°12′ Leo. Nearest degree is 6° Leo, which is the 126th degree of the horoscope wheel.
Neptune 2°34′ Scorpio. Nearest degree is 3° Scorpio, which is the 213th degree of the horoscope wheel.
Pluto 0°41′ Virgo. Nearest degree is 1° Virgo, which is the 151st degree of the horoscope wheel.

We now have a list of horoscope degrees to search for and see if any are on a magical point or within five degrees of one. The magical degrees we seek are —

Elemental Earth from 49th degree to 59th degree.
Elemental Fire from 121st degree to 131st degree.
Elemental Air from 193rd degree to 203rd degree.
Elemental ETHER from 265th degree to 275th degree.
Elemental Water from 337th degree to 347th degree.

Our planetary list is as follows —
Sun in the 289th degree
Moon in the 18th degree
Mercury in the 292nd degree.
Mars in the 18th degree.
Venus in the 266th degree (active in the orb of Ether)
Jupiter in the 181st degree
Saturn in the 250th degree
Uranus in the 126th degree (active in home degree of Fire)

18

Neptune in the 213th degree
Pluto in the 151st degree

Assessment

We can now see what magical points I have in my favour. The planet Uranus is in the elemental home of Fire and Venus is just within orb of the home of Ether. So when we assess this chart we shall note these two points as being in some way magically charged and of some karmic effect in the native's life. Uranus smack in the home of Fire indicates an interest in science and a burning energy to achieve. Also it is the astrologer's planet. The 2nd active point is Venus, just within orb of the Element of Ether. This is a point that brings art and entertainment to others.

For the rest of the planetary points, which are out of orb, I would refer you to the relevant text which follows for the interpretation of their lesser though necessary energy and so complete our magical picture.

I hope that those who bother to trace the elemental forces at work within their lives learn also to work with them and find the success and contentment that I have. If only a few do so, then I will have fulfilled my karmic debt and satisfied by Angelic Rulers.

Degree interpretation

Before you read the degree interpretations, it is important that you understand the following points —

1. The numerological compatibility, given for each degree, shows how the degrees relate to each other, so you will be able to see how many points you and your friends have which are in tune with each other. The numbers also have similar effects to the planetary forces as follows: 1 Sun, 2 Moon, 3 Jupiter, 4 Uranus, 5 Mercury, 6 Venus, 7 Neptune, 8 Saturn and 9 Mars.

So if when you have collated your planetary picture you find that you have, for example, more 3 points than any other, then the magical energy of Jupiter is strongest. You must therefore read the interpretation of the *solar* energy degree for this planet as it has such a strong effect upon you.

2. The colour given for each degree relates to the numerological effect of the degree and not to the Sign it occupies. It is the colour which will bring you most luck.

3. The degree interpretations are split into two parts. First there is the Sun, or solar energy reading, which applies if your Sun or overall strong point is of that degree. Second there is a planetary point reading, in which one or more examples are given as to how a specific planet present in that degree will affect you. This will give you a pretty good idea how any of the planets not mentioned as examples might affect you, bearing in mind their essential characteristics.

1st degree

Colour: white. *Sign*: Aries. 1st decan. *Qualities*: Cardinal, Fire. *Numerological match*: other 1s.
Positive expression: leadership ability
Negative expression: autocratic nature

Solar point

If your solar energy is in the first degree of the horoscope wheel, you were born with the ambition to achieve in your elemental field even to the point of self-denial.

You are ambitious and have been given the ability to become a great leader if that is what you decide you want. There is little that you are not prepared to have a go at, but there is a tendency to be reckless that could result in your downfall. You are positive, assertive and strong, but it is when you use your best qualities to help others that you find the recognition and praise that you desire more than anything. By all means seek to be special, but try not to be aloof from others. Remember that a king without subjects is like a castle without a wall and is easily attacked.

Planetary point

This degree will project the qualities associated with a particular planet in a more assertive and aggressive manner. It will also give a certain amount of ambition in the field that the planet governs. For example, Mercury here would make the mind, and the tongue, sharper.

2nd degree

Colour: grey. *Sign*: Aries. 1st decan. *Qualities*: Cardinal, Fire.
Numerological match: other 2s.
Positive expression: compassion
Negative expression: selfishness

Solar point

If your solar energy is in the 2nd degree of the horoscope wheel you are forceful though caring. You may be a rough diamond but your intentions are nearly always good. Although not always apparent to others, you are true to your high moral standards or code of conduct. You are actually very compassionate and concerned about other people's problems, but you may not want this to be to widely known for fear that others may try to take advantage of your soft side. You could make a good solicitor, fighting for other people's rights, except that you are gullible and might sometimes support the wrong side. You need to share your problems with others but find it difficult to trust people till they have undergone some form of test of loyalty that you have set them.

Planetary point

This degree's energy gives natives a desire to share, though not always the means to do so. Venus here would allow the need to share to be through the arts and creativity. Uranus would make natives unpredictable and prone to mood changes. Although it comes within a Cardinal Fire Sign, the degree gives quite a soft and feminine nature, which modifies the influence of each of the planets.

3rd degree

Colour: violet. *Sign*: Aries. 1st decan. *Qualities*: Cardinal, Fire.
Numerological match: other 3s.
Positive expression: knowledgeableness
Negative expression: inquisitiveness

Solar energy

People born with the Sun in this degree have the ability to mix easily. The mind is curious to the extent of being too nosy in some cases, though it is the natives' curiosity that helps them attain what they seek.

Playing games, having a good joke and a good social life in general are essential if natives are to work at their best, as they can work only as hard as they play and must relax from the responsibilities of the workplace and the home.

They tend to be excellent teachers and communicators, but a career involving salesmanship and where there is no close supervision would also suit.

A religious disposition is likely to develop around the mid-forties.

Planetary point

If you have a planet here, you will have the ability to let go and unwind from social stresses. You will also study deeply subjects that you were unable to come to terms with during your schooling. Your hobbies and social activites will be in the fields relevant to the planet, e.g. the Moon here could see you becoming a voluntary worker or student of the occult, while Saturn at this point would make you accept the responsibilities thrust upon you.

4th degree

Colour: orange. *Sign*: Aries. 1st decan. *Qualities*: Cardinal, Fire. *Numerological match*: other 4s.
Positive expression: constructiveness, protectiveness
Negative expression: destructiveness

Solar point

As a solar point the 4th degree gives the ability to build and construct on behalf of society at large not just for self-interest. Politicians, civil servants or large corporations would use its energy for the protection of us all. The terrorist, however, may try to enforce that which he feels is right upon us whether we want it or not. This degree can give much unpredictability to the lives of those who have it, as they often have little control over events. The lesson of the degree, if you were born with it, is to accept what control and responsibility you were given to influence your own destiny — the decisions you make affect not only yourself but those who come into contact with you.

Planetary point

If you have a planet here, its effect is to bring to your attention the energies that you have at your disposal but perhaps fail to utilise. Patience must be developed and success will follow. Mars here would make you understand how you can physically protect others, while Mercury would give you the mental energy to overcome any hurdles you encounter. The Moon is ill-placed in this point; your intentions may be good but your reasoning is affected by emotions that you cannot express or explain.

5th degree

Colour: scarlet. *Sign*: Aries. 1st decan. *Qualities*: Cardinal, Fire. *Numerological match*: other 5s.
Positive expression: love of travel
Negative expression: instability

Solar point

This fifth solar degree is given to the adventurous. Overseas travel, an interest in the history of times and places and the writing of new chapters is the destiny of the natives of this degree.

There is an inability to stay in one place for very long and those of you born with this degree will encounter many changes of friends, partners and environments in the first half of your lives. Eventually you will settle down and make use of the things you have learned. Soldiers, mercenaries or those linked with the travel industry would be well placed with this degree. You heed no warnings and learn only through your own mistakes. Indeed, hard lessons in life that you have learned enable you to laugh in the face of adversity and create anew from the ashes like the phoenix.

Once you have conquered that which you set out to master you become bored and must seek a new challenge. You may get a desire to rest and settle down, but to do so before the age of 35 would be your downfall.

Planetary point

The energy present allows you to rest from the task at hand in order that you may begin anew that which you desire. For example, Venus here allows you to enjoy social company, while Saturn gives you the time to reassess your directions and motives.

6th degree

Colour: green. *Sign*: Aries. 1st decan. *Qualities*: Cardinal, Fire.
Numerological match: other 6s.
Positive expression: passion
Negative expression: fickleness

Solar point

This degree inspires social harmony. The possessors require to establish in their lives that which they feel has been missing in childhood. Much of the natives' energy is directed into establishing and maintaining meaningful relationships, an experience which makes them excellent arbitrators and peace-makers in other people's problems. They are, however, as forceful as they feel is necessary for achieving their aims and ambitions, and if they feel others are not appreciative of what they are trying to do then they will consider them unworthy of their time and take back what they have given.

Creative and artistic, with much energy and vitality, natives of this degree are not as self-contained as they sometimes appear to be to others. If you were born with this solar point, you will frequently require someone to whom you can express your feelings.

Planetary point

This degree adds a creative flair to the planetary body concerned. Natives take a good deal of care in what they are doing and want the right to express themselves. Saturn here can cause natives to overstrain or commit themselves too soon. Venus, however, is well placed here, giving natives the ability to express their feelings.

7th degree

Colour: blue. *Ruler*: Aries. 1st decan. *Qualities*: Cardinal, Fire.
Numerological match: other 7s.
Positive expression: intuition

Negative expression: day-dreaming

Solar point

The 7th degree of Aries gives natives the ability to cultivate intuition and awareness. They can let their intuition guide them to the top of their career or profession, whatever that may be. They can, on the other hand, be their own worst enemies, by allowing unrealistic dreams to blunt their intuition and perceptiveness and fool themselves into thinking they are capable of achieving more than in fact they can.

People with this solar degree actually work at their best when they are under stress, without time to think or plan. This is because such instant decisions stem from the intuitive mind.

Planetary point

The 7th degree has the ability to make known the mysterious forces that occupy it to the individual. As a result, Jupiter would give the native the desire to break free from the limitations imposed upon him or her and seek out new truths or philosophic ideals.

8th degree

Colour: black. *Ruler*: Aries. 1st decan. *Qualities*; Cardinal, Fire. *Numerological match*: other 8s.
Positive expression: maturity of outlook
Negative expression: irresponsibility

Solar point

Integrity, the acceptance of responsibility and trust, coupled with self-denial while serving others comes with this degree in the native's formative years. This early self-denial beings about the experience and tenacity needed to succeed later in life. If you were born with this solar degree, you may at first have feelings of frustration at your inability to lead the kind of life your friends are leading, but eventually you should develop a patient and persevering attitude that is rare for the sign of Aries. You have been selected to shoulder the responsibilites that others cannot and it is the acceptance and commitment to these which should bring you considerable rewards by your mid-thirties.

Planetary point

A planet in this degree gives the native responsibility of some
sort. Saturn is well placed here, putting an old head on young
shoulders. Uranus, on the other hand, is ill-placed, and natives
tend to put forward the right ideas but at the wrong time or
without sufficient planning. Mars is the ruler of Aries but the
energy of this planet can be self-destructive. Mercury here
would increase the learning and memory capacities.

9th degree

Colour: crimson. *Ruler*: Aries. 1st decan. *Qualities*: Cardinal,
Fire. *Numerological match*: other 9s.
Positive expression: dynamism
Negative expression: laziness

Solar point

If you were born with your solar energy in this degree, you are
independent, adventurous and not content with playing second
fiddle to anyone who has not earned your respect. You can be
very forceful in manner and have no time for those who do not
pull their weight. You work better for yourself or in positions of
responsibility as you are self-motivated and do not like others
breathing down your meek. Your demand for instant attention
and action can be your making or your undoing.

 You were born to lead rather than to be led, but you must
earn the respect of your superiors rather than being too self-
assertive if you are to succeed.

Planetary point

The energy present in this degree acts as a battery charger for
the planet placed there. If you have a planet here, you will be
revitalised or given a second chance if you should fail in certain
tasks. Uranus here would make you volatile. Venus would give
you the chance to overcome romantic problems. Mars is well
placed for soldiers or people in uniforms.

10th degree

Colour: white. *Sign*: Aries. 2nd decan. *Qualities*: Cardinal/
Fixed, Fire. *Numerological match*: other 1s.
Positive expression: idealism

Negative expression: stagnation

Solar point

This degree sits on the cusp of the 2nd decan of Aries which is subruled by Leo. The solar energy here is very strong for the creation of new ideas, projects and inventions. There should be leadership ability, because natives can communicate new ideas and allow them to blend with the old. Many reformist politicians or research scientists would find that this degree is active within their charts.

Natives are inventive, original and creative but they must be in charge of their own direction if they are to achieve their goals in life. Marriage and romance may be put aside for ends that they consider more important. They are somewhat lonely at times and always too busy to bother with what they consider to be trivial. Napoleon's 'Not tonight, Josephine' is typical of this degree, for while there is work to be done the native finds it very hard to unwind.

Planetary point

A planet placed in this degree gives natives inventiveness and an ideology by which they can sort out their solutions to life's problems. The Moon is ill-placed here, as it causes too much emotional friction. Mercury adds a sharp edge to the intellect, allowing the native to express his or her ideals in an understandable way.

11th degree

Colour: grey. *Sign*: Aries. 2nd decan. *Qualities*: Cardinal/ Fixed, Fire. *Numerological match*: other 2s.
Positive expression: healing of others
Negative expression: self-pity

Solar point

The 11th degree gives natives great energy and the ability to put right the emotional, physical and material wrongs of others. Nurses, social workers, probation officers or environmentalists may have this degree at birth. The nature, though outwardly bombastic and brash, is in reality highly sensitive to the plight of others, and in helping them they gain a knowledge of their own worth which they find reassuring. In fact these natives are seldom fully appreciated by their fellows for quite some time or even after their departure from this world. Yet without their behind-the-scenes work society as we know it today could not exist. Fixed in their ideals, there is little that will change their planned direction, be it for good or bad, and they should at times ask those they assisting if they want that assistance.

Planetary point

The energy of this degree tends to soften the planet in residence, giving the native a more compassionate and sympathetic outlook. The Moon is well placed in this degree, as is Jupiter and Venus. But Saturn can find no expression here, and Uranus can cause the native to use physical violence to impose his will.

12th degree

Colour: violet. *Sign*: Aries. 2nd decan. *Qualities*: Cardinal/Fixed, Fire. *Numerological match*: other 3s.
Positive expression: adaptability
Negative expression: old-fashioned outlook

Solar point

This degree gives the person born under it the capacity for independent thought and action coupled with compassion and caring.

The natives are creative thinkers who plan and map out their futures step-by-step, so that they rarely go wrong. If they should happen to do so, they have the ability to recognise where and how, so that they do not make the same mistake again. They are fond of travel and the unknown, and like to find out about the history and background of the things which appeal to them.

Town planning, technical drawing, advertising or jobs which require responsibility but allow the worker to approach and conquer new ground will suit people born with this solar degree. Full of fun when relaxing but with the desire to get on when at work, these people are archievers in whatever they do. They are born with the ability to adapt to their surroundings.

Planetary point

The energy present allows a planet here to act positively in the life of the natives. Those with Mars here can put their excessive energies to constructive use while natives with Saturn learn to control their emotions. This planet furthers mental ability, allowing natives to choose their own direction. The volatility normally associated with Uranus can be turned into positive bursts of energy for creating anew.

13th degree

Colour: orange. *Sign*: Aries. 2nd decan. *Qualities*: Cardinal/Fixed, Fire. *Numerological match*: other 4s.
Positive expression: creative flair
Negative expression: self-destruction

Solar point

A native of the 13th solar degree is highly strung, and fluctuates between being a creative genius, who readily solves problems and goes through life with apparent ease, and the self-destroyer, who sets himself tasks too hard to accomplish but rather than take help from others ruins that which he has built. If you were born with this degree, it is not an easy one to live with because it means you must build your own empires as you cannot inherit them. You may leave home early in life and wander from job to job and place to place, seeking the perfect combination of home and work. Those of you who learn to control the energy of this degree, rather than let it control you, will find that which you seek on the material plane in the joy of a real home and family. This may not come about, however, until quite late in life. Meanwhile you must learn through your own rash mistakes.

Planetary point

Uranus is well placed here, giving natives the answers they require with flashes of insight. If you have Venus here, on the other hand, you would tend to look to other people to solve your problems, which they cannot do; you will have to come to terms with yourself. The energy of this degree does not mix well with the Water planets as they tend to make the native aware of what he or she desires and yet cannot yet possess.

14th degree

Colour: scarlet. *Sign*: Aries. 2nd decan. *Qualities*: Cardinal/Fixed, Fire. *Numerological match*: other 5s.

Positive expression: instigation of projects
Negative expression: deception

Solar point

The 14th degree endows natives with the ability to communicate with the masses. Large long-term projects which require management ability and perseverance would suit these people as they not only are able to conceive such projects and plan them out but they like to see the foundations firmly laid. There is, however, a tendency to take risks. Also, the views and ideals of the natives may not altogether comform to those held by most other people. It is the desire to change and rebuild anew that sees these people achieve in the long term.

If you were born with this solar degree, get-rich-quick schemes are not for you as it is long-term projects that will lead to success and enable you to live in style and comfort. You also need to unwind from time to time. But do not regard your exuberant energy as an indication of a need for a change of direction. It is merely a time for letting off steam.

Planetary point

The energy of this degree allows the occupying planet to consolidate its energy; natives can therefore find an outlet or direction for their ambitions. Saturn is well placed here, giving the patience that is required. If you have Venus here, you are likely to think you will achieve your goals without too much effort, which could bring about your downfall.

15th degree

Colour: green. *Sign*: Aries. 2nd decan. *Qualities*: Cardinal/Fixed, Fire. *Numerological match*: other 6s.
Positive expression: artistic ability
Negative expression: laziness

Solar point

Natives of this degree have the ability to communicate to others through the arts, either as a hobby or as a career. A star of the stage, a pavement artist or the office comedian might have this point in common. A love of nature and the outdoors can also be present and most people with this degree will be animal lovers even if they don't keep pets themselves. Apt to being rather sensitive, people with this degree have in fact a great deal to offer anyone who is able to see beneath their impatient exteriors. This degree can also be related to the healing arts.

Planetary point

The energy present will effect the planet it attends, and allows a fair amount of social activity or gives an outlet for the native's energy. Mars here makes a person very ambitious though not forceful, while the Moon gives someone the expression for their sensitivity. With Uranus here, the native will be as volatile as can be the case with that planet and so may more likely to able to take the advice of others.

16th degree

Colour: blue. *Ruler*: Aries. 2nd decan. *Qualities*: Cardinal/Fixed, Fire. *Numerological match*: other 7s.
Positive expression: intuition
Negative expression: worry

Solar point

A person born with this solar degree has more intuition than most of us. There can be some psychic or clairvoyant ability too, yet this may never be utilised or recognised and simply be put down as good guesswork. There is a fear or mistrust of the unknown, be it spiritual or material, yet all this is hidden beneath the brash Aries cloak. These people require to find within themselves the qualities that they seek in their partners, mates and friends, and then all the fears and anxieties that they keep bottled up in themselves fade away and disappear. They find their best expression in helping others in some way for in so doing they feel wanted and receive the reassurance of their worthiness that they need. They tend to reflect the environments they find themselves in and therefore should avoid mixing with negative types as this makes them feel as bad as they are and gives them no future direction.

Planetary point

Uranus here tends to accentuate phobias and fears. In general, though, natives are able to break down their mistrust of others by the use of the energy of the planet placed in this point.

17th degree

Colour: black. *Sign*: Aries. 2nd decan. *Qualities*: Cardinal/Fixed, Fire. *Numerological match*: other 8s.
Positive expression: business ability
Negative expression: inactivity

Solar point

Natives of the 17th degree have much innate ability in both business and management, but they do not acquire the necessary experience to do anything with their talents until the mid-to-late twenties. If you are one of these people, your time meanwhile is best spent in doing all you desire and seeing as much of the world as you can, for when you begin your task in life in your mid-to-late twenties you may well still have the desire to travel but will no longer have the time. You are likely to be a materialist once adolescence is passed, whose philosophy can be summed up: 'a bird in the hand is worth two in the bush'. There may, however, be a burning ambition to recreate that which inspired your dreams in your early travels.

Colder and more aloof in later years, the longer the native of this degree waits to settle down the more difficult he or she will find it to do so.

Planetary point

The degree adds a certain amount of ambition, coupled with patience learned through the passing of time. Planets placed here enable natives to accept responsibility early on and they will learn by their first mistakes rather than repeat them. Saturn in this degree makes for too much of a loner, while Venus here could see an early marriage. If you have the Moon here, you can be too logical in later life while Uranus may make you predictable. Mercury is well placed here for a career in sales.

18th degree

Colour: crimson. *Ruler*: Aries. 2nd decan. *Qualities*: Cardinal/Fixed, Fire. *Numerological match*: other 9s.
Positive expression: energy
Negative expression: burn-out

Solar point

The 18th degree epitomises all that the sign of Aries encompasses. If you have this solar degree, you may be bursting with energy and the desire for positive action. You make a better leader than a follower and will push ahead in an independent fashion regardless of opposition or advice from others. You will be a seeker of high achievements in order that you may win the acclaim of your fellows, even though your ideals are at times too lofty, best suited to yourself and not to be imposed on others.

Your failure to reach a compromise between your desires and those of your associates is all that stands between you and the success that you seek. Learn this lesson sooner rather than later, for it is the key to success in any field you choose.

Planetary point

This degree energises and increases the abilities of the planet present and will give some indication of how to direct the energy of the degree. If you have Mercury here, it would indicate that travel, the Army or communications will be important in your life. The Moon would indicate the influence your mother may have exerted over you or the intensity of your emotional feelings. If you have Mars in this point you are virtually unstoppable and will win by conquest.

19th degree

Colour: white. *Ruler*: Aries. 2nd decan. *Qualities*: Cardinal/ Fixed, Fire. *Numerological match*: other 1s.
Positive expression: justice
Negative expression: injustice

Solar point

The 19th degree will bring people who possess it the ability to arbitrate and adjudicate in all kinds of problems, be they on a domestic level or in the larger context of the law or even the planet upon which we live.

Those born with this degree really seem to care and through their strength and perseverance bring into our lives the justice we seek. The native is not always understood by his fellow men who wonder what it is he gets out of his actions. So the native often has a lonely crusade before he achieves his goals. He or she is forceful when necessary though capable of being gentle, is feared for the wrong reasons and is seldom really loved. Such a person could make an excellent politician, having the desire to work for the betterment of all through self-sacrifice.

Planetary point

The energy at play brings the faults associated with the occupying planet to the natives' attention. They can thus bring into balance that which is askew. The Moon here would emphasise that effort is needed to stabilise the home. Venus would imply that they seek too lavish a lifestyle and must rethink their plans with regards romance.

20th degree

Colour: grey. *Sign*: Aries. 3rd decan. *Qualities*: Cardinal/ Mutable, Fire. *Numerological match*: other 2s.
Positive expression: sharing
Negative expression: attention-seeking

Solar point

This degree imparts a compassion and sensitivity not actually rare for the sign of Aries but rare in the way that this sign shows them. Aries is not usually a sign for the open show of emotion, but this particular degree can produce a native who is at times hurtfully honest. He or she needs to share everything with someone special but has neither the time nor the patience for anyone who does not respond or give as they receive. The TV advert 'would you give someone your last Rolo' must have been written with these people in mind, for if you are in their confidence they are generous to a fault but have no time for users or liars and will let you know if you are neglecting them.

Home and family are very important to natives of this degree and will play a major part in determining their initial direction. There can be a tendency to marry out of the class or culture they were born into because of a desire for something a little different.

Planetary point

If you have a planet in this degree it gives you the ability to share with those you choose gifts and abilities associated with that particular planet. Mercury here could make you a writer or poet while Venus could give you artistic abilities. Saturn helps you attract maturer mates.

21st degree

Colour: violet. *Sign*: Aries. 3rd decan. *Qualities*: Cardinal/Mutable, Fire. *Numerological match*: other 3s.
Positive expression: literary ability
Negative expression: extravagance

Solar point

If you have this solar degree, you will be able to combine both leadership and individuality. These qualities are best brought out through education and the cultivation of the higher mind.

People born with this degree may not be university dons but they do have the kind of shrewd mind that can spot a bargain — and the ability to turn it to good use. They have versatility, being able to tackle all manner of projects. They are also good mixers, being socially active and popular, but they settle quickly once they have found their soul mate. Their biggest problem is that they become quickly bored with repetitive situations and jobs. They require plenty of change and mental stimulation to progress.

Planetary point

The energy present in this degree allows for adaptation to and acceptance of change. If you have the Moon here, this could mean early upheavals and many changes of home during adolescence. Mercury would indicate changing attitudes and ideals.

22nd degree

Colour: orange. *Sign*: Aries. 3rd decan. *Qualities*: Cardinal/Mutable, Fire. *Numerological match*: other 4s.
Positive expression: originality
Negative expression: braggart

Solar point

The 22nd solar degree does not create shy or timid natives. The energy at play will bring them into the public eye for one reason or another from robbing a bank to saving the world. Unpredictable and little understood by their fellow men, people with this degree tend to be the planners and instigators of great schemes for which they require to take credit.

Although self-critical to an extreme, they won't take criticism from others, unless they have great respect for what they have achieved. Their morals can be either very strong or practically non-existent. A person with this degree is likely therefore to be remembered by posterity for either being particularly good or terribly bad.

Fame can be yours if you were born with this degree of solar energy, if the planetary points in your chart are supportive. Take care not to be infamous!

Planetary point

As a planetary point the 22nd adds a certain amount of publicity or public awareness to the life. If the planet placed here is Mercury, for example, you would be known for your sharp mind, while Mars could make you competitive in business or sport. Uranus here can make you highly strung but very creative, and Saturn puts a wise head on your shoulders, though Aries is a sign associated with rashness.

23rd degree

Colour: scarlet. *Sign*: Aries. 3rd decan. *Qualities*: Cardinal/Mutable, Fire. *Numerological match*: other 5s.
Positive expression: knowledgeableness
Negative expression: illiteracy

Solar point

This solar degree gives a thirst for knowledge, so the natives are always searching for answers to their many questions. It is a great degree for the research scientist or market analyst. If possessed by the ordinary man in the street, tell him no lies for he will certainly find you out. Like a terrier down a rabbit hole, such a person will never let go until he or she finds what they are after, be that money, love or anything else.

This would be a better degree for a detective rather than a policeman as the natives do not work at their best when closely supervised and their methods are not always orthodox.

Strong, wilful and assertive, you should avoid coming into conflict with natives of this degree; it would be far better to have them on your side.

Planetary point

The 23rd degree adds a touch of curiosity and a desire to know the whys and wherefores of everything. For example, Mercury here would make natives want to know the reason for learning things, while Mars could spur them into investigating the physical realms. Venus in this degree could lead them to a career on the stage.

24th degree

Colour: green. *Sign*: Aries. 3rd decan. *Qualities*: Cardinal/Mutable, Fire. *Numerological match*: other 6s.
Positive expression: home building
Negative expression: fear of sharing

Solar point

As a solar degree the 24th has all the ingredients for building a happy and stable home. Women born with this degree will be mothers and housewives or they may work from home or be concerned with home-related products. Men may be builders, bricklayers, plumbers and electricians. For them also there will be no place like home. DIY enthusiasts and those with lots of plants about the house or a garden to put the neighbours to shame are likely to have this energy working for them.

People born with this degree are the stabilisers of society, the devoted mother or father, or the proud house owners who devote all of their spare cash and resources to the home and family. Intensely loyal, these people take traumas in the home harder than most and if their mate lets them down they find it hard to trust others again.

Planetary point

This degree indicates where the strife or problems will occur in the home and family, by the planet placed in it. Mars here can bring problems through the father or other males and makes the native very possessive, while the Moon applies to females and the mother. The native with Venus can make the home too much of a show-place, where you can never feel really comfortable.

25th degree

Colour: blue. *Sign*: Aries. 3rd decan. *Qualities*: Cardinal/
Mutable, Fire. *Numerological match*: other 7s.
Positive expression: imagination
Negative expression: tendency to worry

Solar point

The 25th solar degree is that from which dreams are made. The
natives have the ability to communicate and share their dreams
with others, and to convert them into reality. They tend to be
loners in their formative years, but they come into their own
when they use the energy of Aries to plan constructively in
order to bring about their aims.

Travel and the desire for change from childhood till the
mid-twenties result in the native of this degree gaining a good
deal of experience for one so young. This experience is put to
good use, enabling him or her to create and build with the
power of the imagination. Inventors, writers, poets and artists
would be well on the road to success if born with this degree.

Planetary point

A planet in the 25th degree allows natives to expand beyond
what they know and what they possess into that which they wish
to be. Uranus here is well positioned for an inventive mind,
while the Moon could bring happiness out of strife in the home.
Mars could see the native becoming a great sportsman or
competitor. Whatever the planet placed here, it will have
positive rather than negative effects.

26th degree

Colour: black. *Sign*: Aries. 3rd decan. *Qualities*: Cardinal/
Mutable, Fire. *Numerological match*: other 8s.
Positive expression: wealth through partners
Negative expression: inability to share

Solar point

The Sun in the 26th degree has much to do with the way the
native forms his or her ties with others. Though outwardly
materialistic and logical, this person is in fact highly sensitive
and easily hurt.

The need for material wealth to establish the security that the natives desire, however, can only be attained through partnerships and it is not until they recognise this and learn to share with others that they find what they truly seek. Emotionally they need a mate who is demonstrative in affection but who does not need their partner to be similarly demonstrative (the natives would feel open to attack if they showed their deep feelings). They are however able to relax and become more emotionally expressive and appreciative of their partner's efforts once they feel financially secure.

Planetary point

A planet placed in this degree is an indicator of how natives may find the security that they seek. For example, Saturn here would be by accepting a responsible job, or by taking the hermit's path. Mercury would indicate a mental rather than physical partnership would work better for the native.

27th degree

Colour: crimson. *Sign*: Aries. 3rd decan. *Qualities*: Cardinal/Mutable, Fire. *Numerological match*: other 9s.
Positive expression: spiritual growth
Negative expression: self-seeking

Solar point

The 27th degree is characterised by the necessity of the native having to experience some form of spiritual and karmic lesson. The life may never be very settled, with many things to be done, places to be seen and lessons to be learned. This degree, however, offers an opportunity to put right in this life all that the native failed at in previous existence; though the path may be hard it is worth keeping to. If you are one of these people, you will have a life of self-denial, giving to others that which you wished for yourself and seeing others achieve that which you would have liked to have achieved. But in so doing you may wipe clean the slates of time and enter your next existence with many owing you favours that you may call upon to grant your wishes.

Soldiers who defend their countries, dedicated nurses who care for the sick, or ministers of the church are the kind of people likely to be learning this degree's karmic lesson.

Planetary point

Any planet placed in this degree means that the native has a karmic lesson to learn. The particular planet should indicate where that debt lies. If you have Saturn here, it means you must rely upon yourself and not seek the help of others, while the Moon means you must care for others' emotional needs while sacrificing your own. This is not a negative degree, but rather one which helps you to spiritually evolve.

28th degree

Colour: white. *Sign*: Aries. 3rd decan. *Qualities*: Cardinal/Mutable, Fire. *Numerological match*: other 1s.
Positive expression: business acumen
Negative expression: wastefulness

Solar point

The 28th degree gives natives business and political acumen to be used for the benefit of the masses. Work in the Civil Service, politics or large business organisations which provide jobs and income for others as well as community service is highlighted.

People born with this degree can become involved with charities or similar large institutions which help people in some way. Wealth can be acquired but only so that it can be used for the benefit of all, and not squandered.

If you have the Sun here, you should have marked leadership qualities, though you may tend to be quite insular. Marriage or partnerships are made for life and if vows are broken you could be quite vindictive. Prosperity should come to you during your mid-thirties.

Planetary point

The 28th degree brings the energy of the planet placed in it out into the open, and makes natives take on some form of responsibility. Saturn here can cause imprisonment or restrictions in the lifestyle, while Jupiter makes the native self-reliant and a high earner. The Moon is badly placed here as the energy is too emotional while Mercury sharpens the mind and the wit and is great for self-expression.

29th degree

Colour: grey. *Sign*: Aries. 3rd decan. *Qualities*: Cardinal/Mutable, Fire. *Numerological match*: other 2s.
Positive expression: protectiveness
Negative expression: destructiveness

Solar point

A person born with the Sun in the 29th degree is somewhat of a contradiction for the sign of Aries. Outwardly assertive, strong and competitive (characteristic of the sign), the native is in fact shy and sensitive, and always on guard against what might in fact never happen. On the positive side, the native is fair and just and will always stick up for the underdog. But this may well be because of a fear that he or she might become an underdog one day. Or, that by assisting others he or she quells his or her or own feelings of inadequacy.

Natives work best when under stress, for then they have no time for thought, only action. They are very protective of what they consider theirs and are hard workers when defending their rights and possessions. They are also quick to take offence, though often none was meant.

Planetary point

If you have a planet in the 29th degree, you will have the ability to share with others the energy to that planet. The Moon here would indicate that you must learn to share other people's inner feelings, while Venus would help you to find someone who wants to be protected — or will protect you. Jupiter is well placed here, bringing out a philosophical frame of mind and self-understanding.

30th degree

Colour: violet. *Sign*: Taurus. 1st decan. *Qualities*: Fixed, Earth. *Numerological match*: other 3s.
Positive expression: gracefulness
Negative expression: impatience

Solar point

A person born with the Sun in the 30th degree has grace and sensitivity and is polite, courteous and generous. He or she always give others the benefit of the doubt when judging them.

Natives are perhaps a little too slow to act at times but are careful in thoughts, words and action. They make friends easily and keep them, and are renowned for their reliability (they always keep a promise). They can be very stubborn when their mind is made up and set upon a course of action, but their charm is such that you just cannot help forgiving them when they do wrong.

Work with people of any sort is the most suitable for natives as they need to mix more than most. Hairdressing or serving at the bar of a public house would be ideal, giving both social activity and a place where they can be admired.

Planetary point

The 30th degree makes the effects of whatever planet is placed here appear to be good rather than bad. For example, Mars would make natives appear strong and courageous rather than brash and bombastic. If they have Mercury here, you would be given the impression they knew what they were talking about even when they do not. Venus would give considerable physical beauty while Uranus would allow natives to mix with others in strange surroundings.

31st degree

Colour: orange. *Sign*: Taurus. 1st decan. *Qualities*: Fixed, Earth. *Numerological match*: other 4s.
Positive expression: self-motivation
Negative expression: lack of practical sense

Solar point

The 31st degree gives a person the ability to plan and direct his or her own career. People born with this degree have a head start over the rest of us, as they have the imagination and foresight to decide what they want to do, where to do it and with whom. And with determination and effort they achieve what they desire. Approachable and gregarious, natives of this degree build from the firm foundations laid by themselves and, although they do not often achieve early success in life, their long-term projects bring great rewards. Long lasting marriages, business partnerships and friendships are important in the eventual success of natives of this degree, and they would be wise not to forget those that have helped them on their way.

Planetary point

If you have a planet in the 31st degree, it will impart to you the qualities of stability and individuality. If you have Jupiter here, you will learn to deal with one idea at a time instead of spreading yourself too much. The native with the Moon here finds a foundation from which he or she can develop and project the emotional self. Women with Mars here are likely to be attracted to strong-willed men who present a challenge to them.

32nd degree

Colour: scarlet. *Sign*: Taurus. 1st decan. *Qualities*: Fixed, Earth. *Numerological match*: other 5s.
Positive expression: duality and creativity
Negative expression: gloom

Solar point

People born with the Sun in the 32nd degree are never quite sure what they want until they have it, and then it may be too late to hold onto it. They are nearly always in two minds about what they want to do and where they want to be, and often try to be in both places at once which can cause them to over-commit themselves. Extremely lazy one moment and hyper-active the next, they need a strong partner to give them a sense of direction and meaning in their life, though without taking away their personal freedom.

You will often find that natives of this degree are very strict and sanctimonious with others while themselves breaking their own moral code. They never actually mean to hurt anyone, but they usually end up hurting themselves and must find some stability if they are to avoid this.

Planetary point

The energy of the 32nd degree gives natives the ability to project more than one facet at a time of the planet resident here. A person with the Moon here may run a home and be an agony aunt at work. If Mars is here, natives could hold down two jobs or have two partners. With Mercury, they will tend to vacillate in their decisions or opinions.

33rd degree

Colour: green. *Sign*: Taurus. 1st decan. *Qualities*: Fixed, Earth.
Numerological match: other 6s.
Positive expression: healing ability
Negative expression: miserliness

Solar point

Anyone born with this solar degree is blessed with the ability to heal the troubles in other people's lives but not necessarily in their own. This incarnation could be one of self-sacrifice for the benefit of others rather than the selfish impulse to look after 'Number One'. That may be through the bringing up of a family or, in a wider context, through service to human kind in general.

Many people with this birth degree become involved in charities or with the disabled or less gifted, and if they should stop to reflect, it is this work which brings them the recognition and respect which they particularly need. Failure to express themselves can result in this type hoarding all they can lay their hands on for fear of having nothing. They must learn that the love of others is the greatest wealth of all.

Planetary point

The 33rd degree softens the effect of any planet placed in it. For example, Saturn could bring the native into some form of care for the elderly, and Mercury at this point might make a librarian or a historian.

34th degree

Colour: blue. *Sign*: Taurus. 1st decan. *Qualities*: Fixed, Earth.
Numerological match: other 7s.
Positive expression: artistic ability
Negative expression: thoughtlessness

Solar point

People born with the Sun in the 34th degree have unusual powers of perception. Whatever they apply themselves to, be it in the arts, the world of commerce or personal relationships, they utilise their intuition. They seem to understand how others feel, often reacting with uncanny timing. Their biggest problem is their fear of themselves and of not being able to help themselves. They make great actors, being able to play a part as if they are completely identified with it. As artists, they could paint a picture of a place from a photograph and make it seem that they had actually been there, such is their exceptional interpretive faculty in the realm of the imagination.

Planetary point

A planet in the 34th degree gives natives a special ability to plan for the future.

They will be thus well prepared for any eventuality. Mercury here is specially good for planners and designers.

35th degree

Colour: black. *Sign*: Taurus. 1st decan. *Qualities*: Fixed, Earth.
Numerological match: other 8s.
Positive expression: business travel
Negative expression: secret fears

Solar point

Natives of the 35th solar degree tend to be shy and inhibited. Perhaps for this reason it is their lot in life to learn to acquire and maintain material possessions and partnerships through some form of risk or adventure which is likely to be totally against their normal inclinations. They have to learn to break away from the mundane, tried and tested routines by which they probably earn their living, but not the sort of living that deep down they desire. This can only be obtained by strengthening their individuality and taking on a self-supporting role. In fact many of those born with this degree who have found success are self-employed or have attained some form of promotion or recognition for their initiatives in their jobs.

Although not emotionally demonstrative, natives of this degree are, however, full of feeling and demand total loyalty from their partners and associates.

Planetary point

Maturity and patience are qualities that this degree adds to the effects of planets placed in it. For example, natives with Mars here are less brash than normal. If the Moon is here they can be a little eccentric but very loving, while Saturn can bring wealth early in life instead of later.

36th degree

Colour: crimson. *Sign*: Taurus. 1st decan. *Qualities*: Fixed, Earth. *Numerological match*: other 9s.
Positive expression: ambition
Negative expression: sloth

Solar point

People born with the Sun in the 36th degree are capable of achieving almost anything they wish to do, but quite frequently they end up doing nothing much at all. They are extremely gifted, adaptable to change and able to persevere when they really want to. The trouble is, they do not always make the necessary effort to accomplish something, hoping that they will find someone else to do the donkey work.

If you have this degree, don't expect others to carry you all the time. People who are always looking for free rides soon lose friends. Take no notice of anyone who tells you that you have little capability. You have the ability to turn your hand to almost anything, so long as you have the patience to see the job or project to the end without your attention being diverted elsewhere. Once you have achieved your aim, you should get great satisfaction in having proved to yourself and others that you could do it.

Planetary point

The energy present in this degree adds the drive and versatility of Mars to a planet placed here. The Moon is not well placed in this degree as it makes the native emotionally volatile and insecure. Venus here would give a liking for the arts and of luxurious surroundings, while those who have Mercury here are extraordinarily creative or inventive — and also excellent liars!

37th degree

Colour: white. *Sign*: Taurus. 1st decan. *Qualities*: Fixed, Earth.
Numerological match: other 1s.
Positive expression: love of children
Negative expression: immaturity

Solar point

The energy at play in this degree is ideal for mothers who want large families, or for people who work with or for the young in any way, from children's story writers to baby-sitters. The natives when adult have a great affinity with children, maybe because a part of themselves never grows up or simply because they find their emotional outlet with the young. They also tend to marry someone younger than themselves, perhaps desiring to re-experience the joys of youth through their partner or their children.

If you were born with this degree, you are a good mixer and very likeable. You enjoy games and amusements and TV programmes meant for children, because you like to be childlike at times. A father who plays with his son's train set may have this degree active in his chart.

Planetary point

A planet in the 37th degree gives natives the ability to carry their childhood dreams into the realities of adult life. Examples are the station-master who used to play with toy trains as a child, or the nurse who played doctors and nurses. Someone with Venus here could become a model or artist, while with Mercury he or she could become a writer.

38th degree

Colour: grey. *Sign*: Taurus. 1st decan. *Qualities*: Fixed, Earth. *Numerological match*: other 2s.
Positive expression: compassion and maturity
Negative expression: self-seeking

Solar point

The 38th solar degree gives natives a desire for a peaceful and contented life and the wish to avoid the pressures and stresses that most of us experience.

You would not call a person with this degree a recluse. He or she does enjoy social activity, provided it is with someone he or she specially cares about, at the theatre or a quiet restaurant, rather than at the local disco or nightclub with its loud music and lack of intimate surroundings. Such persons are home builders who sacrifice all for their offspring or families yet are rarely fully understood by those who come into contact with them. They are often ardent dreamers. Their dreams are for them a form of relaxation and an escape from the mundane aspects of their existence; they do not try to transform them into realities. Many people born with the Sun in this degree become involved with nursing and the care of the aged while still raising a family of their own.

Planetary point

This degree adds some sympathy or understanding to the effects of the planet resident in it. Saturn can bring early responsibility in childhood, especially in one-parent families. Mars gives the energy to overcome obstacles that the degree can create.

39th degree

Colour: violet. *Sign*: Taurus. 1st decan. *Qualities*: Fixed, Earth. *Numerological match*: other 3s.
Positive expression: laughter and change
Negative expression: lack of responsibility

Solar point

Anyone born with the Sun in the 39th degree is full of energy and likes to relax and have fun. Job and home moves can be frequent as he or she does not like to be held down in one place for too long and gets bored with repetitive circumstances.

Work in the arts or the theatre would suit natives of this degree as they love to bring laughter and would do well to combine work and pleasure. They will become well known wherever they work because of their practical jokes and frivolity. Ardent in love and quick to fall for the opposite sex, the person born with this degree can, however, quickly disappear, leaving a trail of broken hearts with fond memories, in a search for another fun-seeking partner.

Planetary point

The energy present adds some light-hearted frivolity to the planet placed here. Someone with the Moon here would be less emotionally serious. Pluto would give less fear of death and the unknown. If you have Saturn, you would learn to play after work, and if Uranus, you would not be in such a rush to break away. Mars' energy in this degree can make a formidable person who oozes charm and creativity, causing immediate jealousy in competitors.

40th degree

Colour: orange. *Sign*: Taurus. 2nd decan. *Qualities*: Fixed/
Mutable, Earth. *Numerological match*: other 4s.
Positive expression: empire building
Negative expression: selfishness, insecurity

Solar point

As a solar point the 40th degree gives natives the creative
genius to create much out of nothing. They are strong willed
and ardent planners but they actually make their fortune
through flashes of insight which give them the edge over their
competitors. Success is attained by following through these
flashes of insight, in particular in fields related to the sciences or
in commercial markets such as the commodities on the stock
exchange. Producing and marketing new inventions and promoting new ideas could also be a path to success for these
people. Also any large institution such as a bank may well have
been founded by a native of this degree.

A good stable home is necessary for natives to rest in after
the stresses of their lifestyle.

Natives have a strong urge to leave something behind them
after they have gone by which they will be remembered.

Planetary point

The 40th degree gives a person with a planet here insight into
how best to make use of that planet's energy. The planet would
indicate where his or her fortune lies. Saturn here would indicate work to do with the land, such as farming, or in mineral
extraction. Mars would indicate a military or uniformed career,
or some occupation having a connection with the armed forces.

41st degree

Colour: scarlet. *Sign*: Taurus. 2nd decan. *Qualities*: Fixed/
Mutable, Earth. *Numerological match*: other 5s.
Positive expression: political leadership
Negative expression: rebelliousness

Solar point

A person born with the 41st solar degree has the ability either to
make good his or her birthright or to help bring about the

necessary conditions to create a new organisation, institution or social revolution. Reformers, politicians, social workers, teachers and communicators of every type fall under this degree. Natives are born leaders, with the ability to make others understand the views they hold. They become involved in the decision-making departments of our governments, factories, churches and places of learning. They are often derided and scoffed at until, with the passage of time, their predictions and ideals have become realities.

People born with this degree have much to do with the very making or breaking of the moral laws which govern our society without which we would all live in fear. The energy of the degree can be used in an extreme way and could result in revolution and public disorder because of attempts to enforce ideas or systems on others who cannot accept them.

Planetary point

A planet is the 41st degree brings about in the native a desire to change or replace that which is no longer required. For example someone with Saturn at this point may put aside self interest and work for the betterment of all.

42nd degree

Colour: green. *Sign*: Taurus. 2nd decan. *Qualities*: Fixed/Mutable, Earth. *Numerological match*: other 6s.
Positive expression: romantic nature
Negative expression: failure to trust others

Solar point

As a solar point the 42nd has much to do with domestic situations and environments. A strong emotional need to belong usually results in the native of this degree settling down to building a home and raising a family early in life. Almost always such a person is an old fashioned romantic at heart.

Dating agencies and lonely hearts clubs fall under the agency of this degree, as natives get satisfaction out of finding emotional happiness for others. Children are usually abundant and as spoilt as their parents' income allows. They shower them with all the things that they lacked in childhood.

People born with this degree are always ready to lend a helping hand to a friend in need. Indeed, they build their life upon partnerships and friendships. They are often found in occupations involving the care of others, e.g. as home helps.

Planetary point

If you have a planet here, you will want to share with others the benefits that the particular planet brings. Jupiter in this degree will probably make you financially generous with money. If you have Mercury here, you will always have a friendly word of advice for those who will listen. The Moon or Venus is good for the nursing profession, while Saturn would prompt the native to shoulder the responsibilities of those less able to do so themselves.

43rd degree

Colour: blue. *Sign*: Taurus. 2nd decan. *Qualities*: Fixed/Mutable, Earth. *Numerological match*: other 7s.
Positive expression: poetic creativity
Negative expression: despondency, depression

Solar point

The Sun in the 43rd degree produces a person who is able to communicate feelings and emotion in an expressive way. The intuition and insight is sharpened and can bring forth flashes of creative genius.

Natives of this degree need to find an outlet for their creativity and could best do so through poetry, music or painting. They are gifted in being able to capture the mood of the times they are living in and to bring to expression the feelings of those who come into contact with them. At the very least, this degree gives natives an appreciation of the finer things in life coupled with the desire to share them with others.

Planetary point

The 43rd degree adds to the person who has a planet placed in it an appreciation for the finer qualities given by that particular planet. For example, someone with Venus here can be quite vain about their personal appearance. If they have the Moon in this degree, they will have sympathetic understanding verging on the psychic. Jupiter causes a person to seek out philosophic solutions to life's problems and Mars makes the native learn to understand the planet's energies and direct them into positive and useful enterprises.

44th degree

Colour: black. *Sign*: Taurus. 2nd decan. *Qualities*: Fixed/
Mutable, Earth. *Numerological match*: other 8s.
Positive expression: business flair
Negative expression: greed

Solar point

The 44th degree gives a strong business sense coupled with the
ability to build upon what others think is already complete. You
just cannot help admiring the ability of the person born with
this degree to make a profit out of very little. If his gold mine
turned out to be exhausted when he bought it, he would be sure
to discover oil on the land or else turn the place into an
amusement centre. The mind is very inventive and original and
though the native may be slow to start you can be sure he is one
of the first to finish. Don't try to pull one over on him for he
never forgets what others have done to him no matter how
trivial and will be sure to repay the deed at some time whether
good or bad.

Club or social ties through business are the best expressions
for the native of this degree as this way he or she is able to mix
business and pleasure — and it is always a pleasure for him or
her to do business.

Planetary point

The 44th degree adds to anyone with a planet placed in it the
ability to use that planet's energy in the most constructive way.
For example, the planet Mars here can give tireless ability
though cause the native periods of physical burn-out. But
Saturn brings natives the spoils of their ambitions before they
reach the age of 35. Jupiter can make natives extremely generous to those less well off.

45th degree

Colour: crimson. *Sign*: Taurus. 2nd decan. *Qualities*: Fixed/
Mutable, Earth. *Numerological match*: other 9s.
Positive expression: teaching ability
Negative expression: rebelliousness

Solar point

The native of the 45th solar degree will be rebellious against whatever hinders his ambitions and personal freedom. Suspended between that which he desires to accomplish and that which he was given at birth, he sets out to find the balance between what he can have easily and what he must strive for. This lesson is long and fraught with many trials and tribulations which leaves people born with this degree with a wealth of personal experience which they find themselves passing on to others in the hope that their path to success is shorter and easier. So they therefore tend to become the teachers of the next generation, though not necessarily in orthodox ways.

This is a hard solar degree to be born with, but the life will never be boring and will certainly have plenty of excitement and a chance to expand through personal endeavour.

Planetary point

The 45th degree gives to anyone with a planet placed in it the ability to break free from the limitations imposed by that planet. If you have Jupiter here, you will learn through travel and the higher mind, while with Mars you will learn to control the planet's explosive energy and put it to constructive use.

46th degree

Colour: white. *Sign*: Taurus. 2nd decan. *Qualities*: Fixed/Mutable, Earth. *Numerological match*: other 1s.
Positive expression: home-building
Negative expression: inability to settle down

Solar point

As a solar point the 46th has to do with the constructing and maintaining of homes, not just in the sense of the family home but in the larger context of society as a whole. Building societies, banks and the construction industry would provide suitable occupations for natives of this degree as they are the organisations concerned with financing and building homes for us all. Some people with this solar degree become involved in marriage counselling or the welfare services and it is in creating happier and better conditions for others that they express their real needs. By making everyone safe and secure they build their own sense of security and fulfilment. They have leadership and compassion coupled with the drive to build firm foundations for their children.

Planetary point

The 46th degree gives to persons born with a planet placed in it the ability to adapt or to build upon new and untested areas of their lives. For example, the Moon here could see the native emigrate or move to an area quite different from the birthplace to begin anew.

47th degree

Colour: grey. *Sign*: Taurus. 2nd decan. *Qualities*: Fixed/Mutable, Earth. *Numerological match*: other 2s.
Positive expression: compassion, humanitarianism
Negative expression: insecurity, depression

Solar point

The 47th solar degree has much to do with a humanitarian approach to life. However, many people born with their solar energy here will be great lovers of plants, the countryside and pets and do not particularly want to make contact with the less desirable elements of their own species. On the positive side they are warm hearted romantics, seeking peace and tranquility for both themselves and for those who need assistance. But they are not the toughest of people psychologically speaking and their good intentions are often misused by people who seek to exploit them.

Natives are charitable people, happy just to know that what they have done for others was of use. They desire little else apart from a safe haven to retreat to with someone who understands their needs.

Planetary point

The 47th degree gives natives a desire to share with others the benefits associated with any planet placed in it. The Moon here makes a person emotionally responsive to the needs of others, while someone with Mars will lend his physical strength to his friends and neighbours. With Saturn, natives learn to share their secrets with others; with Mercury, they share their literary knowledge with anyone with the same interests.

48th degree

Colour: violet. *Sign*: Taurus. 2nd decan. *Qualities*: Fixed/Mutable, Earth. *Numerological match*: other 3s.
Positive expression: love of tradition
Negative expression: old fashioned outlook

Solar point

The 48th degree has much to do with the maintenance of tradition while still moving forward into the future. People having this solar degree are the keepers of the cultures and traditions they were born into. They help others to adapt to the changes society imposes upon them without making too radical a change. Quite conservative in their views, natives can be found in most walks of life. However, they are far from being the boring types you may think them to be. They are well able to let their hair down when their work for the day is done, while having the sense to know when enough is enough.

The native can be the ordinary man on the street, placidly going about his own business. But when revolutionary minded individuals threaten that which he considers sacred, this turns him into a ferocious lion who goes about attempting to bring things back to what he considers normal. He wants neither medals nor recognition for his deeds.

Planetary point

The 48th degree gives anyone who has a planet placed in it responsibility for the actions that planet governs. Mercury here makes the native self-critical in anything to do with mental activity while someone with Mars physically punishes himself for his wrongdoings. With Saturn, the native accepts heavy duties; and with Uranus he or she learns to control his or her unpredictable outbursts.

49th degree

Colour: orange. *Sign*: Taurus. 2nd decan. *Qualities*: Fixed/Mutable, Earth. *Numerological match*: other 4s.
Positive expression: originality, energy
Negative expression: dictatorial nature

Solar point

This degree gives persons born with it a great deal of energy and originality but not necessarily the understanding to put it to contructive use. They like to impose or enforce their ideals and ambitions upon other people if they can.

If you have this solar degree, on the positive side you are a creative doer with flashes of brilliance, but problems are apt to occur if your chart lack the maturity of Saturn or intellect of Mercury to give control and order. One or preferably both of these planets would have to be active within the chart if you are ever to achieve much. Let us not paint a picture of gloom here. It is just that the life would be too full of twists and changes without a good, firm direction. A stabilising ingredient must be found if you are ever to finish what you start. (See also the 49th degree.)

Planetary point

This degree gives a person who has a planet here the ability to put great surges of energy and creativity into the projects connected with the planet. Mars, for example, would be good for sporting activities, while Venus would enhance physical beauty and help artistic pursuits. The Moon makes natives emotional and here it can cause violent outbursts.

50th degree

Colour: scarlet. *Sign*: Taurus. 3rd decan. *Qualities*: Fixed/Cardinal, Earth. *Numerological match*: other 5s.
Positive expression: versatility
Negative expression: unpredictability, moodiness

Solar point

The 50th degree creates a person who is adaptable, versatile and communicative. Great energies can be expended in short bursts, so that this type excels in situations where wits and a sharp mind are required, coupled with the ability to adapt to sudden changes. Long-term enterprises and emotional commitments should be avoided in the formative years as the vibrations present need variety and changes in surroundings if the native is to develop into the communicator he or she is destined to be.

Seekers of adventure, searching for the treasures of the past and the future, are born with this degree. They would do particularly well in military service, or as freelancers or scouts for large corporations in any field of endeavour. They can be extremely lazy and work at their best when under pressure.

Self-motivation must be developed if they are to shoulder responsibility. (See also the 54th degree.)

Planetary point

A person who has a planet in the 50th degree has the ability to communicate and project the energies of that planet through physical experiences. If the Moon is here, emotional stress could be overcome and the person will be stronger for it, Mercury would enable a person to conquer a mental problem or to learn from mistakes.

51st degree

Colour: green. *Sign*: Taurus. 3rd decan. *Qualities*: Fixed/Cardinal, Earth. *Numerological match*: other 6s.
Positive expression: beauty, grace
Negative expression: vanity, self-indulgence

Solar point

As a solar point the 51st typifies all that Venus in Taurus means — a strong love of music and the arts, with slowness in committing the emotions though these are intense when they do. Natives are money-conscious, with the desire for some degree of comfort and luxury, and are also somewhat fixed in their views. They prefer to take their own counsel rather than heed the advice others. If you have this solar degree, remember that your ability to appreciate the finer things in life is given in order that you may communicate a feeling for beauty to your less gifted or able associates. By denying them this part of yourself you may find bad luck dogs your life. The angelic ruler of this degree wants all to share what it has to offer but looks without favour on those who misuse his gifts for self-satisfaction and their own vanity. (See also the 54th degree.)

Planetary point

The 51st degree allows a fair amount of artistic expression to be added to the energies of a planet placed there. Mercury, which is associated with logic, may spur someone to write verse, or business memos. And someone born with Saturn here, which is normally cold, will warm to the company of others under the effects of this degree. With Jupiter, much can be learned from the study of history or the arts, while with normally energetic Mars, the native can slow down enough to appreciate fully whatever he or she is doing.

52nd degree

Colour: blue. *Sign*: Taurus. 3rd decan. *Qualities*: Fixed/
Cardinal, Earth. *Numerological match*: other 7s.
Positive expression: sympathetic listening
Negative expression: self-regard

Solar point

The 52nd degree gives natives great sympathy with people
suffering misfortune, especially when they have emotional up-
sets and psychological problems. They are born with the ability
to sense or know what is causing the unhappiness of others as
well as the patience to try to get to the bottom of their problems
and to try to heal them.

When used in its higher role this energy of the 52nd is the
bringer of peace to peoples and nations, but its effect upon the
individuals born under it is to give them the time to listen to
others and to share their joys and heartbreaks. Nurses, social
workers or kindergarten attendants could make great use of this
degree. So too can people in the business world, if they are, for
example, arbitrators or company personnel officers.

People born with this degree find it rather difficult to trust
others, because of their own emotional hang-ups, but it is only
by assisting others that they learn to cope with their own
particular problems. (See also the 54th degree.)

Planetary point

The 52nd degree gives persons with a planet placed in it the
ability to put right whatever they failed to accomplish in a
previous existence. This may be considered a karmic debt that
must be paid if the native is to progress. For example, the
intensity of emotions given by the Moon should be a spur to
help those in need.

53rd degree

Colour: black. *Sign*: Taurus. 3rd decan. *Qualities*: Fixed/
Cardinal, Earth. *Numerological match*: other 8s.
Positive expression: possession of wealth
Negative expression: misuse of power

Solar point

As a solar degree the 53rd is only one degree from the magical energies or home base of the ruler of Earth, Auriel. This placement at birth prepares the native for the responsibility of supporting others through material means and in so doing make moral progress. If you have the Sun in this degree it matters not whether you are a begger or pauper, in this life you must do arduous work for the well being of others. Work well at your task and you will reap financial rewards in this life; if you fail to provide for others, on the other hand, you will bring about future retribution.

Managers or owners of land and property are often born with this degree; it is how they use the assets of the earth to assist others that decides whether they pass this test or not. Be it a large family to care for or a nation, natives must learn to shoulder the responsibility. (See also the 54th degree.)

Planetary point

A planet placed in the 53rd degree indicates how the native may best serve his or her fellow man. Someone with the Moon would be emotional, and be home-orientated. Mercury gives mental powers and Jupiter provides material comforts.

54th degree

MAGICAL HOME DEGREE OF THE ELEMENT EARTH
(*Strongest effect*: 5 degrees on either side)

Colour: crimson. *Ruler*: Taurus. 3rd decan. *Qualities*: Fixed/Cardinal, Earth. *Numerological match*: other 9s.
Positive expression: practicality, material possessions, defence of land, property and large corporations
Negative expression: use of material wealth for own ends, greed, financial collapse

Solar point

As a solar point the 54th is to be considered special. It is the home of the angelic ruler of the element Earth and where his strengths are at their most potent. Up to five degrees from his base are within his immediate view and are therefore likely to be affected by this degree. He rules lands, mines, farming and material possessions, and if you were born with your solar energy in this degree he has selected you to be one of his link-pin workers in these matters when they are connected with the care of others. You could on one level be a council worker, repairing and maintaining the property in your town. On another level, you could be Chancellor of the Exchequer, taking care of the finances of the whole country.

The energy present has many, many outlets, but all people with the Sun in this degree have in common the ability to manage or service the needs of the environments they live in. This is point two of the pentagram, and while important in the scheme of our existence it does, however, tend to work behind the scenes rather than in the limelight. We all carry cash around with us but rarely consider where or how the money came into existence and who maintains its flow behind the scenes.

Many ecologists have this degree active in their charts as well as keen gardeners and anyone who works with the land and plants, for this is the kingdom of Auriel and, as every gardener knows, the soil will only give you back what you have put into it and if you do not care for it properly you are left with a barren waste.

Planetary point

If you have a planet in this degree it indicates which energies may best be put to the service of the angelic ruler Auriel; as he receives so he gives.

Moon: caring services to the society in which you live, nurse, social worker, parent etc.
Mercury: the use of the practical mind to work out solutions to the problems in the society in which you live.
Mars: defence of your fellow men, and adapting all to the changes that occur.
Venus: protecting the arts and bringing them to all people.
Jupiter: protecting the wealth, social status and history of the society you live in.
Saturn: maintenance of land, farms and mines; governing institutions.
Uranus: destroying the outdated; heralding of the new era; future planning for society.

It must be remembered that this is the house of the angelic ruler of Earth and as in all things the owner is stronger and more at ease in his own home than in any other environment. But he also has an affinity or natural ease when active in other degrees in the chart which have a numerological match in the

60

number 9, or the lesser numbers 5 and 4. All things must have foundations upon which they are able to manifest and it is through the element Earth that Water finds a body and Fire a base from which to burn, while Air can carry Earth from one area to another, creating fertility or desolation. Study the elements which combine with this degree for its true purpose.

55th degree

Colour: white. *Sign*: Taurus. 3rd decan. *Qualities*: Fixed/Cardinal, Earth. *Numerological match*: other 1s.
Positive expression: leadership in communication
Negative expression: misrepresentation

Solar point

The 55th degree has much to do with how we, through leadership and authority, disseminate all the knowledge and learning of our race; it could be considered the degree of intellectual responsibility. That which is remembered now is that on which our children base their future decisions and developments and we should preserve this heritage with care. The degree is also concerned in part with the antiques and treasures that we keep in our museums to show those that follow us how we and our ancestors lived. Teachers, museum curators, historians and the like have this degree active whose effects are to create nostalgia and a love of the past and all things to do with it.

If you were born with this degree, you may be a collector of antiques or have a house full of memorabilia. (See also the 54th degree.)

Planetary point

The 55th degree teaches again the lessons of a past existence which were not then correctly learned, and the planet resident here indicates what that lesson is. For example, Mercury here would indicate that a higher level of intellectual energy is to be developed through study, while Saturn would indicate the native must bear the consequences of his or her own past deeds.

56th degree

Colour: grey. *Sign*: Taurus. 3rd decan. *Qualities*: Fixed/

Cardinal, Earth. Numerological match: other 2s.
Positive expression: cooperation, compassion
Negative expression: mistrust, helplessness

Solar point

A person born with the Sun in the 56th degree has a caring and compassionate nature that may best be directed through the arts or literary pursuits. A certain amount of public bravado is present, but the chief desire is to give out a message of peace for all through cooperation.

Natives of this birth degree enjoy sharing with others all they have rather than being alone and they gather their strength from the knowledge that they are not alone. They are found in all walks of life.

This type of solar energy is likened to the charge of the Seventh Cavalry which appears out of the blue just when you thought all was lost.

The natives tend to be worriers. They are also great listeners till they feel really secure, and then they become the talkers and motivators in partnerships. Actors who are flamboyant on stage while being quiet and reserved at home ideally represent this degree. (See also the 54th degree.)

Planetary point

The 56th degree says, if you have a planet in it, that you have something to share with others, and the particular planet placed there indicates what that is. Saturn would indicate some kind of responsibility along with others, not just your own, while Venus would indicate an artistic gift to be shared with those you come into contact with.

57th degree

Colour: violet. *Sign*: Taurus. 3rd decan. *Qualities*: Fixed/Cardinal, Earth. *Numerological match*: other 3s.
Positive expression: artistry, fun and laughter
Negative expression: laughter at others' expense

Solar point

The energy of the 57th degree gives the ability to enjoy the lighter side of life and to help others do the same. Natives of this degree are found usually in the office rather than on the stage. They are the comedians and jokers who liven up both our social and work environments. You will find that they are not prone to travelling great distances unless necessary for work or health, and that they are liable to gain fortune through wills or legacies. They are prone to vivid dreams, psychic experiences and premonitions which often come true.

Having a broad philosophical mind capable of reasoning and reflection upon events that have happened and are to happen, this type learns from the experiences they have gathered how to face up to and conquer all the problems that they encounter on life's path. (See also 54th degree.)

Planetary point

The energies of a planet placed in this degree are indications of what the natives have achieved in their past lives, but there is energy to spare to help them overcome and laugh at what caused them worry previously. Neptune here strengthens the psychic faculties while Venus gives musical or poetic talent. Jupiter would allow natives the inner security to be fearless in the face of death.

58th degree

Colour: orange. *Sign*: Taurus. 3rd decan. *Qualities*: Fixed/ Cardinal, Earth. *Numerological match*: other 4s.
Positive expression: reasoning power, good memory
Negative expression: forgetfulness, illiteracy

Solar point

The 58th degree has much to do with the memory and reasoning capacities. People born with the Sun in this degree would tend to succeed in matters requiring tact, patience and diplomacy. They achieve in such fields as literature, teaching, hygiene and the railways, or in the employment of others.

The native is likely to follow in his father's footsteps, taking up his job or career as his own. The mind is logical and practical and unable to rest or relax until the task at hand is completed which can cause periods of depression or that feeling of 'I'll never get it done'. But with patience and perseverance and the use of what has been taught, all avenues lead to eventual success. (See also the 54th degree.)

Planetary point

The 58th degree imparts the capability of logical thought to the energies of any planet placed here. Anyone born with Uranus here may find expression for his creative energy and inventiveness. Someone with the Moon here learns to be more objective, and put emotional bias aside. Love is put before pride, thus avoiding arguments and quarrels.

59th degree

Colour: scarlet. *Sign*: Taurus. 3rd decan. *Qualities*: Fixed/ Cardinal, Earth. *Numerological match*: other 5s.
Positive expression: alertness, wit and humour
Negative expression: sarcasm, resentfulness

Solar point

The 59th degree creates an individual who is lively, alert, dexterous, witty and ingenious. Enthusiastic and magnetic, he or she will display great energy and drive when they have an interest in any particular project. At times the tongue is just as sharp as the mind. Often there is talent in music, drawing, sculpture or designing on the artistic side. There can be marked ability too in the sciences, as the mind leans towards investigation and the application of new methods. The person born with this solar degree needs a well educated mate so that there can be communion on the intellectual plane as well as on the emotional, spiritual and intellectual planes. Repetition or boredom, however, will cause this type to disappear over the horizon in search of new wonders. (See also the 54th degree.)

Planetary point

This degree gives natives a desire to investigate and to conquer the energies of the planet in it. Mercury here would make a great student of the human mind — a psychiatric nurse, perhaps — while Saturn would produce an individual discontented with old-fashioned views and customs and who would seek to change them.

60th degree

Colour: green. *Sign*: Gemini. 1st decan. *Qualities*: Mutable, Air. *Numerological match*: other 6s.
Positive expression: creative thought
Negative expression: hypochondria, duality of mind

Solar point

The 60th degree is on the cusp of Taurus and Gemini and you would be wise to read the effects of the Sun in the preceding degree also as it can have some influence upon this one. The degree itself has much to do with family life and careers related to it. Strong emotional links are maintained with family and friends made in the past, and even if the native should emigrate to the other side of the world, he or she would frequently write home and sometimes make the long journey to see the family and old friends.

The natives of this degree are deep thinkers who never truly show their inner thoughts to others, holding their own counsel rather than seeking the opinion of others. Workers in furniture stores, or those working on home repairs or improvements, people in the rag trade, nursery teachers and parents of large families will frequently be found to have the Sun in this degree as all deal with products from the home. Warm and compassionate, with the desire for company and someone special, they are popular with all they come into contact with.

Planetary point

This degree gives the native a desire to think things through, in a manner specific to the planet placed in it. Uranus here is less reactive and the native is more likely to consider his actions. With Mars, the native learns to control his temper and direct his energy constructively.

61st degree

Colour: blue. *Sign*: Gemini. 1st decan. *Qualities*: Mutable, Air.
Numerological match: other 7s.
Positive expression: Literary talent, defence of the weak
Negative expression: Self-seeking emotionally

Solar point

People born with the 61st degree active tend to be fighters for the underdogs. A sense of fair play and justice is important to them and if they learn to promote it through literary channels, they will achieve their aims. Good occupations for people born with this degree would be as agony aunts, solicitors or their clerks or policemen. But above all they would excel whenever they have the chance to use the intuitive edge they have when it comes to communicating a feeling into words. They are people whose pets obey them without a verbal command being given (all it needs is a look).

Their failing is that they appear to retreat under stress and should learn to utilise their intuition to help them find the solutions to the problems that the world throws at their feet.

Planetary point

The 61st degree imparts to people with a planet resident in it intuitiveness which will help in solving problems relating to that particular planet. Someone with the Moon in this degree may have psychic warnings through dreams and thereby avoid emotional turmoils. Mercury here could see the creative mind being used in the writing of books, maybe novels or poems, or at least there should be the ability to communicate the subconscious into the conscious.

62nd degree

Colour: black. *Sign*: Gemini. 1st decan. *Qualities*: Mutable, Air. *Numerological match*: other 8s.
Positive expression: loyalty
Negative expression: reclusiveness

Solar point

People with the Sun in the 62nd degree grow up sooner than most, both physically and mentally. They are extremely loyal to those they consider worthy and want only one partner in life, though they seem to go through some form of trauma in their forties which can result in a second marriage. They are inwardly businesslike with casual acquaintances but show intense passion when alone with the one they love.

Careers generally tend to be for life or they will spend long periods in the same place of employment. But if the boss should ever give them cause they will leave with a bang, feeling it was unfair after the loyal service they had given. Most careers are open to them as they have both the patience and learning potential to achieve success in whatever field takes their fancy, but some form of employment leading to authority and with scope for promotion would be best suited.

Planetary point

The 62nd degree gives people with a planet placed in it the

patience to apply the energy present in that planet in the seeing through of long-term projects. The Moon or Venus placed in this degree could indicate emotional support is required in romance if the native is to be happy in marriage or partnerships. Saturn here could indicate that the route to success is through acceptance of responsibility for others.

63rd degree

Colour: crimson. *Sign*: Gemini. 1st decan. *Qualities*: Mutable, Air. *Numerological match*: other 9s.
Positive expression: great mental and physical energy
Negative expression: fickleness, destructiveness

Solar point

People born with the solar energy in the 63rd degree are both physically and mentally active and very competitive. They are much sought after on the social scene, being both entertaining and adventurous. They also have a fine community spirit and involve themselves in voluntary work of all kinds. Usually keen on sports and outdoor pursuits, they also love to be at home with a loved one or a pet, around the fire, or be involved in some indoor activity. However, they are quite hard to tie down to one project for very long, though they commit all they have to their chosen activities while they remain of interest. As far as romance is concerned, they can wander from partner to partner, remembering each for the fun they had with them but never quite finding what they were truly seeking.

Planetary point

The 63rd degree allows natives to have some adventure or relaxation from the tasks normally connected with the planet placed here. Venus in this point, however, can lead to negativity and self-indulgence, or even promiscuity. Saturn, on the other hand, relaxes his sterness so that natives can have frequent periods of pleasure and leisure.

64th degree

Colour: white. *Sign*: Gemini. 1st decan. *Qualities*: Mutable, Air. *Numerological match*: other 1s.
Positive expression: inventiveness, DIY ability

Negative expression: crying wolf too often

Solar point

The 64th degree creates good leaders — and also good liars. People born with this degree can be inventive and energetic when necessary but they are liable to talk their way out of something they don't want to do and to blame someone else when things go wrong. Positively, though, they shirk from obtaining assistance from others, seeking to do everything alone and unaided. DIY activities at home are just up their street. It is only as they grow older and learn to trust others with some of the responsibilities either at work or in the home that they find the time to really enjoy life.

Planetary point

When there is a planet in the 64th degree it indicates that the native needs to learn to share the gifts given by that planet with others. If you have the Moon here it means that you can achieve an emotional rapport with others, while Mercury would indicate you have knowledge to share.

65th degree

Colour: grey. *Sign*: Gemini. 1st decan. *Qualities*: Mutable, Air.
Numerological match: other 2s.
Positive expression: strong partnerships
Negative expression: failure to share

Solar point

The 65th has a lesson to teach, that the native must learn how to share and care in a positive relationship.

If you were born with this solar degree and find you have had more than one marriage or business partnership, especially if the partnership ended with tears or anger, then you are in trouble and will have to come back and do it again till you get it right. The angelic ruler of this degree teaches those who have it the need totally to trust and share with another. You have the freedom to choose your mate and it is your responsibility not to make the choice a purely mercenary one if you are to pass this test. Your outwardly bombastic nature must be conquered and the real you released in order that you may experience the ultimate and complete relationship necessary for your spiritual development.

Environments are many and varied as are careers for persons born with this degree. No matter whether they be rich or poor, the lesson to be learned is not to cling to material things but to share them with others.

Planetary point

If you have a planet in the 65th degree, it gives a clue to the area of your life in which you failed in a past existence. Venus means you were too vain and choosy while Mercury means you failed to communicate etc.

66th degree

Colour: violet. *Sign*: Gemini. 1st decan. *Qualities*: Mutable, Air. *Numerological match*: other 3s.
Positive expression: artistic talent
Negative expression: vanity and fickleness

Solar point

As a solar point the 66th has much to do with artistic expression and the leisure industry. This does not mean that all people born with this degree run hotels, holiday camps, sports centres or such like. Rather it projects the natives' need to have leisure time for hobbies and other activities quite apart from their careers. People with this solar degree can be found in many jobs but they need to have some special aptitude for or enjoyment connected with their work if they are to maintain steady employment. Holidays or breaks from the stresses generated at work and home are a must for them if there is to be domestic peace and contentment; boredom can be the death of them. These people are good social mixers and are generally well thought of. They usually achieve their ambitions through friends and associates or contacts made through leisure.

Planetary point

The 66th degree adds to the energy of a planet placed in it a certain amount of artistic expression. For example, Mercury adds guile or a persuasive tongue to the already sharp mental abilities associated with this sign.

Colour: orange. *Sign*: Gemini. 1st decan. *Qualities*: Mutable, Air. *Numerological match*: other 4s.
Positive expression: adapabity to change
Negative expression: living in a fantasy world

Solar point

As a solar point the 67th degree gives the ability to convert futuristic dreams into realities. People born with this degree have strong imaginations but they also have the ability to work upon and form their ideas into a concrete plan and to communicate this to others in such a way as to make it acceptable even to stick-in-the-muds. Technology in electronics, computers or any similar field tends to appeal to this type, either at the mundane level, for use at work or home, or, on the more creative side, in research and experimentation.

The natives of this degree are good home builders. However, they are often away from home in the course of their work or because of a desire to travel, though they still maintain family ties when far away. Frequently you will find they have a marked aptitude for picking up languages or skills but not necessarily those taught at school, as they tend to learn from practical experience rather than through scholarship.

Planetary point

If there is a planet in the 67th degree, it allows natives to adapt to and work with the element it is placed in, namely Air. People born in the early part of this century, up until May 1914, will have Pluto here. This planet would have helped them to understand their fears and inhibitions.

68th degree

Colour: scarlet. *Sign*: Gemini. 1st decan. *Qualities*: Mutable, Air. *Numerological match*: other 5s.
Positive expression: teaching ability
Negative expression: all talk and no action

Solar point

The 68th degree gives the ability to communicate, teach or explain to others who do not understand. People with this degree are often mature beyond their years, with an under-standing and patience which allows them to pass on to others that which they themselves find simple to grasp. They can make the most complex matter seem clear and straightforward, so that they should find fulfilment through some form of teaching or advisory service. This need not be at a school or university. For example, they would make good personnel officers, union officials, or even driving instructors.

In the home, natives are patient, caring parents who will always find time to answer their children's questions.

Planetary point

The 68th degree gives people with a planet placed in it the ability to share their knowledge and understanding with others. Those with Saturn here could develop maturity through service to others; they should do for other people whatever they are unable to do for themselves. Jupiter here could make the native shoulder the financial burdens of family members.

69th degree

Colour: green. *Sign*: Gemini. 1st decan. *Qualities*: Mutable, Air. *Numerological match*: other 6s.
Positive expression: love of adventure
Negative expression: irresponsibility

Solar point

As a solar point the 69th produces daring explorers who set out early in life in search of their dreams. They are independent types but often prone to periods of loneliness until they find an adventurous mate, who could well come from a totally different background or culture. If you were to meet a native by chance on one of their frequent visits home from travels afar, you might think it strange that he or she could suffer from loneli-ness. Their bubbly personality makes it easy for them to make friends, though one might feel envious of all that they tell you they have seen and done. Because natives are gifted with the ability to enliven others and can easily make friends you may think this is a desirable fun degree. But beware, they are very footloose and can leave many broken promises in their wake as they search for whatever can give them the contentment they ultimately desire.

Planetary point

The 69th degree allows the planet placed here to project its energies into areas where it would not normally be apparent. So someone with Saturn here can be a speculator, though normally he would not be. He will take risks that would normally be considered unthinkable, or have a boistrous lifestyle quite unlike the quiet one expected from Saturn. Someone born with Uranus here could set out to destroy the world and end up saving it.

70th degree

Colour: blue. *Sign*: Gemini. 2nd decan. *Qualities*: Mutable/Fixed, Air. *Numerological match*: other 7s.
Positive expression: peacemaking
Negative expression: cowardice

Solar point

The 70th degree gives the ability to arbitrate and communicate and an intuitive canniness beyond the normal. People with this degree can come up with practical solutions to problems, whether they be trivial, everyday domestic quarrels or national political crises, which satisfy all parties but which nobody else thought of. They make excellent diplomats, politicians and salespeople, having the ability to sell the most outrageous products or get treaties accepted while giving the impression that the idea came originally from the other side.

As they are idealists and lovers of peace and tranquillity, they tend to reside out in the country areas and commute into town to work. Very often they have a keen interest in gardening. They are prone to giving in to the wishes of others in order to have a peaceful existence.

Planetary point

The 70th degree gives people born with a planet placed in it the ability to see both sides of any question or situation. Therefore they should know how to make the best use of their talents or gifts. For example, if the planet is Venus, they can choose either to be generous or selfish with their artistic gifts; they can either show off their ability or teach others how they might develop an artistic sense. Someone with Saturn can either become a recluse, or share his wisdom, and so on.

Colour: black. *Sign*: Gemini. 2nd decan. *Qualities*: Mutable/Fixed, Air. *Numerological match*: other 8s.
Positive expression: promotion of the arts
Negative expression: discontentment

Solar point

The 71st degree gives natives the ability to utilise and promote the artistic gifts of others rather than their own. Intuition and artistic sense can be strong but the desire for material security and independence will be stronger. Women born with this degree can, if they are so inclined, wind people around their little fingers, but that is a negative use of this degree. Most artistic people need agents or promoters as they are not good at selling themselves or their work, generally finding that aspect of things stressful and difficult to handle. A person with this degree has the ability to be an agent coupled with the essential understanding of the artistic temperament of their clients.

Not all people born with this degree become agents, artists or actors. What they do have in common, however, is that in some way they have the ability to bring out into the open the imaginary fears and secret problems of their mates and give them the strength to conquer them.

Planetary point

People who have a planet in this degree have the ability to express the more sensitive side of that planet without guilt or shame. For example, the Moon here can allow a person to be emotionally demonstrative, while Jupiter enables a person to share his wealth both in the material and spiritual sense.

72nd degree

Colour: crimson. *Sign*: Gemini. 2nd decan. *Qualities*: Mutable/Fixed, Air. *Numerological match*: other 9s.
Positive expression: energy, compassion
Negative expression: self-destruction

Solar point

People born with the Sun in the 72nd degree have a karmic lesson to learn. They have great energy to accomplish chosen tasks but tend to tackle too many things at a time. During childhood, they do not follow the advice of their elders.

There is also a danger that the child with this degree, through lack of sufficient stimulation at school, can lose interest in academic subjects and seek other outlets for his or her energy. If the teachers do not notice that the child is bored, he or she will be held back in their learning even though they are quite gifted. Then, as adults, the natives have problems because although they know they are capable of certain jobs, having failed to see their education through, lack of written qualifications prevents them following the careers they desire. If this energy is properly directed in youth these people become high earners and achievers in later life, but if it is not they tend to lag years behind their fellows, having to gain their qualifications the hard way.

Planetary point

Having a planet in the 72nd degree means you are allowed to have a second go at the things you fail at if they are connected with that planet. The Moon here could indicate a second chance at marriage. Mercury gives a second shoot at exams or a further chance in education, and so on.

73rd degree

Colour: white. *Sign*: Gemini. 2nd decan. *Qualities*: Mutable/Fixed, Air. *Numerological match*: other 1s.
Positive expression: independent thinking
Negative expression: trying to do the impossible

Solar point

The 73rd degree gives natives the ability to both generate and communicate new concepts and ideals. The mind is sharp and so is the tongue at times, though they take note of criticism and act upon it even if they do not like to admit it. They are best left to themselves while they think of their next project or path and are far better off working for themselves or in a position of authority rather than under others. However, they are more than ready to mix on a social level.

People with this birth vibration also like to have an intellectually strong partner to discuss their ideas with, and are sexually aroused through mental stimulation as much as physical. You will find them in many walks of life. The karmic lesson of the degree is to incite close associates or members of the family to do better while at the same time shouldering responsibility for them.

Planetary point

The 73rd degree gives persons with a planet resident in it the ability to be original in anything connected with that planet. For example, the Moon here can bring about unusual ways of expressing emotions.

74th degree

Colour: grey. *Sign*: Gemini. 2nd decan. *Qualities*: Mutable/ Fixed, Air. *Numerological match*: other 2s.
Positive expression: dependable partners
Negative expression: dependence upon others

Solar point

People born with the Sun in the 74th degree thrive when attached to someone they respect or when they have a career they really enjoy. They need to have a real love for what they are doing or else they find it very hard to accomplish what they set out to do. Born romantics who are a little bit more sensitive and caring than is the average, they generally become involved with the welfare of others in some way. In romance they make adoring and caring partners though they are prone to being possessive through fear of losing that which they love. If they work in commerce, they are best employed in the service industries, or better, to be in a business partnership with their spouse. Their creative ability is enough for them to become designers or actors. But I feel the ward sister caring for both her staff and patients better personifies this degree.

Planetary point

Having a planet in the 74th degree disposes that person to share with others the gifts connected with that particular planet. For example, Mercury here can create a chatterbox, or someone always ready to share his knowledge with others.

75th degree

Colour: violet. *Sign*: Gemini. 2nd decan. *Qualities*: Mutable/

Fixed, Air. *Numerological match*: other 3s.
Positive expression: literary ability
Negative expression: squandered education

Solar point

The 75th degree gives natives the ability to turn imaginative, forward-looking ideas into realities. These individuals are capable of finding imaginative ways of communicating their ideas or for that matter the ideas of others to both close associates and the masses. They would make very good teachers, advertising executives, writers, journalists, salespeople, newsagents or postmasters. They sometimes have difficulty in distinguishing what can be achieved from that which is not feasible or practical. Natives are great social mixers who constantly seek out new outlets for their own and their friends' leisure time, and have a good sense of humour, so they are rarely alone.

Planetary point

The 75th degree gives persons with a planet resident in it the ability to put the energy of that planet to practical use. Saturn in this degree means the native has the opportunity earlier rather than later in life to take on responsibility and attain a position of power. Someone with Venus here will be able to put his or her artistic ability to some practical use, such as painting scenery for a theatre or for amateur dramatics.

76th degree

Colour: orange. *Sign*: Gemini. 2nd decan. *Qualities*: Mutable/Fixed, Air. *Numerological match*: other 4s.
Positive expression: social conscience
Negative expression: emotional instability

Solar degree

The 76th degree's energy has many and varied applications. The native's imagination and sensitivity is, however, usually directed into some form of public service or social activity. Civil servants, policemen, social workers or firemen are the kind of people likely to have this degree active in their natal charts, but whatever the outlet they find they will in some way be of service to others. By owning a factory or business firm, for example, a native would supply goods or services for the rest of us.

At home, and away from the responsibility of their work the natives of this degree prefer a quiet life, yet even here they prefer to do their own chores, such as cooking or cleaning. Marriage for a person with this degree tends to be of the long-lasting type, as will be his or her career.

Planetary point

If there is a planet in the 76th degree natives are enabled to assist others according to the nature of that planet. The Moon here makes great parents and arbitrators, as they will have the emotional understanding to assist others. Someone having Mars here can use his physical energy to assist those less able to help themselves or to defend those who are oppressed.

77th degree

Colour: scarlet. *Sign*: Gemini. 2nd decan. *Qualities*: Mutable/Fixed, Air. *Numerological match*: other 5s.
Positive expression: humanitarian ideals
Negative expression: self-righteousness

Solar point

As a solar point the 77th is typified by the desire to save the world, the whale and other endangered species — and by the need for self-preservation. The energy present is best directed into some form of quest, task or adventure which will help safeguard the future of the living world and also give the native public recognition for his or her work. It is not so much that persons with this degree are self-centred, they just need to feel that what they do is of use to themselves. In saving the whale, or an endangered species, they are in reality saving themselves by finding a cause which in some way reflects how they feel others treat them. Ecologists and vegetarians, who refuse to eat meat, in reality fear that society may devour them unless they can communicate to society that such behaviour is wrong. This vibration finds its best expression through humanitarianism.

Planetary point

The 77th degree indicates by the planet resident in it where the native's insecurities lie. Mercury may indicate an inability to explain logically his or her fears or find a reason for them. With Jupiter here, natives may find it difficult to trust others with their money or possessions.

78th degree

Colour: green. *Sign*: Gemini. 2nd decan. *Qualities*: Mutable/
Fixed, Air. *Numerological match*: other 6s.
Positive expression: protectiveness, ambition
Negative expression: manipulation of others

Solar point

The 78th degree gives natives the ability to manipulate others
for good or ill. Those who put this birth energy to constructive
use become the managers, supervisors and organisers of our
society, but the temptation to misuse it is too strong for many to
resist. If you were born with this degree, no matter what walk of
life you find yourself in, be you rich man, poor man, beggarman
or thief, you will find yourself saddled with the responsibility of
organising and managing not only those close to you but also
those you come into contact with both socially and at work.
Managers rather than leaders, politicians rather than prime
ministers, those of you born with this vibration take on the
karma of many, but the public recognition will always tend to
go to others. Accept these responsibilities and the Kingdom of
Heaven is yours in the next world.

Planetary point

If you have a planet in the 78th degree, it shows in which area of
your life responsibility for others will manifest. Jupiter here
could indicate that a large sum of money or estate is left in your
hands, while the Moon would indicate loving care of others,
especially as a mother. Saturn in this degree is indicative of
moral responsibility for society as a whole.

79th degree

Colour: blue. *Sign*: Gemini. 2nd decan. *Qualities*: Mutable/
Fixed, Air. *Numerological match*: other 7s.
Positive expression: imagination, energy
Negative expression: self-destructive energy

Solar point

People born with the Sun in the 79th degree are both highly
imaginative and energetic. They can use this energy to create a
lifestyle of their own design and choice through enthusiasm and

hard work, turning the dreams of childhood into adult realities.

The native of this degree will use persuasion or even force to obtain their wishes if others should oppose them. Eventually they reap as they have sown. One only need remember that if the seeds are sown on fertile soil, i.e. desirable projects are nurtured, then success will come with a little effort. However, if seeds are sown on infertile land, or natives seek to obtain what was meant for others, then they will find only disappointment and isolation, for others will avoid them.

People with this degree are to be found in all walks of life. A native can be born a pauper and become rich, or be born rich and die poor; the choice is in his or her own hands.

Planetary point

A planet placed in this degree indicates in what direction success may be found. Saturn here would indicate success through City stocks, the mining industry, or farming, while Mercury would indicate success through higher education and communications such as the press, advertising or travel.

80th degree

Colour: black. *Sign*: Gemini. 3rd decan. *Qualities*: Mutable/Cardinal, Air. *Numerological match*: other 8s.
Positive expression: financial success
Negative expression: extravagance

Solar point

Those born with the Sun in the 80th degree become mature at a young age and are gifted with much patience and perseverance and an ability to communicate their wishes and desires.

If you were born with this degree you may have caused concern during your childhood as you would not have mixed readily with others of your own age group and therefore could have been a loner. Such a start in life, however, can give one determination to suceed in adult life. Your aim would be to achieve material security early on and to retire at an age when you could still enjoy it.

Marriage for natives of this degree is usually late rather than early; the late thirties onwards is most usual. But even though the marriage may be late it is nearly always long-lasting, for when a person born with this vibration makes a promise it is binding.

Planetary point

The 80th degree brings the energies of a planet resident in it to natives' attention in such a way as to develop a mature or serious disposition. For example, Venus here produces loyal devoted parents and partners, while Jupiter can produce a financial wizard or philosopher. Saturn here is ill placed and sometimes produces an eccentric loner who finds it hard to trust others.

81st degree

Colour: crimson. *Sign*: Gemini. 3rd decan. *Qualities*: Mutable/Cardinal, Air. *Numerological match*: other 9s.
Positive expression: inventiveness, purposeful action
Negative expression: childish pranks

Solar point

As a solar point the 81st creates a hive of activity both mental and physical. People born with this solar energy are both inventers and planners, and like to do their own chores. But they have a tendency to be impatient both with themselves if things do not go right and with others for not doing things quicker. Dynamic and forceful, they are capable of directing their energy so that it is of assistance to others. Independent managers of their own affairs, they can become aggressive, if they feel people are interfering when it isn't their business.

Long-term careers such as with the Army or in large corporations where there is some scope for advancement and promotion suit people with this degree. They have ambitions to fulfill and also seek an income to match.

Planetary point

Whoever has a planet in the 81st degree should have the energy and inventiveness to put that planet to good use. For example Uranus here enables a native to learn to handle one task or idea at a time rather than dissipating his energy on many projects.

82nd degree

Colour: white. *Sign*: Gemini. 3rd decan. *Qualities*: Mutable/Cardinal, Air. *Numerological match*: other 1s
Positive expression: care for others

Negative expression: self-preservation

Solar point

As a solar point the 82nd creates an individual with moral strength. Persons with this gift are required not only to use it to the benefit of their fellow men but to set other people an example in the way they conduct their lives.

Outwardly often brash or bombastic and stern when necessary, people born with this degree are little understood by those who fail to measure up to their high standards. This is, however, of no importance to them and they should learn to think of their greater task in life rather than dwell on how they feel others see them. Being independent types who work at their best when left alone or under pressure, they are suited for professional occupations such as accountancy or banking.

If you happen to be married to someone born with this solar degree, you have a faithful partner who expects equal loyalty in return and, although your spouse may appear to let you have the upper hand at times he or she is always in charge of his or her own destiny.

Planetary point

Most people born with a planet in the 82nd degree have the ability to discriminate between the good and bad uses of the planet. Jupiter here prompts the native to share his wealth and knowledge with others rather than hoard it all for his own benefit. The energy of Mars can be put to use by building something rather than tearing down what others have created.

83rd degree

Colour: grey. *Sign*: Gemini. 3rd decan. *Qualities*: Mutable/ Cardinal, Air. *Numerological match*: other 2s.
Positive expression: care and compassion
Negative expression: greed

Solar point

As a solar point the 83rd offers people born with it the ability to care for others and in so doing look after their own interests. Although businesslike, they actually have one predominant motive — to attain enough material security so that they may find their mate and live out a peaceful existence. They are found in many walks of life though generally thrive in any occupation which allows them to show their kindness and sensitivity. They will not allow spongers or cheats to take advantage of them, however. Nursing would be a very suitable occupation for these people.

On the negative side, persons with this birth degree may act in a spiteful manner if they feel that their chosen companion is playing around or betraying their trust. They are great mothers and fathers who shower their children with affection.

Planetary point

People with a planet in the 83rd degree care about what others think or feel about them and what they do. With the Moon here, there would be a need for others to recognise their caring for others or they would lose the desire to do so. With Saturn, they need others to recognise their material achievements.

84th degree

Colour: violet. *Sign*: Gemini. 3rd decan. *Qualities*: Mutable/Cardinal, Air. *Numerological match*: other 3s.
Positive expression: guardianship of inherited wealth
Negative expression: boasting, self-satisfaction

Solar point

The 84th degree gives people born with it the ability to gain success through their historical past. It may be that they take over the family business or follow in their father's footsteps, or simply are inspired to do what someone else in their family had done before. A love of the arts, philosophy and history motivates these people to read a good deal and to be well informed, and this gives them a firm bed on which to build their futures. They are by no means stick-in-the-muds, however. With anything to do with history, their enjoyment comes from either reliving it in the imagination or visiting and exploring old buildings.

Children are much loved by natives of this degree though some tend only to work with them rather than have their own, but most do enjoy a full and happy marriage or partnership.

Planetary point

Having a planet in the 84th degree makes natives more mature and experienced, and furthers spiritual development. Someone with Mercury in this degree can have an excellent memory and much common sense even while still young. And the normally wasted energy of Mars may be concentrated to tackle one task at a time for greater success.

85th degree

Colour: orange. *Sign*: Gemini. 3rd decan. *Qualities*: Mutable/Cardinal, Air. *Numerological match*: other 4s.
Positive expression: strong intellect
Negative expression: cunning, guile

Solar point

The 85th degree gives the native a sharp intelligence and a good memory. Providing there is early parental encouragement, the mental faculties should develop much above the average bringing success as an adult through research and the sciences. If, however, the abilities are not recognised and become stifled, then the native can become involved in other outlets where a sharp mind is needed to avoid being caught by those in authority. This does not mean that the negative use of this energy is criminal in the legal sense, but it could be morally questionable.

On the domestic side, this energy will manifest itself through management of the housekeeping and finances of the family, but this would be only using the energy at a quarter of its potential.

The self-made millionaire or businessman with no academic qualifications who manages to become self-employed after unsuccessful employment with others can also be attributed to this type of energy.

Planetary point

The degree sharpens the energy of the planet in residence. For example, natives with Saturn here could mature and succeed earlier in life, but on the other hand they might tend to overestimate their own ability. If Venus is here, their artistic talents could be put to good use, though vanity might cause a downfall.

86th degree

Colour: scarlet. *Sign*: Gemini. 3rd decan. *Qualities*: Mutable/Cardinal, Air. *Numerological match*: other 5s.
Positive expression: persuasiveness, stability.
Negative expression: self-aggrandisement

Solar point

As a solar point the 86th gives natives the ability to communicate through the arts or literary pursuits. The imagination and wit are versatile though not always in good taste. They are sometimes prone to wheedling their way into people's confidence, causing them to part with money or sign contracts that they will later regret.

One of the chief characteristic of people with the sun in this degree is that they crave stability and are prepared to use everything at their disposal to achieve their aims short of openly breaking the law of the land, and even that is possible if they feel they can get away with it. Selling, advertising and similar work would best suit these people, giving them the satisfaction that they require as well as good money — which may run through their fingers, though very often it is invested wisely for future expansion.

Planetary point

People who have a planet in the 86th degree are prone to conceal facets of their personality until the time is right to reveal them. Someone with the Moon here, for example, can appear to be hard boiled at work but be soft at home. A person who has Mercury here could be chatty with clients at work but be taciturn at home.

87th degree

Colour: green. *Sign*: Gemini. 3rd decan. *Qualities*: Mutable/Cardinal, Air. *Numerological match*: other 6s.
Positive expression: innovation, sensitivity
Negative expression: introversion

Solar point

People born with the Sun in the 87th degree get wonderful new ideas, and it is then left to others to follow them through. On the mundane level the person with this degree can be extremely lazy and yet show a remarkable ability for motivating others to do his or her own work. At a higher level, however, natives of this degree become originators or inventors, benefiting or affecting all of us in some way. Work in offices rather than outdoors suits them as they require a base to operate from. Union leaders or officials, town planners and party political workers often have this degree's energy. They are the motivators or planners of others, though this does not mean they will not work in a physical sense at achieving their aims; if they can organise others to do the work for them, they will.

Planetary point

The 87th degree adds inventiveness and organisation to the energy of the planet placed in it. Someone with Mercury here could discover or invent different ways to communicate old ideas. Those older people among us who have Pluto here may have set out in the course of their lives to update the laws of their day, or to seek different modes to sexual expression.

88th degree

Colour: blue. *Sign*: Gemini. 3rd decan. *Qualities*: Mutable/Cardinal, Air. *Numerological match*: other 7s.
Positive expression: creative management
Negative expression: karmic debts to pay

Solar point

As a solar point the 88th has two possible expressions: either failure or dissatisfaction, due to the karmic consequences of a previous life; or the capacity of one who has learned from mistakes made in past lives to teach others not to err in the same way. So people of this degree may be either spiritual leaders in the positive sense or karmic prisoners in the negative.

If you have this solar degree and you tend to fail or have only moments of joy in your life, then the indication is that you have a karmic debt to pay. But if you pay it to the full you will overcome your failings sooner. On the other hand, if you shy away from the responsibility you have brought upon yourself you will carry it on to your next existence. On the positive side, you can further the spiritual growth of others through doing work with young people or for religious orders or similar activities in your spare time.

Planetary point

The 88th degree indicates by the planet resident in it where a person either failed or succeeded in a previous existence. Venus here indicates whether natives gave love and companionship to those in need, while Jupiter indicates that they saved or squandered their wealth, and so on.

Colour: black. *Sign*: Gemini. 3rd decan. *Qualities*: Mutable/
Cardinal, Air. *Numerological match*: other 8s.
Positive expression: business acumen
Negative expression: mismanagement of others

Solar degree

If you were born with your solar energy in the 89th degree you
are gifted with the ability to both manage your own life and that
of others in some way, be it at home, work or play. Others look
on you as being bossy. This, however, is not always the case, as
you tend to work for the betterment of all which sometimes
makes it necessary to crack your whip. Just make sure that
those you employ or work with respect and understand what
you are trying to accomplish and then the problems you encounter should fade away. Try to avoid those moments of
despondency when you feel that all are against you. It is only
because they don't understand what you are trying to do for
both them and yourself.

People with this degree often come to own a business, and
may acquire considerable wealth.

Planetary point

If you have a planet in this degree it is an indicator of where you
may find the success you seek or the help you require. Mars
would indicate travel or short-lived business projects rather
than long-term employment in one job. Mercury would indicate
that higher education or a return to study would further your
prospects.

90th degree

Colour: crimson. *Sign*: Cancer. 1st decan. *Qualities*: Cardinal,
Water. *Numerological match*: other 9s.
Positive expression: responsiveness
Negative expression: irritability

Solar point

The 90th degree produces natives who are full of activity but
also are highly emotional. They are bold, fearless, ambitious
and industrious, but they tend to be irritable, have frequent

emotional outbursts and are easily offended. They are inclined to bear grudges against those who do them wrong. Other characteristics that they have in common are sensuality and luxury.

If you were born with this solar degree you may rebel against those in authority, feeling that they are not interested in knowing abour your point of view or what your real needs are. Problems usually stem from insufficient attention from your mother in your early childhood or a quarrel which forced you to leave home before you were really ready. You must learn to overcome your inadequacies and develop your individuality, for it is the lesson of this degree that you should build your own foundations in life rather than have others provide them for you.

Planetary point

If you have a planet in the 90th degree you would have the ability to use the energy of that planet to break free from environmental restrictions. For example, Mars or Jupiter here could suggest travel could bring success that is unobtainable where you were born.

91st degree

Colour: white. *Sign*: Cancer. 1st decan. *Qualities*: Cardinal, Water. *Numerological match*: other 1s.
Positive expression: authoritative care.
Negative expression: inability to mix

Solar point

The 91st degree gives natives the ability to take charge of other people, offer them advice and solve their problems. They are neither the greatest listeners nor the most patient of people, yet they always seem to find themselves in some way drawn into the emotional entanglements of friends and neighbours. This propensity leads to these people becoming the managers and supervisors of care related industries. You frequently find the degree active among solicitors, hospital matrons and civil servants.

People born with this degree do not work well when closely supervised or dominated in partnerships. If they do seek out a partner, it will be one who can help them bear the load of responsibilities they sometimes carry.

Although well able to solve other people's emotional problems, natives can have difficulty in expressing their own.

Planetary point

The 91st degree indicates by the planet placed in it how a person is best suited to help care for others. The Moon here would indicate emotional support in domestic situations, while Saturn would suggest managerial or business skills. Uranus here nearly always indicates that that native will learn through his or her own mistakes.

92nd degree

Colour: grey. *Ruler*: Cancer. 1st decan. *Qualities*: Cardinal, Water. *Numerological match*: other 2s.
Positive expression: moral strength
Negative expression: psychological distress

Solar point

Natives of the 92nd solar degree have much to learn on the domestic front. Disharmony, unpleasantness and quarrels in the early home life cause them to set out to build all the things they imagined their home should have been. This creates an imbalance which can only be remedied through personal experience. Those who are strong win through, realising that such dreams are for bedtime and nothing to do with the realities of the world we live in. Those, however, who chase their dreams and fail to find what they seek, can become mentally or emotionally unstable and perhaps suffer a nervous breakdown.

The karmic lesson is quite straightforward: use the strengths acquired during your tough childhood to build up a new future and you should attain all you desire; but dwell in the past, trying to create the home that never was, and you will find it never really can be.

Planetary point

If you have a planet in the 92nd degree it indicates how you might attain domestic contentment. Mars would indicate a strong partner to protect you from future bangs and knocks, while Venus would indicate a more tolerant partner who is able to understand and cope with your emotional insecurity.

Colour: violet. *Sign*: Cancer. 1st decan. *Qualities*: Cardinal, Water. *Numerological match*: other 3s.
Positive expression: adaptability, philosophic interests
Negative expression: perpetual wandering

Solar point

The 93rd degree has two clear cut expressions. Either early experiences teach the natives of this degree to look upon the bright side of life and to adapt to changing environments and situations. They are optimistic, quickly forget past troubles and soon overcome any obstacles in their path. They thoroughly enjoy all the good things in their lives and don't burden themselves too much with guilt about their failings. These people can be found in most walks of life and tend to greet all with a happy smile.

Or, on the negative side, there are natives who will spend so much time brooding over what they have failed to accomplish that they have no energy left for tackling anything else and there is the constant fear of failing yet again. This type finds it difficult to settle down and is apt to wander through life from place to place.

Planetary point

The 93rd degree gives to anyone with a planet resident in it optimism and a philosophic outlook to overcome the problems that planet may cause. If Neptune is here, it allows the native to draw from the positive imagination and the psychic senses rather than dwell in negative thoughts and feeling. If Saturn is resident, natives are helped to face up to the responsibilities placed upon them by the planet.

94th degree

Colour: orange. *Sign*: Cancer. 1st decan. *Qualities*: Cardinal, Water. *Numerological match*: other 4s.
Positive expression: home building
Negative expression: domestic tyranny

Solar point

Those born under the 94th degree use much of their time and

energy in constructing a stable base or home from which to operate and which they will then protect. Many proud home owners, construction workers, people in the furniture industry and building societies have links with this degree as they are involved in institutions which make secure homes possible. But this does not mean that everyone born with this degree will work in similar fields. The source of income is immaterial; it must merely satisfy the native's financial needs, allowing them to lay the foundation for future stability. Once this has been achieved those of you born with this degree are more than able to go out and enjoy the rest of the world knowing that your castle is always there should problems occur.

The negative side of this degree causes natives to seek others to provide their security.

Planetary point

The 94th degree indicates by the planet placed there how natives may build a secure base. Venus would point to careers connected with the arts or literature, while Mercury would suggest office-type environments or work in communications.

95th degree

Colour: scarlet. *Sign*: Cancer. 1st decan. *Qualities*: Cardinal, Water. *Numerological match*: other 5s.
Positive expression: compassion, understanding
Negative expression: irresponsibility, selfishness

Solar point

A characteristic of people born with the Sun in the 95th degree is that they have much to say and do but rarely enough time to do it. Many of them tend to travel away from the place of birth, marry and settle down overseas or wander for years before returning home to find their roots. Although somewhat adventurous for the sign of Cancer, they still retain a deep affection for the place of their birth and the old family home. However, they are just as eager to explore those places of childhood dreams from which some may never return.

They are articulate and expressive when communicating with people. Foreign diplomats, journalists, travel couriers and romantic novelists, who explore within their minds rather than on the land, are likely types to have an affinity with this degree.

Natives are often outwardly bombastic with a caustic tongue to go with their sharp wit but, if you trouble to look beneath the surface, you will find beneath it all a heart of gold.

Planetary point

People with a planet in the 95th degree are allowed to explore and communicate to others an understanding of that particular planet's energy. Jupiter here allows natives to expand their horizons through getting to know other cultures, while Mercury would allow them to introduce foreign concepts to their own circles.

96th degree

Colour: green. *Ruler*: Cancer. 1st decan. *Qualities*: Cardinal, Water. *Numerological match*: other 6s.
Positive expression: good taste, energy
Negative expression: vanity, laziness

Solar point

Those born with the Sun in the 96th degree have been endowed with a love of the arts, though often not participating in any of them. There may be an interest in poetry, literature, music and the fine arts, or just enjoyment of a good play on the television. Their homes are normally tastefully decorated and their furniture, though perhaps antique and valuable, is still of practical use in the home.

Natives with this degree tend to fluctuate between periods of great activity and of utter laziness where even the housework can become neglected. Partnerships, though strife-torn at times, tend to be long lasting and the children can be spoiled beyond belief.

Art critics, quality controllers, art dealers or antique collectors are often born with this degree active in their birth chart. Many females with this degree can show marked physical beauty.

Planetary point

When someone has a planet in the 96th degree, they are able to bring artistic expression or interpretation to the effects of the planet placed in it. For example, with Pluto here, they can laugh in the face of adversity, while with Mars the planet's energy can be turned to artistic construction. When the Moon is here it can indicate marriage to an older person.

97th degree

Colour: blue. *Sign*: Cancer. 1st decan. *Qualities*: Cardinal, Water. *Numerological match*: other 7s.
Positive expression: intuition
Negative expression: anxiety

Solar point

The 97th degree gives a fondness for curiosities and travel, for occult and metaphysical subjects and favours marine activities and aquatic sports. It increases the generosity, strengthens the emotions and enthusiasm and creates a desire for mysticism, romance and adventure. It is a positive degree for those connected with water, liquids, beverages, oil, drugs, chemicals, hospitals, sanitariums, the sea and with the occult in a practical manner.

The degree can cause changes of residence and a peculiar domestic life or secrets regarding the home life. Inheritance through the parents or mystical gifts are typical benefits brought about by this degree. The health of natives can be affected through the nervous system, especially in later life, so they should endeavour to avoid stressful occupations. Being highly impressionable, they can become the dupes of unscrupulous salesmen. If you were born with this degree make sure you check the small print in contracts. Partners are often unresponsive to the deep emotions of the natives.

Planetary point

As a planetary point the 97th indicates where the natives may suffer danger or loss. Mars here would suggest by bribery or false accusation or arrest, whereas Jupiter indicates loss of property.

98th degree

Colour: black. *Sign*: Cancer. 1st decan. *Qualities*: Cardinal, Water. *Numerological match*: other 8s.
Positive expression: confidentiality, determination
Negative expression: material losses

Solar point

As a solar point the 98th teaches the native to deal with land, wealth and property. Gain can come in business through the acquisition of land, mines and any property that is valuable because it is old or antique. If the Sun is well aspected in the chart, this degree is favourable for the attainment of positions of trust and responsibility, notably in public life, through persistent effort. The approval of parents, friends and superiors, is important for success, however.

The negative application of this degree can cause loss through speculation. Also, the native may feel persecuted or become involved in some scandal, which results in loss of approval and the withdrawal of the support of his or her peers. Natives can marry more than once with consequent loss of property and possessions.

Planetary point

The 97th degree indicates by the planet resident in it how the native may acquire security. Jupiter would indicate that service to others would bring financial rewards and the attainment of executive positions. Mars would indicate military service or any kind of officialdom, but there is always a danger of sudden loss.

99th degree

Colour: crimson. *Sign*: Cancer. 1st decan. *Qualities*: Cardinal, Water. *Numerological match*: other 9s.
Positive expression: bravery, ardour, resolution
Negative expression: foolhardiness

Solar point

The 99th degree offsets many of the supposedly emotional problems of Cancer. People born with the Sun here are ambitious, energetic, firm and resolute. The degree makes the body strong, increases the vitality and is good for those whose work requires strength or for outdoor occupations. Success and promotion come through resourcefulness and enterprise in business. Good results are more likely to be achieved by quick action on the spur of the moment rather than through decisions made in a planning department. Unlike many Cancerians, people born with this solar degree possess common sense and, through hard work, inspire confidence and trust in others. The negative use of this solar energy can make natives brave but headstrong. Their rash actions and words may subsequently cause them deep regret. The degree is also associated with unusual sexual appetites.

Planetary point

A planet in the 99th degree indicates the area in which natives should channel their energies. Uranus here denotes spiritualism, psychism, healing and telepathy, electronics and computer technology, while Venus or Mercury points to the fine arts, instrumental music or singing.

100th degree

Colour: white. *Sign*: Cancer. 2nd decan. *Qualities*: Cardinal/ Fixed, Water. *Numerological match*: other 1s.
Positive expression: sincerity, loyalty
Negative expression: over-confidence

Solar point

As a solar point the 100th degree gives natives sincerity and loyalty, and strengthens the constitution in both sexes, while allowing them the adaptability and strength of character necessary to realise their ambitions. If you were born with this degree you are unlikely to have difficulty in obtaining employment or mixing socially. Your pleasant personality inspires confidence in others and through the use of influential friends you should be able to obtain a job with a high salary, especially as you have a good managerial ability.

People with this degree are good savers. They can make financial gains through speculative ventures, investments and enterprises in conjunction with their marital partner. They usually get what they want in the long term but should never be considered easy prey for, although slow to anger, once aroused and they take action it is in a decisive manner.

The negative effect of this degree is difficulty in maintaining worthwhile employment. The natives may make rash decisions based on over-confidence.

Planetary point

The 100th degree gives whoever has a planet resident in it the personal qualities, such as leadership, for them to succeed.

With Saturn here, promising areas would be land, stocks, shares, large corporations or work with the aged. Jupiter denotes achievement through religion, philosophy and the higher mind.

101st degree

Colour: grey. *Sign*: Cancer. 2nd decan. *Qualities*: Cardinal/ Fixed, Water. *Numerological match: other 2s.*
Positive expression: popularity, success
Negative expression: deception, mental strain

Solar point

People with the Sun in the 101st degree are well placed for gaining benefit through parents, the home and domestic life and from the opposite sex. They are popular and make friends easily. This is a good thing as there can be many changes of residence before they settle down.

Typically, the native is agreeable and kind to all, and in some instances may become elected to some position of prestige or honour. There can be a love of travel but the native of this degree is always happy to get home again. There can be heightened sensitivity, which can be good or bad, for although the natives can laugh hard and joyously, when they cry their grief can be very deep indeed. They tend to choose work in the medical field or the welfare services or in any form of service to others that can bring them honour or reward.

Negative use of this energy can cause mental disorders or breakdown or an inability to maintain relationships.

Planetary point

The 101st degree shows by the planet placed in it how natives may serve others and also attain their own success. Jupiter here can indicate this is by making contributions to charities or in management of the home, while with Mercury's communicative gifts, domestic disputes can be readily settled.

102nd degree

Colour: violet. *Ruler*: Cancer. 2nd decan. *Qualities*: Cardinal/ Fixed, Water. *Numerological match*: other 3s.
Positive expression: fertility, resourcefulness
Negative expression: misplaced confidence

Solar point

As a solar point the 102nd increases the native's imagination, intuition and appreciation of beauty. It indicates usually an ability to make sound judgements through logic and reasoning power. It also increases the native's vitality, fertility and resourcefulness and inclines him or her towards honesty, benevolence and compassion, creating a sociable and generous individual who is therefore popular.

People with this degree are found in most walks of life. Success can come through literature but is more likely to come through the House that the Sign of Cancer occupies at birth. Happiness in marriage and good health, with financial gain through the mother and family later in life, is also indicated.

The negative effect of the degree leads the native to misplace his or her confidence in others, with resulting losses, lawsuits and adverse circumstances.

Planetary point

The 102nd degree indicates where individuals failed to exert themselves in previous existences. The Moon here denotes a need to become more emotionally stable or expressive in this life. Jupiter is indicative of natives' need to support both themselves and others financially rather than relying on others.

103rd degree

Colour: orange. *Sign*: Cancer. 2nd decan. *Qualities*: Cardinal/Fixed, Water. *Numerological match*: other 4s.
Positive expression: scientific leanings, originality
Negative expression: impulsiveness, abruptness

Solar point

Someone with the Sun in the 103rd degree is characterised as being active, firm, enterprising and scientific, and also very fond of the opposite sex. There may be interest in the occult sciences such as astrology and numerology but even if this is not present the mind can be intuitively sharp in solving problems. The degree favours work for larger corporations while still maintaining a certain amount of personal freedom and choice of environments. An example is the work of a lorry driver who hauls for a large firm and journeys to stimulatingly different places but still has the freedom to drive to his destination in his own time by his chosen route. Computer technology, electrical engineering and similar fields could be good areas of employment for the native.

This is one degree of the sign of Cancer in which the natives can feel at home in many different places. Home is often where they find themselves at any particular time.

Planetary point

The 103rd degree gives anyone who has a planet resident in it the ability to accept new ideas and technology, according to the particular planet. For example, with Pluto here they are well placed for accepting the sexual changes society has seen of late, while with Mercury they are able to climb down and admit they can be wrong and accept the viewpoints of others, and so on.

104th degree

Colour: scarlet. *Ruler*: Cancer. 2nd decan. *Qualities*: Cardinal/Fixed, Water. *Numerological match*: other 5s
Positive expression: perceptiveness
Negative expression: over-sensitivity

Solar degree

The 104th endows those born with the Sun here with exceptional mental powers. Natives possess a quick wit and are keen to know about what is happening around them. They are also diligent when set a problem to be solved, resting only when the task is completed. Versatile and expressive, people born with this degree learn easily and seem to pick up languages with particular ease.

People born with this solar degree are also fond of change and respond readily to suggestions of adventure from others, which is always less of a risk for them with their ability to weigh up the consequences of their actions better than most.

If you were born with this degree and suffer anxity, worry and turbulent states of mind, then you are failing to find outlets for your mental abilities and should do so quickly if you are to keep your sanity.

Planetary point

Having a planet in this degree sharpens whatever ability is especially connected with it, allowing natives to find new avenues of expression. Uranus here could help a person to hold down two jobs or run two homes, while Saturn enables a native to loosen his belt, relax a moralistic attitudes and rekindle lost youth by having a good time with others.

105th degree

Colour: green. *Sign*: Cancer. 2nd decan. *Qualities*: Cardinal/ Fixed, Water. *Numerological match*: other 6s.
Positive expression: good nature
Negative expression: careless habits causing strife

Solar point

The 105th degree bestows on any person born with the Sun here a kind and cheerful disposition, pleasing manners and good taste in clothes. There can be a fondness for nature, pets, music and artistic expression. Natives with this degree can also have a fondness for light literature, drama and social engagements. They get on well with the opposite sex. They enjoy social outings, have many friends and are generally popular.

Found in most occupations, their success tends to come through an engaging personality and cheerfulness at work. They have a flair for knowing what the public needs and wants and would do well in work connected with confectionary, and in hotels, restaurants, boarding houses and catering for others in general. Work involving the buying and selling of houses and land could also suit them.

Planetary point

The 105th degree shows where gains could be made according to which planet is placed in it. Mars here could indicate legacies or the commodity markets. Jupiter in this degree is favourable for the acquisition of possessions through marriage and possible gain through areas connected with the occult, spiritual matters or publishing.

106th degree

Colour: blue. *Sign*: Cancer. 2nd decan. *Qualities*: Cardinal/ Fixed, Water. *Numerological match*: other 7s
Positive expression: inspiration, artistic ability
Negative expression: nervous disorders

Solar point

The 106th solar degree gives natives strong inspirational qualities and a good imagination. There can be pronounced mediumistic qualities, too, which may draw the native into investigating spiritualism, psychism and the mysteries of nature, or
perhaps go in for some form of occult study. They would make
particularly good psychometrists, being sensitive to impress-
ions, though they can be too sensitive and over-emotional at
times, when they sense something is wrong without understanding why.

If this degree is well aspected in the natal chart there can be
an aptitude for music, art, public speaking or acting. If aspects
are bad, there can be nervous disorders which may affect the
body which result from a reaction to environmental stresses. A
tendency to let impulse override reason, with consequent acts
of indiscretion, can eventually lead to eccentricity and irrational
behaviour if not checked.

Planetary point

The planetary placement shows how psychic faculties or the
imagination may be best utilised, or indicates where problems
may occur. Pluto here can indicate a tendency to moodiness or
depression because of a lack of physical expression. Venus or
Jupiter here point to artistic ability which may be utilised to
bring some degree of success.

107th degree

Colour: black. *Sign*: Cancer. 2nd decan. *Qualities*: Cardinal/
Fixed, Water. *Numerological match*: other 8s.
Positive expression: industriousness, thoughtfulness
Negative expression: fault-finding, sanctimoniousness

Solar point

As a solar point the 107th creates serious, thoughtful natives
not given to gaiety and social interaction with others till they
feel they have acquired material security. Nevertheless they are
popular and respected by their peers for the industrious and
productive example they set. They tend to achieve results by
diplomacy and careful attention to detail rather than by impulsive gambles.

Most people born with this solar degree attain some position of authority and respect in recognition of their hard work be that as head of a household or of a business concern. As far as their deep inner feelings are concerned, this is a side of themselves they rarely express openly or reveal to others unless they have earned their trust and respect. Loners in their early years, natives of this degree tend to make up for lost social activity after the age of 40.

Planetary point

The planet placed in this degree indicates in what way the native must learn to be self-reliant. The Moon here would indicate that the person relied too heavily on others for emotional support in a previous existence, while Jupiter would indicate that he or she must learn to cope with their own financial problems.

108th degree

Colour: crimson. *Ruler*: Cancer. 2nd decan. *Qualities*: Cardinal/Fixed, Water. *Numerological match*: other 9s
Positive expression: ambition
Negative expression: hasty temper

Solar point

As a solar point the 108th gives to natives a physical strength and versatility not normally associated with the Sign of Cancer. Confidence replaces the shyness usually found with this Sign and the natives may be seen far away from the place of birth, home and family safety. Resourceful and enterprising, they have the ability to pick themselves up and begin anew if they should fail in business, romance or any area of their lives. Being highly self-critical but not able to take advice from others can often cause people to misunderstand them and even avoid them. However, they do have the emotional qualities of Cancer though it may be that they rarely have the time to express them. Being Jacks of all trades or at least willing to have a go results in these people being found in various kinds of occupation.

People with this degree tend to possess romantic partners and they expect them to keep their vows. If they do not, their love will turn to hate.

Planetary point

As a planetary point the 108th shows where natives may best

direct their energy, according to which planet is in residence. Saturn would indicate a steady rise to success and the acquirement of land and property. Mercury would show that travel will bring rewards.

109th degree

Colour: white. *Sign*: Cancer. 2nd decan. *Qualities*: Cardinal/Fixed, Water. *Numerological match*: other 1s.
Positive expression: sincerity, adaptability
Negative expression: over-protectiveness

Solar point

The 109th solar degree makes sincere, loyal and prosperous natives who, if they utilise all they have been given, soon rise to a position of influence and authority and reach the top earning bracket in their field of work.

This degree gives the native the chance to put to good use all that was learned in previous incarnations. Those lessons that were not well learned have to be gone through again this time round.

If you were born with this degree, you will be well rewarded for your hard work and fruitful endeavours. If, however, you find you are having no success in your life, then you have nobody to blame but yourself. You have all the ingredients for a happy and contented life and the realisation of your dreams and ambitions, but you are not using your gifts and abilities to the full.

Planetary point

The 109th degree indicates by the planet in residence how a native may reap rewards. Venus here could see someone as a collector or dealer in the arts or antiques, while Jupiter could shower a person with money through luck alone.

110th degree

Colour: grey. *Sign*: Cancer. 3rd decan. *Qualities*: Cardinal/Mutable, Water. *Numerological match*: other 2s.
Positive expression: home building
Negative expression: emotional instability

Solar point

Those of you born with the 110th degree active prefer to walk along the lines of least resistance. You are sociable and friendly, and, more than is found in most birth degrees, attached to the home or family.

Natives are sensitive and have warmth of feeling. However, they should choose their friends with care as they tend to be all too readily influenced by them. They often have some acting ability, and indeed are inclined to dramatise too much in daily life. There is also a danger of insincerity, not showing others how they really feel. It is better to express emotions as they are rather than how you feel others would like to see them.

The sensitivity of this degree finds its best expression through service to others.

Planetary point

The 110th degree indicates by the planet placed here what natives have in most abundance and are capable of sharing with others. Mercury here would indicate an intellectual understanding of others' needs and problems and would point to some form of advisory career. Venus would suggest that the arts could be used to help others forget their troubles for a while.

111th degree

Colour: violet. *Sign*: Cancer. 3rd decan. *Qualities*: Cardinal/ Mutable, Water. *Numerological match*: other 3s.
Positive expression: generosity, benevolence
Negative expression: egocentricity

Solar point

The 111th solar degree creates ambitious and enterprising individuals. They are also good humoured, sympathetic and charitable, and their sociable nature makes them popular with their fellows and also with those above them who are in a position to advance them.

People with this degree tend to have an intellectual outlook and a fondness for fine arts and cultural entertainments. They are patriotic and interested in public welfare, and many have been noted for their investigations into the occult and psychic fields.

While showing a fondness for the family home, there is also a likelihood of travel to distant parts. Best gains are made for natives in public work through mental ability and, if the planetary aspects in the chart agree, through investment, inheritance, property or marriage.

Planetary point

If there is a planet in the 111th degree it indicates where the native should direct his or her mental energy. With Uranus here, the native can turn his inventive mind to great new discoveries through the sciences, while Mercury would indicate some form of teaching, governmental or welfare work, and the keeping of records.

112th degree

Colour: orange. *Sign*: Cancer. 3rd decan. *Qualities*: Cardinal/Mutable, Water. *Numerological match*: other 4s.
Positive expression: originality, inventiveness
Negative expression: unpredictability, moodiness

Solar point

As a solar point the 112th degree creates a sensitive nature that is easily moved and at times this can make the natives eccentric, cranky, restless, impatient, peculiar or radical. They are generally under the shadow of some sort of domestic upheaval or estrangement yet they love the home and children. They are also patriotic, love travelling and are capable of original expression, thought and action. Losses and difficulties can occur through the dwelling place, land or property. Many people with this birth degree become involved in legal affairs, either as rebels who try to enforce the changes that they feel are necessary or as guardians of the old standards that they feel should be kept. If there are good planetary aspects, the natives' courage will see that they win through in the end.

Planetary point

Whoever has a planet in the 112th degree is inclined to be unpredictable. Also, that planet, whichever it is, indicates how natives can shape or rebuild their lives. For example, the Moon here would suggest a return to the family roots.

113th degree

Colour: scarlet. *Sign*: Cancer. 3rd decan. *Qualities*: Cardinal/ Mutable, Water. *Numerological match*: other 5s.
Positive expression: tact, diplomacy
Negative expression: impressionability

Solar point

The 113th solar degree makes natives diplomatic, tactful, discreet, faithful and generally good natured. There is also a good intelligence and a retentive memory, and they are quite able to adapt to changes and circumstances within their own environments though less able to adjust in strange surroundings,

One of the greatest weaknesses of natives of this degree, however, is that they are suckers for flattery. Most people who are born under this degree have a tale of woe to tell about how they were done down by some individual or other such circumstance, but if the truth be known their undoing was their own fault because of their failure to hear anything except about the good they were doing at that time. However, they make loyal friends and faithful companions for those who return their good deeds in like manner.

They would be best employed in entertaining others in some way, which could be standing behind a bar, calling the bingo or performing on the stage.

Planetary point

As a planetary point the 115th has something to teach natives, and the planet residing here will indicate what it is. Saturn shows the need to learn self-reliance and the procuring of some form of long-term stability. Jupiter prefers natives to be footloose and fancy-free.

114th degree

Colour: green. *Sign*: Cancer. 3rd decan. *Qualities*: Cardinal/ Mutable, Water. *Numerological match*: other 6s.
Positive expression: strong affections
Negative expression: immoral attitudes

Solar point

A person who has the Sun in the 114th degree has a strong love of the home and the things that go with it. The nature is firm but sympathetic, kind hearted and receptive to the needs of others. There can be some mediumistic ability. Many natives of this degree have been known to have numerous love affairs in their search for their eventual soul mate. However, once the mate is found they settle down to build the home and family of their dreams. The only other obstacle they then have to overcome is their over-possessive and demanding nature which their mate may not be able to satisfy. Eventually this could lead to secret love affairs as they will then seek what they want elsewhere.

With regards employment, they are capable of doing a wide variety of jobs but they do not enjoy heavy or dirty physical work. In fact, they would prefer to keep a home rather than a job.

Planetary point

People with a planet in the 114th degree have a great need to fulfil themselves emotionally and the particular planet placed here indicates how they might achieve this end. The Moon would suggest through the care of the home and family, while Pluto would indicate a strong physical requirement.

115th degree

Colour: blue. *Sign*: Cancer. 3rd decan. *Qualities*: Cardinal/Mutable, Water. *Numerological match*: other 7s.
Positive expression: refinement
Negative expression: discontentment

Solar point

As a solar point the 115th degree brings delicacy, refinement and idealism to the lives of those born under it.

It matters not what background the natives of this degree are born into or whether they be rich or poor, as the energy of the degree will find a way of refining and improving upon what they were born with. The degree is conducive to a love of nature, plants and the life outdoors, and would be excellent for landscape gardeners. There can be some scientific ability and there is also present a love of the home and domestic comforts, and if a native should ever manage to combine the two he or she would have found his or her ideal niche in life.

With a romantic yearning to see far off places, those born under this degree usually do much travelling to foreign parts;

some will even settle down permanently abroad.

In health there can be a tendency to get stomach disorders.

Planetary point

The 115th degree refines the energy of any planet placed in it so that it manifests in a more acceptable manner in the native. For example, the authoritarian Saturn native is less cold or indifferent in how he rules his kingdom or business empire. Someone with Jupiter here is more careful in how he spends his money, or looks after the finances of others.

116th degree

Colour: black. *Sign*: Cancer. 3rd decan. *Qualities*: Cardinal/Mutable, Water. *Numerological match*: other 8s.
Positive expression: moral development
Negative expression: feelings of dissatisfaction

Solar point

As a solar point the 116th has a lesson to teach those born under its power. They can feel great dissatisfaction with what they were born with and with what they have achieved, always seeking more than they really need. Similarly, they may have a desire to be away from wherever they happen to be. The lesson of the degree is for the native to make practical use of what he or she has rather than always seeking for the unobtainable, for only by so doing can natives hope to develop on their karmic path. They must learn to rid themselves of feelings of jealousy and resentment about what others may have, and learn to spend more time appreciating what they themselves can achieve. They should concentrate on developing the higher self through personal sacrifice, for the good of others. It is only through this life of self-sacrifice that any of us are able to develop spiritually. Service through religious orders or charities would best serve this end.

Planetary point

The 116th degree shows by the planet placed in it how natives may best serve others (and in so doing reap rewards for themselves). Saturn here could indicate service in places of solitude such as prisons or remote lands, and so on.

Colour: red. *Sign*: Cancer. 3rd decan. *Qualities*: Cardinal/ Mutable, Water. *Numerological match*: other 9s.
Positive expression: courage, boldness
Negative expression: hiding behind others

Solar point

The 117th degree makes natives bold and couragous, preferring to lead a life full of excitement, travel and adventure before settling down for good. Not all born under this degree actually run away from home or go to sea, but many do. Those who remain behind will move from job to job or house to house, having the same kind of urge for constant change of environment as those who actually leave home.

If the great physical energy of this degree is harnessed and put into one task at a time rather than being spread over many, then the person who does this can become a formidable character. People with this degree are inclined to be brash and physical. However, they are capable of great bursts of emotional expression which they should learn to sustain over longer periods rather than in occasional flashes that they show to those they love. A marriage can be short-lived for the natives of this degree, unless they find a mate who has a very tolerant nature.

Planetary point

The 117th degree shows by the resident planet where natives should project their physical strength and courage. With the Moon here, the emotions could play a part, urging natives to protect those less able to look after themselves, while Mercury would indicate intellectual experience gained through some kind of physical confrontation.

118th degree

Colour: white. *Sign*: Cancer. 3rd decan. *Qualities*: Cardinal/ Mutable, Water. *Numerological match*: other 1s.
Positive expression: patience, tenacity
Negative expression: pride, resentment

Solar point

Any person born with the Sun in the 118th degree will be

changeable, sensitive and have a retiring disposition. He or she will experience many ups and downs in life and changes of occupation.

Natives have generally a fertile imagination, and are prone to be somewhat sentimental and talkative. They are fond of their home and family and have a retentive memory, especially for family or historical events. They can be industrious when necessary but tend to be diffident whenever they feel their position or status could be threatened. They are very anxious to acquire the good life but suffer from a fear that others may take from them what they have worked for.

Emotions are strong and natives with this degree delight in romantic or strange adventures. They are conscientious and receptive to new ideas and have the ability to adapt to a new environment as long as someone is there to help them on their way. Long-term employment and jobs involving the welfare of others suit them best.

Planetary point

The 118th degree shows those born with a planet here how they may avoid dependency on others, by the use of the energies of that particular planet. Venus would indicate an artistic hobby or occupation, while Saturn would help natives take on responsibilities and make decisions.

119th degree

Colour: grey. *Sign*: Cancer. 3rd decan. *Qualities*: Cardinal/Mutable, Water. *Numerological match*: other 2s.
Positive expression: domesticity
Negative expression: self-deception

Solar point

The 119th solar degree is typified by benefits and gains through the home, parents and domestic life. Favours can be obtained through the opposite sex and for some there could even be an unexpected inheritance. Although there may be many changes in residence and fluctuations in affairs of the heart and financial matters, these constitute a learning process which prepares the native for an ultimate rise to success and independence through possessions, such as landed property.

If this degree works out negatively, much disappointment

will be encountered, with great difficulties in financial matters, even poverty, largely owing to family affairs. Although difficulties and hardships will eventually be overcome, a level of success depends on how well the native manages family matters. The larger the number of dependants the more disappointments there are likely to be.

Planetary point

The placement of a planet in the 119th degree indicates how natives' dependants may become a drain on their resources. Uranus here or Mars can indicate sudden accidents or fraud and deception, while the Moon may drain a person's emotional energy so that he or she cannot carry on.

120th degree

Colour: violet. *Sign*: Leo. 1st decan. *Qualities*: Fixed, Fire.
Numerological match: other 3s.
Positive expression: balanced personality
Negative expression: unheeding of sound advice

Solar point

Whoever is born with the Sun in the 120th degree is good natured, noble, lofty minded, loyal, generous and compassionate. The body and constitution is usually strong and the fertility generally higher than that of natives of other degrees. A woman born with this degree is likely to have a large family while a man will probably be the father of strong children.

The natives of this degree learn best from first-hand experience which sets them well onto the path of career advancement and eventual success. Their minds are intuitive and they are attracted towards pure mathematics and the sciences, philosophy, fine arts, religion and various cultural pursuits. There is often a love of nature. Not being scared of taking a calculated risk, many people with this degree are successful in the money markets or wherever matters of investment and speculation are concerned. Benefits can come through contacts made on long journeys or in connection with sports and hobbies.

Planetary point

The 120th degree gives to whoever has a planet placed in it the ability to think logically and put to use the energies of the planet in question. Mercury here can see the refinement of artistic expression by working in the entertainment world, while Venus can bring benefit and pleasure through the offspring, and by children supporting their parents in later life.

121st degree

Colour: orange. *Sign*: Leo. 1st decan. *Qualities*: Fixed, Fire.
Numerological match: other 4s.
Positive expression: sensuosity
Negative expression: unconventional sexual partnerships

Solar point

People born with the 121st solar degree are to say the least rather unconventional, especially with regard to sexual matters. Unions, partnerships or romance may not be as considered the norm though this does not necessarily mean that the natives are gay or kinky. The positive energy of the degree is extremely sensuous and if it does not find a constructive outlet then the self-gratifying nature is let loose to satisfy its lust upon whatever takes the native's fancy. However, on the positive side, people with this degree are often prepared to have a go at things when others wouldn't dare. They would be well employed in jobs which are unusual or have a degree of risk or even danger. A film stunt man, soldier of fortune and an extremist in a political party are all likely to have this degree in common. (See also the 126th degree.)

Planetary point

Having a planet in the 121st degree indicates where that individual's life is likely to differ from that of the majority. Mars here can indicate that the native has what appears to be a self-destructive urge as he or she requires combat and confrontation to be happy. Someone with Jupiter here can earn great sums of money but will squander it or spend it on unusual pursuits.

122nd degree

Colour: scarlet. *Sign*: Leo. 1st decan. *Qualities*: Fixed, Fire.
Numerological match: other 5s.
Positive expression: refined intellectual
Negative expression: phrenetic behaviour

Solar point

As a solar point the 122nd degree refines the senses. The natives have a predominantly mental nature rather than a muscular or physical one. The intelligence is usually well developed and there is likely to be success and gain through speculation or investment.

Travelling, public amusements and work with children are all areas that could bring beneficial rewards for those born with this solar degree. The natives can show great ambition. Their quick wits combined with long, hard study should enable them to work their way up from the bottom of any trade or profession they choose to the very top. Those with a little less ambition are likely to become the managerial backbones of large corporations or government offices. (See also the 126th degree.)

Planetary point

The 122nd degree indicates by the planet resident in it what fields of work or study would bring rewards. People with Neptune here would tend to have scientific or intuitive abilities and many of them will have been good research scientists or people connected with the theatre. They could also be interested in occultism. Venus here would point to anything to do with feminine qualities or artistic expression as likely to bring success.

123rd degree

Colour: green. *Sign*: Leo. 1st decan. *Qualities*: Fixed, Fire.
Numerological match: other 6s.
Positive expression: hospitality
Negative expression: extravagance

Solar point

As a solar point the 123rd gives a fondness for company and a desire to be hospitable. Natives of this degree delight in the social pleasures, loath confrontation and want a fair amount of comfort in their lives but they hate to be tied to the home and are more at ease in large crowds and social gatherings. The nature is amiable, kind, generous and warm hearted. They like to use their creative skills in hobbies and jobs around the home. There is a liking, and some talent too, for music, opera and the fine arts generally.

When it comes to earning a living they tend to do this

through professional and public occupations. If employed by others, they are generally popular with their colleagues and readily attain promotion.

Their marriage or partnerships may be opposed by other family members yet always appear to work out well.

There can be a tendency to pride and vanity. (See also the 126th degree.)

Planetary point

As a planetary point, the 123rd eases the path and brings forth the refined energies of the planet placed in it. Saturn here brings fruitful conclusions to business ventures and creates a mature reasoning ability, while the normally unpredictable and destructive energies of Uranus can be turned to creative use.

124th degree

Colour: blue. *Sign*: Leo. 1st decan. *Qualities*: Fixed, Fire. *Numerological match*: other 7s.
Positive expression: inspiration
Negative expression: animosity

Solar point

As a solar point the 124th inspires those born under its influence to study philosophy, religion, science and kindred subjects. Some natives may show a marked interest in the occult sciences and may have mediumistic ability. The nature is generally kind and sympathetic.

Those born under the energy of this degree tend to have refined tastes and have an appreciation and often an aptitude for the arts. Many of them have romantic inclinations and dreams of adventures, so you will often see them taking to the sea in a leisure pursuit such as yachting. Some look to the sea for an occupation. The merchant navy or any work connected with the sea of an adventurous nature is highly suited to the pride of Leo.

This degree is not likely to bestow great riches, though most people born under its effects do attain a fair amount of comfort.

Planetary point

The 124th degree indicates by the planet is residence how natives may find the inspiration to achieve their dreams. Those with Mars in this degree attain their wishes through decisiveness and courageous application of their physical energy. They also do their own donkey work. Anyone with Jupiter here is more likely to make gains through share luck, or by social contacts. (See also the 126th degree.)

125th degree

Colour: black. *Sign*: Leo. 1st decan. *Qualities*: Fixed, Fire.
Numerological match: other 8s.
Positive expression: concentration, organisation
Negative expression: selfishness, scepticism

Solar point

The 125th solar degree aids natives to achieve general success in life through their own hard effort, and gives them commendable qualities such as the ability to concentrate, to appraise their options, and to plan and coordinate their efforts in the pursuit of their objectives. The personality is strong and not easily swayed by the opinions of others.

The individual with this degree is authoritative and has organisational flair. If assisted by good practical, planetary degrees in the chart there should be great success through concerns connected with the land, coal or mineral extraction, investments and industrial enterprises.

If politically motivated or fond of coming before the public, natives of this degree can obtain political honours, public appointments or the support of the masses. (See also the 126th degree.)

Planetary point

The 125th degree indicates by the planet placed in it where natives should seek public recognition and esteem. Saturn here favours all the occupations listed under the solar point, while Jupiter would give benefit through travel, voyages and investment overseas.

MAGICAL HOME DEGREE OF THE ELEMENT FIRE
(*Strongest effect*: 5 degrees on either side)

Colour: crimson. *Sign*: Leo. 1st decan. *Qualities*: Fixed, Fire.
Numerological match: other 9s.
Positive expression: constructive energy, building, creating,
achievement, protecting the weak, discipline
Negative expression: destructive use of physical energy, self-
hate

Solar point

As a solar point the 126th is the home base and operating centre
of the magical element of Fire, whose ruler is Michael. He is at
his strongest in this degree and also affects the five degrees on
either side of it. He is the bringer of warmth and joy, the energy
and colour of summer and the strength to accomplish the tasks
of his fellow elements.

Fire is the spirit of the doer and achiever for without his
energy, Air's ideas would remain dreams, Water's emotions
would never be expressed, and Earth's empires would never be
built. Most people who think in magical, spiritual or occult
terms, especially astrologers, seem to place psychic or mediumistic ability within the realms of Water and although Water signs
can indeed show marked mediumistic ability it is Fire which is
the principal element connected will these faculties.

Those of you born under this degree have some special task
to accomplish in this incarnation. You have been blessed with
the capability to lead and adaptability, with a vigorous mind
and strong body in keeping with the energy of the element of
Fire. You are to adventure into new areas and make discoveries
in the sciences and medicine, and revolutionise work practices
and social customs. You are the protectors of all that must be
saved and the bringers of change to all that is out of date.
Responsibility for others will be thrust upon you whether you
desire it or not and it is your acceptance of this responsibility
which will see whether or not you enter the Kingdom of
Heaven. Strong minded and resolute in your tasks, you must
resist the temptation to relax and allow others to take control,
for no matter how arduous the task it is your birthright. Military
leaders, heads of households and of large corporations which
employ thousands, political motivators, explorers of new lands,

scientific researchers, even those who work physically in arduous conditions, may all have in common the ability to draw upon the energy of Michael. But it is their ethical use of his energy which will be ultimately counted, not how much they conquered and took by force.

This is point 3 of the pentagram. It is below the horizon and governs the physical, mental and emotional application of energy behind the scenes for the protection and safety of society. Those born with this degree are the unseen doers whose work and creativity rarely receives the public recognition it deserves but without whom society would grind to a halt.

Planetary point

A planet in the 126th degree indicates how natives may apply this energy for the benefit of others.

Moon: gives energy and vitality to the emotions, allowing natives to pick themselves up after emotional trauma and begin anew, as well as being able to be emotionally supportive to their fellows.

Mercury: sharpens the mind, wit and intellect in order that they may motivate others as well as themselves in academic, business or communicative pursuits.

Venus: softens the physical energy, allowing artistic expression in areas such as entertainment and for relaxation from the stresses of daily life.

Mars: increases the natives' physical energy so that they may apply it to the tasks which face them for the benefit of all rather than the betterment of themselves (Mars in this degree can be destructive).

Jupiter: brings wealth and a philosophical outlook, and increases the reasoning power in order to solve the problems of the day.

Saturn: promotes use of the energy of Michael to maintain the equilibrium between new discoveries and those things which are the old and established.

Uranus: brings flashes of inventive genius and the ability to overcome society's non-acceptance of innovations.

Neptune: through the intuition and imagination, furthers spiritual growth and the ability to accept or adapt to new environments.

Pluto: brings about changes in social attitudes to different types of sexual behaviour.

127th degree

Colour: white. *Sign*: Leo. 1st decan. *Qualities*: Fixed, Fire.
Numerological match: other 1s.
Positive expression: authority, leadership
Negative expression: false pride, dictatorship

Solar point

As a solar point the 127th gives the native inspired leadership
qualities and he or she is able to enlist the help of others with
casual ease. Many natives climb to the highest heights in either
the business or the political world, being ambitious without
appearing to be pushy. Promotion at work comes easily, as does
respect from friends and colleagues and from family members.

Responsibility is almost thrust upon those of you born with
this degree, whether you desire it or not as you exude self-
confidence and awareness and have a firm yet gentle manner.
Hard work brings its just rewards and there is no reason other
than your own foolish pride why you should not succeed in all
that you set your mind upon. (See also the 126th degree.)

Planetary point

A planet placed in the 127th degree indicates to natives where
best they might put their leadership qualities to good use.
Saturn here would indicate a career in property, the mining
industry or the land, or in the handling of the finances of others.
With Mercury here, natives would find more expression and
versatility through politics or the media.

128th degree

Colour: grey. *Sign*: Leo. 1st decan. *Qualities*: Fixed, Fire.
Numerological match: other 2s.
Positive expression: sincerity, loyalty
Negative expression: egotism, irresolution

Solar point

The 128th degree gives those born under it sincerity and loyalty.
Though anxious to better themselves, these individuals never
forget the roots they sprung from and will endeavour to share
any fruits of success that they may achieve with those who
helped them on their way. They make loyal and adoring part-

ners and trustworthy business associates.

Many become self-employed, but natives who work for others tend to be looked on with favour by those in influential positions and are rewarded for their honesty and loyalty. They are good salary earners but not the best savers; nearly all their money is spent on family and home or in assisting family members or friends who are not able to look after themselves sufficiently.

If you were born with this degree you should be popular and liked by all; if you are not it is your own negative ego which is holding you back. (See also the 126th degree.)

Planetary point

The 128th degree indicates by the planet placed in it how natives may best achieve the respect of others and their assistance when needed. The Moon here indicates support in the family through a woman while Uranus gives natives the adaptability to succeed.

129th degree

Colour: violet. *Sign*: Leo. 1st decan. *Qualities*: Fixed, Fire.
Numerological match: other 3s.
Positive expression: success in material things
Negative expression: weakened morals and vitality

Solar point

The 129th degree increases the chance of those born under it of gaining worldly wealth, notoriety and success. The degree confers rewards for good karma; natives are able to relax and enjoy life after previous and more arduous incarnations.

People with this degree are honorable and humane in how they deal with others and even if the planetary degrees in the chart are negative natives will still find rewards and success in this life. In some cases there is a religious tendency or an inclination to investigate spiritual matters and delve into the deep mysteries of existence.

They usually enjoy good health throughout life. Benefits can come in particular from retail trades or in dealing with the public in general.

If you were born with this solar degree you are capable of achieving anything you wish within reason and should live a happy and contented life. (See also the 126th degree.)

Planetary point

When there is a planet in the 129th degree it indicates the abilities the native may have which could help bring about worldly success. Venus here indicates talent in the arts, fashion-design or the entertainment field while Mars would provide success in manufacturing or industry.

130th degree

Colour: orange. *Sign*: Leo. 2nd decan. *Qualities*: Fixed/Mutable, Fire. *Numerological match*: other 4s.
Positive expression: independence, perception
Negative expression: impulsiveness, broken vows

Solar point

As a solar point the 130th denotes natives born with exceptional powers of perception and intuition. Independent and original in the way they think and act, and scoffed at by the more timid for the risks they sometimes take, no matter how near to the precipice they tread they rarely if ever fall off.

Although fond of taking risks they do not realise they are taking a risk at all.

If you were born with this degree, you require the stimulation of physical danger to motivate you if you are to attain the level of success you are capable of. If this stimulation is not found, your novel ideas are never realised or put to good use and the energy of the degree becomes wasted, resulting in broken vows and promises both to yourself and those who put their trust in you. (See also the 126th degree.)

Planetary point

The planetary energy placed in this degree indicates how natives may find the stimulation to best utilise the degree. Someone with Mercury here finds his stimulation in trying to communicate ideals or teach languages to other people. It is also a good position for salesmen and those who work in the advertising or communications fields.

Colour: scarlet. *Sign*: Leo. 2nd decan. *Qualities*: Fixed/ Mutable, Fire. *Numerological match*: other 5s.
Positive expression: communicative ability
Negative expression: abrasive nature

Solar point

Those born with the Sun in the 131st degree are blessed with the ability to communicate emotionally, physically and intellectually. Honest, logical, always sticking to the point and with an ability to plan, these individuals rarely fail at the tasks they undertake as all eventualities have been considered beforehand. Their powers of comprehension are such that they can get to grips with the most complex matters and explain them in a simple way to others who would otherwise find them too difficult to understand. Not surprisingly, they tend to find their friends and partners amongst intellectual people.

They excel under stress situations and in any kind of employment which requires quick decisions. They do particularly well in the educational field where their knowledge and communicative ability can be used. (See also the 126th degree.)

Planetary point

The 131st degree shows through the planet resident in it where natives may find an outlet for their communicative skills. With Saturn here, they would be concerned with land use or the money markets, while with Neptune they could use intuition and imagination in the literary field.

132nd degree

Colour: green. *Sign*: Leo. 2nd decan. *Qualities*: Fixed/Mutable, Fire. *Numerological match*: other 6s.
Positive expression: generosity
Negative expression: emotional insecurity

Solar point

The 132nd degree makes generous, warm hearted individuals who seek out the company of their fellows. The nature is sympathetic to the needs of associates, well mannered and always ready to look on the bright side when the going gets tough. People with this degree are generally creative. They are well placed for gaining a good income through business, in one of the professions or in the social services where people are helped with their problems. There is a likelihood that the native will be popular and get many social invitations. He or she should readily obtain promotion in their employment.

People born under this degree tend to be attractive in their physical appearance and can be fashion conscious or 'snappy dressers'. There can be a liking for music and the arts in general.

Planetary point

A planet placed in the 132nd degree indicates where natives may direct their insight and understanding. Venus here would indicate through the arts, music or entertainment of others be that in the larger context of the stage or as the family practical joker. Mercury would find better expression as a teacher or a civil servant.

133rd degree

Colour: blue. *Sign*: Leo. 2nd decan. *Qualities*: Fixed/Mutable, Fire. *Numerological match*: other 7s.
Positive expression: inspiration
Negative expression: scandal-mongering

Solar point

The 133rd solar degree gives those born under it inspired creative powers and good imagination. There can be a leaning towards philosophy, science, psychic research, photography or the various fields of medicine. If well aspected by the planets in the chart there can be marked literary or musical ability, especially in the playing of stringed instruments. The tendency of the degree is to refine the feelings and emotions, giving natives a keen appreciation of the beauties of nature, and of art or music in their highest forms.

Those born under this degree are kind and generous and usually benefit by the study of mystical or spiritual subjects. In its negative application this energy incmines to lax morality and the inspirational creativity becomes self-destructive, with attempts to realise impossible dreams.

Planetary point

The 133rd degree shows by the planet placed in it where natives may draw their inspiration from. Saturn here would indicate from people or things that are old. With Pluto here they are able to throw off their social conditioning and strive without moral restraint for the attainment of their desires.

134th degree

Colour: black. *Sign*: Leo. 2nd decan. *Qualities*: Fixed/Mutable, Fire. *Numerological match*: other 8s.
Positive expression: strong will
Negative expression: dissolute habits

Solar point

The 134th degree allows natives to achieve success in life in all areas, financial, emotional and material, through their own efforts. There is present the ability to concentrate, and to appraise, organise and coordinate when working to obtain a desired objective. The personality is strong willed and not easily influenced by the opinion of others. The native is capable of pursuing his or her projects even when there is strong opposition to them.

Gains are made by natives of this degree through commercial dealings, buying and selling other peoples' products. Although they have the ability to organise others into working as a group, they become fully involved themselves. Failure or success in this life is linked only to the amount of patience summoned up and the application of the energy present. Long-term projects bring greater rewards.

Planetary point

The placement of a planet in the 134th degree indicates how natives may achieve their independence. Someone with Uranus here uses his or her mind inventively and originally and is likely to become an agent for a large concern. If Mercury is here, natives would think of ways to get others to assist them in getting their projects off the ground.

135th degree

Colour: crimson. *Sign*: Leo. 2nd decan. *Qualities*: Fixed/

Mutable, Fire. *Numerological match*: other 9s.
Positive expression: strong determination
Negative expression: rashness, over-forcefulness

Solar point

The 135th solar degree gives natives a strong constitution and a forceful and direct-to-the-point nature. Many people born under this degree become keen on sport, either as participators or followers. Sport in fact is often developed as an outlet for the excess physical energy at their disposal which would otherwise be hard to cope with. People with this degree have great physical endurance and once they have set their mind upon something they see it through. They should, however, realise that not everyone has such enormous determination and motivation to tackle the tasks at hand as they have, and they should make allowances as they can be very hard taskmasters to work for.

If you were born with this solar degree, learn to control your physical energy and use it for the benefit of all. Whatever you build with it you will defend against those who would destroy it. Your problem can be you can't tell who is your friend and who is your foe.

Planetary point

A planet placed in the 135th degree indicates to natives where their strengths lie and how to obtain the best prospects. Mars in this degree is good for soldiers, sailors and airmen or any in occupations where risk is involved, such as financial speculation. When the Moon is in this degree, more benefit can be found through the home and the family than in business ventures.

136th degree

Colour: white. *Sign*: Leo. 2nd decan. *Qualities*: Fixed/Mutable, Fire. *Numerological match*: other 1s.
Positive expression: ambition, self-esteem
Negative expression: domineering, forceful nature

Solar point

The 136th degree creates a nature which is ambitious and proud (though the native rarely admits it), frank, generous and compassionate.

A position of responsibility will inevitably fall to those of you with this degree be it in the home, at work or, in a broader context, on behalf of the nation. The position of trust and responsibility that you can expect to attain will come to you, however, only after you have earned the respect of your predecessors who will hand over the reigns of power when they feel you are able to cope with them. The hardest thing you have to learn is to wait for those above you to hand over responsibility to you.

If the head of any company, corporation, council or country possesses this energy, he or she should use it wisely to direct the lives of their subordinates. Many union officials and rebels also make use of the energy of this degree.

Planetary point

The 136th degree indicates by the planetary placement how or where natives can attain to a position of authority or responsibility. Neptune here would enable natives to open new sea routes or handle the movement of people and cargo overseas. Or they may be involved in the introduction of nuclear energy. Uranus here could produce the kind of inventiveness required for creating computer handware and software and natives could be concerned with bringing electronic goods into general acceptance.

137th degree

Colour: grey. *Sign*: Leo. 2nd decan. *Qualities*: Fixed/Mutable, Fire. *Numerological match*: other 2s.
Positive expression: warm-heartedness, independence
Negative expression: rigid opinions

Solar point

The sun in the 137th degree makes the native ambitious, self-confident and self-reliant. To others, the native can appear overconfident or to be a know-all, but this is a misunderstanding.

The degree helps develop the intuition and, coupled to the drive of Leo, can bring flashes of inventive genius. Many with this degree become the leaders among us, strict and orderly in conduct yet caring enough to assist others in a time of need.

Having this degree in the natal chart should lead to a rise in the native's social status, through the attainment of positions of respect and trust.

As well as being responsible marital partners, the natives make able managers and supervisors in their work.

Planetary point

A planet in the 137th degree can indicate in what area you may become a leader or earn the most respect for your efforts. Venus here is good for anyone who comes before the public, from the entertainer on the stage to the barmaid at the local. Mercury here gives a harder task, as the mental ability must be used to win the favours of others.

138th degree

Colour: violet. *Sign*: Leo. 2nd decan. *Qualities*: Fixed/Mutable, Fire. *Numerological match*: other 3s.
Positive expression: good nature
Negative expression: eccentricity

Solar point

People with the sun in the 138th degree are good natured, benevolent, compassionate and prudent, knowing when to act or speak their piece and when to remain silent and bide their time. This degree strengthens the constitution, increases the physical vitality and favours those born under its power with large families or at least strong healthy children.

Natives are attracted to intellectual activities rather than physical ones and although they enjoy sports they usually refrain from physical contact or violence. They make better diplomats than soldiers, and would do particularly well in any of the welfare services or service industries. If work in the diplomatic service is being considered, it would be good to have a strong Jupiter in the birth chart for protection while travelling.

Planetary point

If you have a planet in the 138th degree, it could indicate that you will arbitrate between others. Saturn here, for example, is well placed for the settlement of industrial or financial disputes and is also great for accountants. Those of you with Pluto here, on the other hand, will learn to relax and enjoy the increasingly available products of the leisure industry.

139th degree

Colour: orange, *Sign*: Leo. 2nd decan. *Qualities*: Fixed/
Mutable, Fire. *Numerological match*: other 4s.
Positive expression: industriousness
Negative expression: disregard for convention

Solar point

As a solar point the 139th is not the most stable energy to be
born under. On the one hand the native can be industrious to
the point of physical exhaustion, working all hours possible to
fulfil his or her dreams. On the other hand, the energy is used in
confrontation with the rest of society, trying to change the
conventional way people live in conformity with the native's
own idea of what is best for them. However, physical force is
not generally used in the attempt to change people's ideas and
behaviour. The native's great mental energy is used in debate,
discussion and propaganda to try to achieve the desired ends.

The mental energy of people with this degree is often used in
the making of great discoveries, either about their own inner
being or in the new industries, such as electronics, though first
they must learn to concentrate on one project at a time.

Planetary point

A planet in the 139th degree will indicate the best expression
for the native's mental energy. Jupiter would suggest overseas
travel or financial dealings, while someone with Saturn here
would do well as a town planner, public speaker or in local
politics. To whatever purpose it is used, this energy is mentally
expressed.

140th degree

Colour: scarlet. *Sign*: Leo. 3rd decan. Fixed/Cardinal, Fire.
Numerological match: other 5s.
Positive expression: persuasive communicator
Negative expression: stubborn pride

Solar point

People with the Sun in the 140th degree have been gifted by the
elemental forces with the ability to lead others and to attain to a
position of authority. The mind is sharp, as is also, quite often,

the tongue. Their best achivements come from their ability to communicate and promote the ideas and inventions of others. That is not to say that they cannot be inventive themselves, merely that they can best make use of this energy by concentrating upon marketing rather than on creation. They are found in most walks of life, from the advertising and promotion girls, who make products appear so attractive, to the sales executive dealing in world trade and communications. If somebody born under this degree should decide to sell snow to eskimos then he would do just that, as long as he could convince himself that the product is good.

Planetary point

A planet placed in the 140th degree shows natives how they may direct their abilities. Mars here is indicative of marketing in the fields of law enforcement or the armed services, i.e. would benefit those who sell manufactured goods to the Army, Navy, police force etc. If Jupiter is in this degree, natives would do best at promoting the fine arts and entertainments industry.

141st degree

Colour: green. *Sign*: Leo. 3rd decan. *Qualities*: Fixed/Cardinal, Fire. *Numerological match*: other 6s.
Positive expression: affection, charitableness
Negative expression: killjoy

Solar degree

As a solar point the 141st endows those born under its power with a nature which is sympathetic to the needs of others. They are charitable to those less able, kind hearted, generous and sincere and ardent in their affections. These natives are greatly attracted to the opposite sex and are fond of stage entertainment and amusements of all sorts. There may well be considerable talent for one of the activities ruled by Venus, if other degrees in the chart assist, such as music, poetry, singing, acting, or painting.

The entertainments industry is by far the best expression of the energy of this degree and those of you born under it who do not actually work in this field will be avid attenders at performances. You will also be the practical jokers in your work place and at home.

The negative application of this degree is to deny both yourself and those around you the entertainment they require.

Planetary point

The 141st degree indicates by the planet placed in it where natives may best find the relaxation they require. Those with Venus here can lean back and enjoy the arts as a listener or spectator, or actually participate themselves. Those with Saturn here prefer their entertainment to be in a private atmosphere such as the theatre or the countryside.

142nd degree

Colour: blue. *Sign*: Leo. 3rd decan. *Qualities*: Fixed/Cardinal, Fire. *Numerological match*: other 7s.
Positive expression: service to others
Negative expression: unstable home life

Solar point

People born with the Sun in the 142nd degree would like to save the world if they could. They are charitable and generous and their intuitive foresight sees them in the right places in society helping those in need. Capable of intense feeling, they are well able to understand the feelings of others and their hearts are always open to those who need a sympathetic shoulder to cry upon.

Natives of this degree find their best vocation through the caring institutions such as charities, and the nursing profession.

The negative use of this degree is indulgence in pleasures of the senses.

Planetary point

A planet placed in the 142nd degree indicates where natives can be of service to others. The Moon here denotes that the native can provide a stable home and emotional support to others — a type of mother to all in fact. With Jupiter here, a person is better employed in the financial realms, perhaps as a fund-raiser for needy causes.

143rd degree

Colour: black. *Ruler*: Leo. 3rd decan. *Qualities*: Fixed/

Cardinal, Fire. *Numerological match*: other 8s.
Positive expression: hard working
Negative expression: misplaced loyalty

Solar point

The elemental energy of the 143rd degree creates a courageous and indomitable spirit. Determination and a strong will are given in order that the natives of this degree may apply themselves to the problems they encounter with patience and perseverance, and they should learn to avoid sudden emotional outbursts when frustrated or thwarted.

Long-term projects and jobs with the promise of eventual promotion or the gaining of positions of authority are the best for people with this degree. However, they should choose large industries or big organisations such as unions, political parties or local government. Natives tend to marry once only and for life. Children are few, if any.

If you have this degree wealth can be acquired but not until the second half of your life, and then only as a reward for fulfilling your karma. You are not a great social mixer, preferring your own company, though you will socialise if necessary in the interests of business.

Planetary point

If there is a planet in the 143rd degree, it indicates how natives may best apply their willpower and determination. With Mercury here, they would be well advised to gather facts assiduously and utilise the communicative abilities that the planet gives. People with Venus here would be better employed serving a prominent person or celebrity rather than dreaming of stardom.

144th degree

Colour: crimson. *Sign*: Leo. 3rd decan. *Qualities*: Fixed/Cardinal, Fire. *Numerological match*: other 9s.
Positive expression: fearlessness, enterprise
Negative expression: dissipated efforts

Solar point

As a solar point the elemental energy of the 144th degree makes the person born with it candid, independent and fearless. It indicates the free roaming soul, and a rest from the responsibility of previous incarnations.

If you were born with this degree, during the whole of this lifetime you are allowed to exercise free will in the things you do and the events you participate in. If during previous incarnations you were at war in any sense, you are now in a rest period, back from the front line and you need only return if you choose to. You have resources gathered from all your previous existences to draw upon should you still decide to work through this incarnation however.

Many born with this degree become involved in fighting for the rights of others as they feel an affinity with the downtrodden, having vague memories or fears from their previous lives. Independence and ease can be yours during this life if you so choose, but the fight must continue in the next life.

Planetary point

As a planetary point the 144th indicates what lessons natives have learned in a former existence and may benefit them in this one. The Moon here indicates that in previous lives they have learned to share with others, while Pluto has taught them to accept death with equanimity.

145th degree

Colour: white. *Sign*: Leo. 3rd decan. *Qualities*: Fixed/Cardinal, Fire. *Numerological match*: other 1s.
Positive expression: confident leadership
Negative expression: domineering tendency

Solar point

The 145th degree's elemental energy will force those born under it to take on responsibility for other people apart from their own family. In previous existences they relied too heavily upon the help or advice of others and now is the time to pay back the debt. The lives of these natives need not, however, be severe; that choice is their own for when they accept responsibility they also reap its rewards.

If you were born with this degree, you will find that sometimes circumstances are forced upon you that you feel were not of your making. However, if you cope with these properly material success will follow in other areas of your life. So think carefully before you turn down the next cry for assistance that you receive as in the long run you could be the loser.

Planetary point

If you have a planet in the 145th degree, it will indicate in what way others will call upon you for assistance in this life. Jupiter here indicates that you must bear financial responsibility for others. Venus indicates that you must entertain others more often than they entertain you.

146th degree

Colour: grey. *Sign*: Leo. 3rd decan. *Qualities*: Fixed/Cardinal, Fire. *Numerological match*: other 2s.
Positive expression: fairness, honesty
Negative expression: dishonesty, mendacity, theft

Solar point

The elemental energy of the 146th degree works towards the upholding of the laws, traditions and moral values of society. If you were born with this degree you were given a firm foundation at the start of your life which should be of benefit throughout your childhood and years of schooling. Now it is up to you to apply those energies for the good of your family and friends as well as yourself.

A slightly exaggerated use of this energy is exemplified in the factory worker who preaches his gospel to his fellow workers all day; his ideals may be sound but his timing is not. Anyway, it is better to show others the right way to live by setting them an example.

The negative use of this degree produces tremendous thieves and liars, who are sure to be found out in the future.

Planetary point

When there is a planet in the 146th degree, according to which one it is natives are shown how to teach or set examples to others. Someone with Mars here can teach his fellows how to be fearless, independent and self-reliant, giving them the confidence they lack. If Venus is here, the native can teach others not to be embarrassed by the expression of their true feelings.

130

147th degree

Colour: violet. *Sign*: Leo. 3rd decan. *Qualities*: Fixed/Cardinal, Fire. *Numerological match*: other 3s.
Positive expression: philosophical outlook
Negative expression: pessimism

Solar point

As a solar point the elemental energy of the 147th degree is geared towards philosophy, optimism and the advancement of the higher mind by meditation and contemplation.

Natives of this solar degree can look forward to a life of travel and for some even adventure in far off lands and different cultures. It is through these experiences, brought about by karma, that the native learns that, regardless of colour, race or creed, dress, or outward appearance, underneath all people have the same needs, greeds, faults and problems. It is only after this realisation that natives stop their wanderings or fruitless searches for impossible dreams, and settle down to try and communicate what they have discovered by working with or for others. Some born with this degree even become missionaries.

Planetary point

When there is a planet in the 147th degree it indicates to natives where they may journey and the types of learning experiences they will undergo which further their spiritual development. Saturn here, for example, relates to the continent of Asia and its cultures, while Mars indicates the UK and experiences on the home front.

148th degree

Colour: orange. *Sign*: Leo. 3rd decan. *Qualities*: Fixed/Cardinal, Fire. *Numerological match*: other 4s.
Positive expression: easygoing
Negative expression: failure to carry out duty

Solar point

The elemental energy of the 148th degree is geared towards those individuals who take life as it comes. They happily accept gifts or enjoy good times if they come along but will weather the harder times without complaint. The lesson for natives of this degree is to accept the occasional knocks and bruises of life in a calm and responsible manner. They should not let these undermine their lives and prevent them from becoming real achievers.

In their formative years natives may be brash, rash and in a hurry to do and achieve everything, yet it is these same people who, through hard experience, become the backbones of stable institutions and of society as a whole. Sometimes they become the teachers of future generations.

Planetary point

The 148th degree indicates for those who have a planet in it what lessons they may have to learn before they settle down. Saturn here would indicate the need to learn self-reliance and to build and maintain a stable base. The Moon would point to learning experiences through emotional relationships with others.

149th degree

Colour: scarlet. *Ruler*: Leo. 3rd decan. *Qualities*: Fixed/Cardinal, Fire. *Numerological match*: other 5s.
Positive expression: adaptability
Negative expression: forgery, plagiarism

Solar point

People born with the Sun in the 149th degree have the ability to step into the place of others and take over their responsibilities for periods of time. They do not usually become famous or notable people themselves but they are capable of standing in for someone who is taking a rest. This energy can be found in all environments, from the stand-in stunt man for the movie star to the friendly aunt who looks after the kids while mum works. The ability to stand in for others and to mimic them can in some cases lead these individuals to the stage as impersonators of the famous, but in most cases they find an outlet through light-hearted imitation of friends, colleagues and acquaintances. In employment, they prefer to be deputies for the boss rather than the boss himself as this allows them responsibility but without the full pressure that can be the lot of the man at the top.

Planetary point

Anyone who has a planet in the 149th degree will have the

ability to copy others or learn by their example. With Venus here, a person could learn by the artistic examples set by others — or become a copy artist or forger. If Mercury is here the native can grasp the ideas of others and utilise them.

150th degree

Colour: green. *Ruler*: Virgo. 1st decan. *Qualities*: Mutable, Earth. *Numerological match*: other 6s.
Positive expression: sensitivity to the needs of others, organising ability
Negative expression: over-sensitivity to criticism

Solar point

People born with the Sun in the 150th degree have artistic ability and sensitivity and, most of all, organisational ability. In fact they just cannot help becoming involved in the organisation of others, especially in the realms of entertainment and the arts. On one level they can become entrepreneurs in advertising or promotional work while on another they may just be the planners of family holidays. They have to organise their friends' leisure for them and seem to know intuitively what will bring satisfaction. They appear to derive their chief pleasure in seeing them enjoy the events they have organised. They do not, however, respond well to criticism because their motives, as they see them, are purely unselfish and reckon a person is not deserving of their efforts if he or she thinks otherwise.

Planetary point

A planet placed in the 150th degree indicates to natives how they may organise the events of others and receive some form of recognition for their efforts. Those with Mercury in this degree would instigate the ideas and motivate the planners but not become physically involved, while with Jupiter they would find themselves organising the finances of various events.

151st degree

Colour: blue. *Sign*: Virgo. 1st decan. *Qualities*: Mutable, Earth.
Numerological match: other 7s.
Positive expression: tireless work
Negative expression: all work and no play

Solar point

People born with the Sun in the 151st degree have tasks to perform and will take no rest or respite till the job on hand is completed and even then only till the next one comes along. They have a burning desire for financial success and public acclaim though they may not realise this themselves. Not only are they tireless workers, if they become employers they expect the same from their employees, not realising that they probably do not have the same motivations as themselves.

This degree can bring about isolation and seclusion, yet if you were to ask those born under it if they are lonely they would answer that they are not, for they rarely have the time to realise what they may be missing on the emotional plane, being too concerned with acquiring on the physical one. They are great communicators and can turn their dreams into realities through application and hard personal effort. No wonder you often find these people in the top jobs!

Planetary point

The 151st degree indicates by the planet placed in it in what field natives' efforts would reap the best rewards. Someone with Saturn in this degree can found, build or assist institutions or organisations and acquire land or property. With Mars here, a native should use his energies in the sciences or in medicine.

152nd degree

Colour: black. *Sign*: Virgo. 1st decan. *Qualities*: Mutable, Earth. *Numerological match*: other 8s.
Positive expression: money sense
Negative expression: squandering

Solar point

The elemental energy of the 152nd degree helps the native to learn how to handle and control financial resources, whether that person happens to be the treasurer of a local club or group, the manager of a bank or building society or just a frugal housewife.

Those of you born under this degree will have to accept some form of financial responsibility and the trust which comes with it. In some cases this can be connected with the care and welfare of others, such as fund raising activities for charities and organisations for the needy. But first and foremost you must learn to handle your own finances without the support of others. You may not like the idea of risk-taking or speculation, yet it is through these areas that the required lessons are learned.

Planetary point

A planet in the 152nd degree can indicate how financial independence may be achieved. Mercury here can give natives literary talent or the ability to organise others to work for them. Venus in this point would give artistic flair which could be used to help boost the family income.

153rd degree

Colour: crimson. *Sign*: Virgo. 1st decan. *Qualities*: Mutable, Earth. *Numerological match*: other 9s.
Positive expression: mental energy
Negative expression: bad temper

Solar point

The 153rd degree gives natives mental agility and the ability to find their own path in life. They will be able to find the answers to their problems and also those of their fellows.

People with this degree have inquiring minds, wanting to know the whys and wherefores of everything. They become involved in all forms of research. Some will work in the sciences, such as pharmaceutical research, and others may make careers as political analysts, private detectives or accident investigators. The mind is sharp and discerning, and natives often communicate in such a rapid manner that others can have trouble in following them.

It must be said that without the energies of this degree the progress of mankind could long ago have come to a halt. This is because they are able to sort out the good from the bad through research and application and this ensures that the problems of yesterday don't recur tomorrow.

Planetary point

A planet in the 153rd degree indicates in what area research or investigation may bring benefits for the native. Venus here suggests that research into the arts could bring rewards both in the material and the spiritual sense. Someone with Mars here is likely to be the pioneering type, breaking new ground and opening up new avenues in scientific research or in anything connected with the physical environment.

154th degree

Colour: white. *Ruler*: Virgo. 1st decan. *Qualities*: Mutable, Earth. *Numerological match*: other 1s.
Positive expression: social leadership, motivation of others
Negative expression: boredom, dissatisfaction

Solar point

The elemental energy of the 154th degree is that of the social motivator. The strength of the native lies not in being able to do arduous physical labour but rather in the ability to motivate others along such paths for the betterment of all. It is the mental energy rather than the physical which is the stronger and natives would do well to obtain some form of academic qualifications before embarking on a career, as without a certificate to back them up their strong communicative abilities will fall upon fallow ground and success will come later rather than sooner. People with this degree of solar energy need to learn what motivates and inspires them before they can ever put their full abilities to use. They should endeavour to find an occupation which will give scope for fulfilling their eventual ambitions and desires otherwise they will forever be bored and dissatisfied with their job. Local politics or community work is probably the best type of work for natives of this degree.

Planetary point

The 154th degree indicates by the planet placed in it by what means natives may achieve recognition in society. Someone with Mars here would win recognition by conquest and strife in risk-taking ventures, while someone with Jupiter here would be well placed for a financial career, or perhaps become a buyer, an organiser or a trend setter for a large corporation.

155th degree

Colour: grey. *Ruler*: Virgo. 1st decan. *Qualities*: Mutable, Earth. *Numerological match*: other 2s.

Positive expression: caring administration
Negative expression: vindictiveness, rebelliousness

Solar point

The 155th degree creates a person who really cares about the people whom he or she comes into contact with and the needs of society in general.

Not emotionally demonstrative, people with this solar point are easily misunderstood by their fellows. Furthermore, they usually attain some form of administrative position, and by looking after the needs of the many they almost always dissatisfy a few. Some decisions may be difficult, even heart-rending, for the native, but they have to be made.

If you were born with this solar energy you will become involved in some form of social administration which you must use for the benefit of the most needy.

Planetary point

When there is a planet in the 155th degree it indicates for the natives how they may best put their administrative abilities to use. With Saturn or Pluto here, they are best utilised through the law in the defence of peoples' rights; this planetary placement is good for lawyers and policemen. Those with Uranus here can use their inventiveness to help others to forget the troubles they may have, and is good for entertainers.

156th degree

Colour: violet. *Sign*: Virgo. 1st decan. *Qualities*: Mutable, Earth. *Numerological match*: other 3s.
Positive expression: sharp intellect
Negative expression: materialism

Solar point

As a solar point the elemental energy of the 156th degree sharpens the mental faculties and natives tend to be intellectuals with a somewhat materialistic outlook.

If you were born with this degree, you are inclined to have a somewhat cautious nature and are not easily imposed upon by others. You are discreet, prudent and discriminating and would therefore have an aptitude for the applied sciences, psychological or philosophical studies. Your mind is analytical and critical and you tend to be matter-of-fact in your speech. You are also prone to being fussy in your choice of friends or partners. Occult groups or unusual societies with have a fascination for you.

A good income can be acquired in fields concerned with literature and the practical application of the sciences. You should also do well in investments and speculative ventures. Marriage is likely to be to someone who is socially inferior.

Planetary point

A planetary placement here indicates how natives may use the analytical mind to learn essential lessons. Someone with Mars here can learn only through his or her own physical mistakes, and learning is by retrospection. Whoever has the Moon here will seek the answers to the emotional trauma of existence.

157th degree

Colour: orange. *Sign*: Virgo. 1st decan. *Qualities*: Mutable, Earth. *Numerological match*: other 4s.
Positive expression: originality, independence
Negative expression: mutiny, rebelliousness

Solar point

The 157th degree creates a subtle, independent and original mind. Those born under its sway can be both eccentric and stubborn. But they can also display a special aptitude for the sciences, in particular those to do with electricity and electronics, dietetics and chemistry. The intellectual ability can verge on that of the genius. Frequently they are interested in the occult which, if followed up, can bring financial rewards.

Natives would make great teachers or mechanics, and tend to do better as employers rather than as an employees. Most success is found through work in occupations associated with the government or local councils.

There can be a fondness for collecting curiosities which can infuriate their mates.

Planetary point

When there is a planet in the 157th degree it indicates what abilities persons born with it could learn to develop beyond the ordinary. For example, Uranus here (present in the early '60s) is indicative of those who will make the scientific discoveries of the future in both the electronic and the medical fields, while Venus could bring out new forms of artistic expression.

158th degree

Colour: scarlet. *Sign*: Virgo. 1st decan. *Qualities*: Mutable, Earth. *Numerological match*: other 5s.
Positive expression: motivation of others
Negative expression: mendacity

Solar point

As a solar point the elemental energy of the 158th degree gives the native an all-round personality, with good intellect, a careful, prudent, discriminating mind and much practical sense. There is versatility and perceptiveness. When the mind is fully developed the native has the capacity for concentrated study along with a good memory. He or she is generally a fine linguist.

If you have this degree you will know that you have great powers of persuasion, and you can express yourself well.

With all these abilities, natives of this degree keep themselves well informed, especially about any circumstances that may affect them, so they are rarely caught out by others. They are actually of a quiet, somewhat serious disposition although this is hidden under a chatty exterior. At times they can be deeply critical and skeptical of anything which cannot be proven, which can lead them into a study of the occult sciences. Mathematics and literature are their strongest points as well as the ability to motivate or convince others.

Planetary point

This degree indicates by the planet placed in it how natives may go about motivating others for their own benefit. Someone with Venus here can be born with a beauty and grace which inspires others to care for them. If Saturn is in this degree, a native may gain the assistance of elders and those in authority to set them on the path to success.

159th degree

Colour: green. *Sign*: Virgo. 1st decan. *Qualities*: Mutable, Earth. *Numerological match*: other 6s.

Positive expression: sympathetic nature
Negative expression: multiple romantic attachments

Solar point

The elemental energy of the 159th degree endows natives with a deep feeling of sympathy for the needs of others but this is seldom fully outwardly expressed. The outer personality is brisk and efficient, as if the natives are trying to keep themselves busy to hide some form of personal bereavement or loss. Emotional attachments may be formed without any possibility of real fulfilment, and desire for the unobtainable often drives natives into some form of service to others. The efficient ward sister or mistress to the married industrialist are types who may have the energy of this degree in common. The karmic lesson that must be learned is to forsake personal ambitions and serve others, rather than to live the selfish existence expected by so many of us. Work connected with drugs, medicine, nursing or food constitutes the best outlets for this life of service.

Planetary point

A planet in the 159th degree indicates in what area natives can be of service or assistance to others. With the Moon here they make great foster parents, or they might remedy the consequences of emotional failure in others, bringing joy were there was sorrow. Those with Jupiter here will often give financial support to the needy.

160th degree

Colour: blue. *Sign*: Virgo. 2nd decan. *Qualities*: Mutable/ Cardinal, Earth. *Numerological match*: other 7s.
Positive expression: artistic flair, communicative ability
Negative expression: vandalism

Solar point

People born with the Sun in the 160th degree have the ability to communicate on an emotional level and in a sensitive way; they can make the harshest order sound like a mild request. They are able to draw upon the sympathies of those they come into contact with and if they put this energy to commercial use they would have people falling over themselves to place orders with them.

There can be pronounced physical beauty which can draw

admirers from near and far. The best application of this energy is through a subtle show of helplessness, which compels others to go to their assistance. This works much better than brash, confident approach. Many natives have an ability to communicate the emotions through music or the arts and may make a career out of it.

Planetary point

If you have a planet in the 160th degree it will indicate to you in what field others may be persuaded to assist your development. Saturn here could bring the favour of elders, stability in a career or gifts of land or property. Jupiter may provide good tutors in education, travel companions to help you get about, or backers in business ventures.

161st degree

Colour: black. *Sign*: Virgo. 2nd decan. *Qualities*: Mutable/Cardinal, Earth. *Numerological match*: other 8s.
Positive expression: work balanced with recreation
Negative expression: all work and no play

Solar point

The elemental energy of the 161st degree lets natives enjoy a full social life and at the same time retain a worthwhile career. Positions of authority and respect are nearly always attained by natives though eventually most end up working for themselves. Responsible and methodical, when given a task to do, these people work at their best when left to get on with it in their own way.

After a day's work, natives will readily forget the worries of the office and settle back to relax with the hobbies of their choice.

Those of you born under this degree know that there is a time to work and a time to play and endeavour to give each of these activities all you've got.

People with this solar degree make loyal and devoted mates. They earn a good income and enjoy spending it with their mate.

Planetary point

A planet in the 161st degree shows how natives may balance work and play. Someone with Saturn here may work on a farm or with land and property, and as recreation enjoy country walks or mountain climbing. If Venus is here, the person would be better employed in the arts or the entertainment industry, allowing business and pleasure to mix.

162nd degree

Colour: crimson. *Sign*: Virgo. 2nd decan. *Qualities*: Mutable/Cardinal, Earth. *Numerological match*: other 9s.
Positive expression: mental acuity
Negative expression: abusiveness

Solar point

The 162nd degree gives those born with the Sun in it great mental capabilities. There is little that natives cannot tackle mentally and they generally manage to work out solutions to their problems. The mind, however, can become easily dulled by unstimulating environments. Many bright children have regularly played truant from school or left school earlier than they should simply because their teachers failed to recognise that the other, less bright children were holding them back, making them lose all interest in school work. A bright child of six can thus become a dull child by the age of 15. Something similar can happen in adults if varied and stimulating employment is not found. A career in sales or promotion work would suit natives best.

People with this birth degree can appear flirtatious in romance, but they are in fact very loyal.

Planetary point

A planet in the 162nd degree will show natives how their brain power should best be used, if it is ever developed. For example, someone with Jupiter here is likely to develop a philosophical nature, and will try to work out ideal structures for society in the modern world.

163rd degree

Colour: white. *Sign*: Virgo. 2nd decan. *Qualities*: Mutable/Cardinal, Earth. *Numerological match*: other 1s.
Positive expression: leadership
Negative expression: frustrated hopes

Solar point

The elemental energy of the 163rd degree can make those under its sway leaders among men. Many may feel that these people overstep the mark in asserting their leadership either at work or in social situations. But it is the natives' burning desire to put right what they feel is mismanaged that makes them stick their necks out and intervene. Generally they achieve their aim in the end.

If you have this degree, caution should be taken in forming friendships as you often have to upset those around you to set matters right and it is only those who understand your true motivation who will stand by you.

No matter what social class natives of this solar degree happen to be born into, they will always want to exert themselves to achieve a position above those around them in order to attain a better lifestyle for themselves and their loved ones. The path to success and recognition has never been a smooth one and, if one sets one's sights high, the upward climb is likely to be tough.

Planetary point

The 163rd degree shows by the planet placed in it what personal qualities a native possesses that are useful in leadership. Mercury here is very strong for persuasive logic and the ability to sell an idea to others. Someone with Mars here tends to lead more through personal example in such things as military service or sporting activities — or just through brute force.

164th degree

Colour: grey. *Sign*: Virgo. 2nd decan. *Qualities*: Mutable/Cardinal, Earth. *Numerological match*: other 2s.
Positive expression: compassion
Negative expression: lack of confidence

Solar point

The 164th degree blesses the natives with the patience and compassion to assist others in seeing the errors of their ways. They would make great arbitrators, personnel officers or public relations executives. They are able to see both sides of an argument and while retaining sympathy for both parties reach a fair and just decision. Their nature is usually quiet and reserved. They ponder deeply before speaking or when having to make a decision. Friendly counsellors to all people in times of need, their shoulder is always there to cry on.

In the home and in marriage they are more able to give rather than take as long as they feel that what they are building is worth while in the long term. They have long memories and do not easily forgive those who fall foul with them. People with this degree of solar energy are found in most walks of life.

Planetary point

This degree allows a balanced expression of the planet placed in it. When the Moon is here, natives can give emotional succour to others. If the planet here is Venus, natives can help others beautify their surroundings. With Mercury, they can give a balanced rather than a biased, self-interested account of events and deeds and with Mars they learn to help others as well as themselves.

165th degree

Colour: violet. *Sign*: Virgo. 2nd decan. *Qualities*: Mutable/Cardinal, Earth. *Numerological match*: other 3s.
Positive expression: well adjusted personality
Negative expression: irresponsibility

Solar point

As a solar point the elemental energy of the 165th degree is not what one would expect to find in the Sign of Virgo. Natives born under this degree are extremely adaptable to all situations. Indeed, they revel in their ability to survive and will even create problems in their own lives in order that they may adjust to them and thus surmount them.

The mind is sharp and shrewd and they rarely betray what they are feeling — which is great for professional poker players or those that take speculative risks in business. People with this degree do not like to be tied down to one environment and must at least have the option to be elsewhere for a time if they are to settle down in the normal sense of the word. Avid readers in their quest for knowledge or travellers in their desire for new experiences, they leave the family home earlier than most in search of their quest. A career in sales or promotions would suit.

Planetary point

The 165th degree indicates, by the planet in residence, how natives may break free from environmental restrictions and limitations. With Saturn here they can gain the support of elders in their plans while with Mars they would need have perseverance and if necessary use forcefulness to escape.

166th degree

Colour: orange. *Sign*: Virgo. 2nd decan. *Qualities*: Mutable/Cardinal, Earth. *Numerological match*: other 4s.
Positive expression: artistic communication
Negative expression: vanity, insecurity

Solar Point

As a solar point the elemental energy of the 166th degree produces people who are extremely artistic and rather emotional, but somewhat secretive about their real motives and desires. They have a feeling of safety with old tried and tested routines, yet at the same time they feel a vague discontentment, desiring something more though not fully understanding what. There can be great sensitivity to the emotional needs and desires of others yet an inability to discuss their own feelings of insecurity with those close to them. This is largely because of a difficulty in verbally expressing themselves. The best outlet they have for their emotions is through their artistic talents such as painting, singing or playing a musical instrument.

Planetary point

When there is a planet in this degree it indicates there may be mistrust of others. The Moon here could indicate emotional instability caused by the mother or other early childhood experiences. Mars here would be indicative of the father being the prime influence in the native's development. Someone with Saturn here can be forced to grow up too soon because of hardship in the family.

167th degree

Colour: scarlet. *Sign*: Virgo. 2nd decan. *Qualities*: Mutable/Cardinal, Earth. *Numerological match*: other 5s.

Positive expression: business sense
Negative expression: ineffectuality

Solar point

The 167th degree makes the native into either a high flier in the business world or a dreamer who has lots of great ideas but neither the confidence nor energy to implement them.

This degree needs support energy from other Fire elements within the chart if the native is ever to utilise his or her talents to any great effect. Cold logic at the expense of the emotions is not likely to satisfy a marriage partner, who could be expected to demand more than the native has to offer. In business, however, the compensations are great for here the capacity for logical decision making does not have to be combined with any great conscience about how the firm makes its money or what effect this has upon others; profit and efficiency are of paramount importance. But monetary reward is no real substitute for emotional warmth as you will learn if you have this degree.

Planetary point

The placement of a planet in this degree indicates to natives what they must learn in their relationships and attitudes to others. If Saturn is here, the person is happy to remain alone, feeling he or she does not need others and anyway does not trust them. Such a native must learn to change his or her views. If someone has Venus in this degree, he or she can be too demanding of attention from others.

168th degree

Colour: green. *Sign*: Virgo. 2nd decan. *Qualities*: Mutable/Cardinal, Earth. *Numerological match*: other 6s.
Positive expression: adoring parenthood
Negative expression: possessiveness

Solar point

As a solar point the elemental energy is the mother energy of the sign of Virgo. People born with this degree have an unhappy childhood or else lack many of the material luxuries enjoyed by their friends and classmates. This spurs them to do well at school by working hard, so that they can gain qualifications that will enable them to earn a good income and prosper. Once they have established themselves in society there is nothing they would rather do than find their chosen mate and start a family, lavishing love and all the material possessions upon their children that they did not have themselves.

In a wider context, a native with this energy becomes a mother to all and will be found working for the welfare of others in charities, schools and hospitals. An understanding and appreciation of the luxuries of life is the karma of people with this degree.

Planetary point

A planet in this degree will indicate how the native will learn to appreciate what he or she has. Someone with Mars here will, through wanderings and conquest, learn to be humble. With Jupiter, the native learns to appreciate the value of money and its real use in society.

169th degree

Colour: blue, *Sign*: Virgo. 2nd decan. *Qualities*: Mutable/ Cardinal, Earth. *Numerological match*: other 7s.
Positive expression: imagination
Negative expression: over-sensitive reactions

Solar point

The elemental energy of the 169th degree gives natives both the imagination to create their own dreams and the energy and drive to achieve them. There is a marked ability to tune into nature and to sense the needs of others by some form of sixth sense, though they would scoff at the idea if you mentioned it. There is kindness and sensitivity in their dealings with others which often brings them unexpected rewards.

Friends made are remembered for a lifetime though not always with fondness, for persons with this degree also never forget those who misused them. Partnerships are never easy for them as the people who are attracted to them also tend to exploit them, and it is normally too late when they realise that they have been used.

Artistic ability can be strong.

Planetary point

The placement of a planet in this point affects natives more in a spiritual way than materially. Those with Mercury here can have doubts about the religious tenets that they were brought up with and have a desire to find out whether they are true or not. Jupiter here brings discontent with the material world and the searching for better motives than just earning money for doing work.

170th degree

Colour: black. *Sign*: Virgo. 3rd decan. *Qualities*: Mutable/Fixed, Earth. *Numerological match*: other 8s.
Positive expression: acquisition of wealth
Negative expression: extravagance

Solar point

The elemental energy of the 170th degree gives tenacity and the ambition to both make and spend money.

To find the true expression of natives' emotional needs, the Moon's placement must be considered also. If it is in a Water sign (Pisces, Cancer or Scorpio) they are almost entirely driven by their emotions. If it is in Air, their impetus comes from their childhood dreams, while in Earth there is desire for material security. Only when the placement is in Fire can a native really express his or her need to say to the world, 'Look, I've done it, but now I will rid myself of the responsibility of it.'

People with this degree have no great need to seek after and acquire material goods, having sufficient already. Yet they will spend ninety per cent of their time working at adding to their worldly goods, so that others are likely to regard them as somewhat shallow in their outlook and interests.

Natives are usually found in the well-healed social circles. Most of them work when they don't really need to.

Planetary point

The placement of a planet in this degree is connected with natives' desire for financial security. Mars here indicates that they must do things for themselves as they have little faith in others. The Moon in this degree indicates the need to acquire material wealth or stability before full emotional development can take place.

171st degree

Colour: crimson. *Sign*: Virgo. 3rd decan. *Qualities*: Mutable/Cardinal, Earth. *Numerological match*: other 9s.
Positive expression: imagination, leadership ability
Negative traits: inordinate expectations

Solar point

The 171st degree imparts creative imagination and intuition coupled with leadership ability. It also gives a sharp mind, and an acid tongue at times.

Having inexhaustible reserves of mental energy, natives always attain their objectives in the end. One would not call them academically minded, however. They are adventurous types who prefer to be employed in outdoor work. They are also happier when self-employed as they hate to have anyone breathing down their neck. Their best outlet would be found in any adventurous or risky enterprise where they can make use of their mental energy, intuition and drive.

Many people with this degree are clairvoyant or mediumistic, though they are also inclined to scoff at that which they cannot weigh or measure.

Planetary point

A planet in the 171st degree shows where natives are likely to take more risks than most people. Someone with Venus here can have more than one lover, playing one against the other for the thrill of it. With Jupiter here a person will probably be a speculator or gambler, perhaps frequenting the turf accountants shops or the bingo halls.

172nd degree

Colour: white. *Sign*: Virgo. 3rd decan. *Qualities*: Mutable/Cardinal, Earth. *Numerological match*: other 1s.
Positive expression: organising ability
Negative expression: bossiness

Solar point

The 172nd degree gives natives organising ability and a great capacity for enjoyment. They can give it, too. The giving of enjoyment to others ideally should be incorporated into the career in some way.

Love affairs are usually happy and remembered with fondness though the native can take some time to find his or her partner and settle down. People with this solar degree can be very ambitious for their children, often demanding too much of them. This is usually because they feel that they had themselves wasted much of their lives.

Financial success can generally be gained in business. As the natives are generally well thought of and trusted by those they come into contact with, and have such a capacity for enjoyment which rubs off on those around them, they are usually forgiven for any slight misdemeanours or minor scandals that happen in association with their business.

Planetary point

A planet in the 172nd degree is indicative of organising ability. With Venus here, a person can utilise the artistic ability of others and would make a great manager of a rock band or entertainments centre, or perhaps be an artist's agent. The person with Mars here is able to get others to put physical effort into projects.

173rd degree

Colour: grey. *Sign*: Virgo. 3rd decan. *Qualities*: Mutable/ Cardinal, Earth. *Numerological match*: other 2s.
Positive expression: conservation, preservation of the past
Negative expression: rebelliousness

Solar point

As a solar point the elemental energy of the 173rd degree gives the native some form of ability through the father, family or social background. People born under this degree tend to be the guardians of the family history or, on a broader scale, of the larger societies they were born into. Because the native tends to be extremely methodical and painstaking, it could be thought that he or she is a dull stick-in-the-mud. This, however, is not the case. Anyone born under this degree likes to savour all that is good from the past, and seek to learn from it so that the information may benefit us all both now and in the future.

Parsimonious to the verge of meanness, natives tend to accumulate wealth simply by not squandering money.

Planetary point

If you have a planet in the 173rd degree, it indicates what spiritual gifts or abilities you bring with you into this existence. Mercury here shows an intuitive link with previous existences which can very much enhance this life. Pluto here will bring sexually mature partners.

174th degree

Colour: violet. *Sign*: Virgo. 3rd decan. *Qualities*: Mutable/Cardinal, Earth. *Numerological match*: other 3s.
Positive expression: broad outlook
Negative expression: weird lifestyle

Solar point

People born with the Sun in the 174th degree are able to free themselves from the conditioning brought about by the family and society. There can as a result be a liberal attitude to unconventional unions or partnerships, and natives may be drawn to a partner from a different culture or race.

If you were born with this solar degree, you will either experience many different types of employment before you settle down in your chosen career or you will have a job which involves much travel and changes of environment. The karmic lesson of this degree is to let go of all that is safe and secure in the life you were born into and to branch out and encounter new ideas and experience different lifestyles. In so doing you and your fellow natives become the bringers of reform and change to invigorate society.

Planetary point

A planet in the 174th degree indicates how a native may break with convention. Pluto here can point to unusual sexual tastes or partnerships or strange in relationship to death. Saturn here engenders a concern about distribution of the land and wealth in our society.

151

175th degree

Colour: orange. *Sign*: Virgo. 3rd decan. *Qualities*: Mutable/Cardinal, Earth. *Numerological match*: other 4s.
Positive expression: benefits from friends
Negative expression: failure to trust others

Solar point

The elemental energy of the 175th degree has a friendly angelic being who will assist those born under it to benefit through friends.

If you have this solar degree, you should know that this incarnation is one in which you can rest. Friends and neighbours will come to help you when needed. But you must recognise that this is a special favour bestowed on you, so stop questioning peoples' motives for wanting to befriend you. Be grateful for and enjoy what has been offered. If you refuse to trust those who offer assistance your soul will go into its next incarnation alone, as it is the friends of this life who help you in the next. You can, if you want, have a happy though not particularly exciting life with a close-knit family and many good friends; all you have to do is to learn to accept things at face value rather than look for catches which are rarely there.

Planetary point

A planetary placement in this point indicates where others can be of special assistance to natives. For example, the Moon here would indicate that the mother or womankind in general can be of assistance in times of need, while Mars would be more indicative of the father.

176th degree

Colour: scarlet. *Sign*: Virgo. 3rd decan. *Qualities*: Mutable/Cardinal, Earth. *Numerological match*: other 5s.
Positive expression: clear mind, self-confidence
Negative expression: over-forcefulness

Solar point

The elemental energy of the 176th degree gives the native a clear, rational mind and he or she can usually make sense of complex ideas that others tend to be confused by.

If you have this degree you can build the empires that others can only dream of, for you have the original ideas and the energy to accomplish the practically impossible. All the managerial and organising ability that the sign of Virgo relates to is at your disposal. Your dogged determination will also help you obtain whatever you desire. Your only failing is that you may try to organise those who do not wish it, causing ill feeling or even enmity which can bring about your downfall. Avoid becoming a dictator.

Planetary point

If you have a planet in the 176th degree it will indicate to you how you should apply your organising abilities. With Saturn here, you would be best employed in a large corporation or in a political organisation or trade union. If Venus is here you would enjoy organising social activities for your circle of friends. You would also make a good manager in anything to do with the arts or in the entertainment world.

177th degree

Colour: green. *Sign*: Virgo. 3rd decan. *Qualities*: Mutable/Cardinal, Earth. *Numerological match*: other 6s.
Positive expression: emotional responsiveness
Negative expression: vindictiveness

Solar point

As a solar point the elemental energy of the 177th degree gives all the emotional sensitivity that anyone could require.

If you have this degree, it is better that you should let your partner read this text as you are a reflection of your partner's emotional expression. If kindness is shown to a native of this degree, it will be returned ten-fold. If love is shown, then the love is returned, and if joy is received then joy is given. But be warned: all that is negative can also be reflected. Bring pain to a native of this degree and you will invoke a vengeance that is more terrible than Shiva, the Hindu god of destruction.

Persons with this solar degree can show marked physical beauty. Also they should have no trouble in adapting to most environments as they have the ability to absorb themselves into and become a part of the environment, whatever it happens to be.

Planetary point

Having a planet in this degree will show you what energies you are able to absorb and respond to. For example, with Mercury here you will be mentally agile, and this is a good placement for those who mix with people of different cultures. With Mars here you have the capacity to put up with physically exacting environments.

178th degree

Colour: blue. *Sign*: Virgo. 3rd decan. *Qualities*: Mutable/Cardinal, Earth. *Numerological match*: other 7s.
Positive expression: fertile imagination, resourcefulness
Negative expression: lack of caution, absent-mindedness

Solar point

The 178th degree gives imagination, resourcefulness, practicality, a quick mind and versatility bordering on genius at times. Natives are receptive to new ideas and methods. Often they are capable of developing mediumistic and psychic powers such as clairvoyance and psychometry. Either way they are attracted to organisations to do with the psychic and paranormam and become spiritual investigators or use unconventional methods of healing. The degree favours employment connected with liquids, chemicals, oils, drugs, beverages, canned goods, fish, the sea and hospitals.

Sometimes the native has a marked artistic or musical ability in addition to all his or her other gifts.

Planetary point

A planet in the 178th degree is indicative of inspirational resources. With the Moon here a person may gain inspiration through the emotions, the mother or feminine attributes, while with Jupiter inspiration comes through philosophy, the higher mind, foreign cultures and overseas travel.

179th degree

Colour: black. *Sign*: Virgo. 3rd decan. *Qualities*: Mutable/Cardinal, Earth. *Numerological match*: other 8s.

Positive expression: business acumen
Negative expression: squandering, wastefulness

Solar point

The 179th degree gives business acumen and the kind of shrewd, sharp mind that can turn other people's ideas into going concerns. The natives lack any original ideas themselves, however. They sometimes lead a life of self-imposed solitude, fearing others will try to take credit for what they have done. But they have failed to distinguish what they have achieved from the part played by others, bringing about feelings of discontent and guilt.

If you where born with the Sun in this degree you have the tenacity of mind and patience to succeed where others fear to tread, but make sure you recognise the contribution others have made without which your success would not have been possible.

Planetary point

If you have a planet in this degree it will indicate to you what is the source of inspiration that will lead to your future successes. With Pluto here, for example, you will gain inspiration through the changing sexual ideals or views on death that the general masses hold.

180th degree

Colour: crimson. *Sign*: Libra. 1st decan. *Qualities*: Cardinal, Air. *Numerological match*: other 9s.
Positive expression: sense of justice
Negative expression: immorality

Solar point

The elemental energy of the 180th degree can give natives such strong views on morals and the law of the land that they can become active enforcers of them. This trait can sometimes have a religious expression and there may be strong reforming seal. On the other hand, natives may be radicals and rebels, revolting against the laws and beliefs in the society they were born into. Work or involvement in law enforcement agencies, social welfare, military service or religious and political movements would better express this energy as these institutions uphold the law and are guardians of the moral standards of our society.

Misuse of this energy is the vigilante syndrome — taking the law into one's own hands — or enforcing one's ideals on others.

Planetary point

A planet in the 180th degree reflects the views on public morality the native is likely to hold. When the Moon is here the person can hold strong views about family unity or about feminine roles in society. Someone with Venus here might have strong views regarding morality in artistic expression, objecting to nudity in different art forms and so on.

181st degree

Colour: white. *Sign*: Libra. 1st decan. *Qualities*: Cardinal, Air.
Numerological match: other 1s.
Positive expression: general popularity
Negative expression: pleasure-seeking

Solar point

The 181st degree favours the formation of partnerships and gives natives popularity. They have a fondness of pleasure, social activity and amusements, and an affinity with young people; they often work with children or youth organisations.

People born with this degree are good humoured and have an affectionate, agreeable, courteous personality. They are kind and make friends easily. Love, romance and marriage play an important part in their eventual path to success. There is a liking for fine clothes, adornment and in some cases luxury.

Their life is considerably affected by other people and they usually prefer to work as an employee along with others rather than as their own boss.

Natives greatly appreciate music, painting, and beautiful scenary.

Planetary point

A planet in the 181st degree indicates what type of partnerships or associations would be best made. Mars here is indicative of a native who requires somewhat masterful or fatherly guidance from others, while the Moon shows that a sympathetic listening ear is a necessity.

182nd degree

Colour: grey. *Sign*: Libra. 1st decan. *Qualities*: Cardinal, Air.
Numerological match: other 2s.
Positive expression: philosophical outlook
Negative expression: pessimism

Solar point

The elemental energy of the 182nd degree gives natives emotional balance along with intuition and a sympathetic understanding of the plight of their fellow men.

If you were born with this solar degree you would make a
good arbitrator, because you have the qualities enabling you to
make fair and just decisions, taking all aspects into account
rather than just following the letter of the law.

Marriage tends to go smoothly for people with this degree as
they have the capacity to give as well as to take. They also have
the maturity to forgive and forget.

Work in any form which involves the public is the most
suitable.

Planetary point

When there is a planet in this degree, it is indicative of how
natives can best help others and in so doing help themselves.
For example, Neptune in this degree imparts natives with
intuition and psychic gifts so that they can give advice to others
and help them find the balance they seek.

183rd degree

Colour: violet. *Sign*: Libra. 1st decan. *Qualities*: Cardinal, Air.
Numerological match: other 3s.
Positive expression: adaptability to change
Negative expression: failure to accept and adapt to change

Solar point

The 183rd degree gives natives the ability to adapt quickly and
to be one step ahead of competitors. If utilised in the correct
way there is no reason on earth why people born with this
degree should not become top earners and leaders in their
chosen careers. In partnerships they can only really get on with
people with their own type of degree energy, who thrive upon

competitiveness within the partnership.

There can be a fondness for travel which can result in natives settling down in foreign parts. Children are abundant and usually spoilt.

The moral of this degree is that if at first you don't succeed then try and try again, for if you do you will be more than rewarded for your efforts.

Planetary point

If you have a planet in this degree it indicates how you may have an edge over others around you. Mercury gives a mental edge in solving problems. You are often first off the mark, giving you the advantage in the race to success. Venus here allows you to take things easy as you are able to motivate others to work for you.

184th degree

Colour: orange. *Sign*: Libra. 1st decan. *Qualities*: Cardinal, Air. *Numerological match*: other 4s.
Positive expression: romantic nature
Negative expression: bad choice of partner

Solar point

The elemental energy of the 184th degree gives the native all the emotional expression of the true romantic. If fortunately aspected, wealth and success will come through partnerships.

If you have this degree, it is your choice of partner, either in a business relationship or in a marriage, which will decide whether or not you have the success you desire in this life. Choose badly and your partner will hold you back, but if you choose wisely you will be motivated and assisted in your path to success.

This degree creates some interesting and unusual characters and it must be said that often it is this unusualness that attracts the kind of partner needed.

Care should be taken by natives of this degree not to offend those in authority as they could hinder their progress or force them to move on.

Planetary point

When someone has a planet in the 184th degree it indicates that he or she has an unusual ability, or the power to attract others in some way. Jupiter here may indicate that unusual philosophic views could stimulate others. If Mars is in this point, others are drawn to the native for the feeling of caring protection that he or she exudes.

185th degree

Colour: scarlet. *Sign*: Libra. 1st decan. *Qualities*: Cardinal, Air.
Numerological match: other 5s.
Positive expression: balanced mental energy
Negative expression: scattered mental energy

Solar point

The energy of the 185th degree endows natives with a quiet, refined and broad-minded nature.

People born with this degree are often drawn into other people's disputes, and try to settle them. They do, however, prefer a quiet life and will avoid arguments and disputes in their own personal lives. They are attracted towards mental pursuits. In particular they like music; they have splendid natural abilities in this field and should endeavour to learn an instrument. By this means they can temporarily escape from the pressures that society places them under.

Planetary point

A planet placed in this elemental degree is indictive of how the native would benefit by relaxation, especially through music. Someone with Mars here would enjoy music more in the busy disco type of environment and release his or her pent up energy through dance. Whoever has Venus here on the other hand would like to dim the lights and enjoy soft music with a close friend.

186th degree

Colour: green. *Sign*: Libra. 1st decan. *Qualities*: Cardinal, Air.
Numerological match: other 6s.
Positive expression: calm, soft manner
Negative expression: immaturity

Solar point

Anyone born with the Sun in the 186th degree has gentle and refined qualities. Natives are always kind and sociable, and often show marked physical beauty or graceful manners.

If you were born under its sway you will have ability in music and the decorative arts. You are a natural peacemaker, being able to calm the ruffled feelings of others by the very presence of your elemental vibration. You should find satisfying employment in the entertainments industry or as a host to guests, because of your ability to perceive the needs of others and win them over with your charm and grace.

The negative application of the energy of this degree is over-indulgence in physical pleasures. Also, accidents may mar the physical beauty.

Planetary point

If you have a planet in this degree it will indicate to you where you are likely to exhibit a softening touch. For example, if Saturn is here you would be able to employ a softer touch than normal in business transactions. If Venus is in this degree, you should seriously consider embarking on a theatrical career for you could be a star.

187th degree

Colour: blue. *Sign*: Libra. 1st decan. *Qualities*: Cardinal, Air. *Numerological match*: other 7s.
Positive expression: love of life
Negative expression: sensationalism

Solar point

As a solar point the elemental energy is like that of Neptune in Libra, which last occurred between 1942 and 1957. In its positive aspect it brings the love of life itself, and working for the rebuilding of social normality after upheaval, though, as in the Neptune effect, you can only rebuild after tears. The degree promotes developments in the sciences, especially the occult sciences, but it is better that they are developed for peaceful purposes rather than for war. Neptune was last in this degree in October 1945, when World War II was over and people had to look ahead to the long and arduous task of rebuilding the economy.

Those of you born with the Sun in this degree have some similar task to perform within your own social environment, bringing into balance that which is out of tune. The task will be a difficult one and long drawn out, perhaps taking you a lifetime, but rewarding nevertheless.

Planetary point

The 187th degree indicates by the planet resident in it what is out of balance in the native's life and which areas require some attention if the soul is to develop. When Jupiter is here the native may fail to settle down, or may not learn money sense. Someone with Mars here is likely to use his or her physical abilities for self-gain rather than for assisting others.

188th degree

Colour: black *Sign*: Libra. 1st decan. *Qualities*: Cardinal, Air.
Numerological match: other 8s.
Positive expression: personal freedom
Negative expression: contentiousness

Solar point

The elemental energy of the 188th degree is that of the social reformer. Last most active in the 1950s, this degree demands plenty of personal freedom and social expression. There are no class barriers for people born with the Sun here and if they have to work to become a millionaires to make the changes they demand, they will do just that.

This degree can be associated with the growth of union power in the '50s, when men joined together for a fairer share of what they felt was in the offing and attempted to institute the changes required in society.

If you were born under this solar point you can be disputative, voicing loudly the changes you desire to take place. There can be losses through romance or at least some difficulty in that area, for your aspirations are wider ones than just contentment in the home. People in the professions, such as lawyers, doctors and teachers, use this degree to best effect by working for the good of society.

Planetary point

When there is a planet in the 188th degree it indicates where natives would like to see changes occur. With Pluto, they will bring changes in the sexual tastes of the general masses, while if Uranus is here they will bring new scientific development.

189th degree

Colour: crimson. *Sign*: Libra. 1st decan. *Qualities*: Cardinal, Air. *Numerological match*: other 9s.
Positive expression: observational powers
Negative expression: over-heated passions, rashness

Solar point

The elemental energy of the 189th degree promotes the development of the abilities of observation and perception. It gives clear vision or objectives, refinement of taste and an idealistic outlook.

People born with this degree are enterprising and will be often found in positions where they exert some authority over others. In early life they are often rash and impulsive, trying to accomplish too much too soon. Only by the learning of hard lessons and with the coming of maturity are the ambitions fulfilled and real satisfaction attained. Further education is generally sought late in life, when the native needs to keep abreast of new developments. Children of this degree can in some cases show genius or high intellect. Friends or partners are best found among professional people.

Planetary point

Whoever has a planet in the 189th degree must learn patience before they can achieve very much. If the Moon is here the native must learn through the experience of emotional upheaval the true value of his or her partner. With Mars in this degree the native learns through combat and personal defeat before he is able to build his castles of strength.

190th degree

Colour: white. *Sign*. Libra. 2nd decan. *Qualities*: Cardinal/ Fixed, Air. *Numerological match*: other 1s.
Positive expression: love of justice
Negative expression: over-bearing manner

Solar point

Whoever is born with the Sun in the 190th degree has a love of justice, peace and harmony. They are courteous, agreeable and, as a rule, even tempered.

If you have this solar point, you are affectionate and sympathetic to those around you so you should choose your friends and associates with care least you find yourself knee-deep in other people's problems.

Office work or a clean environment is desirable for people with this degree as they like order and to keep everything in its place. Romance, however, can be a problem because they tend to reflect back the mood of whoever they are with; if the partner selected is bad tempered they will become the same and may eventually seek newer and more peaceful pastures.

Any of the fine arts could be developed to a high standard by persons with this degree.

Planetary point

With any planet here, the 190th degree is an indicator of natives' ability to share with others. If that planet happens to be Saturn, the native will have a wise head before his or her years, and have an interest in antiques and history in general. Someone with Mars here will be energetic and forceful and would make a good lawyer or doctor.

191st degree

Colour: grey. *Sign*: Libra. 2nd decan. *Qualities*: Cardinal/Fixed, Air. *Numerological match*: other 2s.
Positive expression: compassion, caring
Negative expression: suppressed emotions

Solar point

People born with the Sun in the 191st degree have sensitivity, patience and compassion for all. They are also quiet, hard-working types who keep everything going smoothly. They are wise counsellors who listen with a sympathetic ear and soothe troubled souls. Though basically peaceable, if ever roused to anger they will endeavour to end disputes in the shortest manner possible, be that by direct conflict or by walking out and closing the door behind them.

The best kind of employment for persons with this degree is

that involving the care of others, such as nursing or welfare work. Many hairdressers have this degree and people working behind the bar in public houses; they will lend a sympathetic ear to the stranger who needs to unload his worries.

Planetary point

A planet in the 191st degree will indicate to the person born with it how he or she can give joy and comfort to others. Venus here would indicate places of entertainment or even amusing people on a social level. Saturn could bring natives into work with the aged and socially deprived.

192nd degree

Colour: violet. *Sign*: Libra. 2nd decan. *Qualities*: Cardinal/Fixed, Air. *Numerological match*: other 3s.
Positive expression: mild manner, temperate habits
Negative expression: lack of concentration

Solar point

The elemental energy of the 192nd degree gives natives a mild, sincere, earnest and kindly disposition. They prefer to see the good in things rather than look for the bad. There is a love of peace, justice, mercy and harmony in their lives and they will go out of their way to attain just that.

There can be a fondness for travel and many people with this degree will cover the globe in the course of their lives, with holidays in far off and exotic places. Benefits come through the opposite sex and powerful friends made in the course of their travels.

Scientific, philosophic or spiritual organisations, groups or clubs also tend to attract people with this degree, and many a mason will have it in his chart. Marriages or partnerships can be somewhat unconventional.

Planetary point

The elemental energy of the 192nd degree modifies the influence of the planet placed in it in such a way that it is much milder than usual. Someone with the Moon here will be less prone to extremes of emotion. With Mars, a person is less aggressive in manner, and with Saturn less cold.

Colour: orange. *Sign*: Libra. 2nd decan. *Qualities*: Cardinal/ Fixed, Air. *Numerological match*: other 4s.
Positive expression: preservation of tradition
Negative expression: rebellious nature

Solar point

A person born with the Sun in the 193rd degree will have the unrewarding and arduous task of ensuring that social reforms do not take place too quickly or before their time.

Natives of this degree are the preservers of our heritage and may have strong views about Green Belt areas, look up to Royalty and tend to be right wing in their politics. They generally have a great love of freedom and independence and abhor those who try to enforce changes upon them. Difficulties in the home life or the loss of one of the parents in the formative years make people with this degree cherish the tried and tested traditions which they will do all in their power to protect should they be threatened.

The negative working of this degree can result in the native becoming a tyrant or despot who wants to force his views of what is right on others by violent means. (See also the 198th degree.)

Planetary point

If you have a planet in the 193rd degree it indicates in which particular area of life you stick to old habits and tradition. For example, if you have the Moon here, you will most likely take the view that one must marry before having sex or starting a family, and you will be against extra-marital relationships. Those born with Uranus here, however, are likely to break with traditions.

194th degree

Colour: scarlet. *Sign*: Libra. 2nd decan. *Qualities*: Cardinal/ Fixed, Air. *Numerological match*: other 5s.
Positive expression: communicating new concepts to society
Negative expression: gossip

Solar point

The 194th degree has a touch of eccentricity about it. Natives are often leaders in setting new trends of conduct, but tend, especially in later life, to cling on to outdated fashions and customs too long. They may be the first to accept new concepts in music and to sport new fashions in clothes, but they may be reluctant eventually to let go of them. Examples are the rocker at 40, still dressing up as he did in his teens, and the couple still living together now that it is fashionable to marry. Or, someone may be the first to try a microwave oven and the last to let go of his old record collection. (See also the 198th degree.)

Planetary point

If you have a planet in the 194th degree it will indicate what area of your life you will totally change. With Uranus here, you are a young person who can accept new scientific discoveries and applications with ease. If Venus is here, you would quickly latch on to new music or forms of artistic expression.

195th degree

Colour: green. *Sign*: Libra. 2nd decan. *Qualities*: Cardinal/Fixed, Air. *Numerological match*: other 6s.
Positive expression: sincerity
Negative expression: snobbery

Solar point

The 195th degree gives natives a fondness for pleasure and social life and they will do whatever is necessary to obtain it. Old when young and young when old, they are just as at home in an expensive restaurant or hotel as in the local working men's club, as long as the company is stimulating. They could be described as intuitive, philosophical and generous, and they do not judge other people too hastily.

There is a fondness for romance and pleasure which make it difficult for them to settle down even if other parts of the chart indicate that they desire it. Marriage is much better left to the middle years when natives have the experience and maturity to enjoy it.

Gains are best made through companies, firms, partnerships and by association with others. (See also the 198th solar degree.)

Planetary point

A planet in the 195th degree is an indicator of what environment would provide the best social activities for the native. Someone with Uranus here would enjoy the bizarre and unusual and like surprises, while if the Moon is here he or she would prefer to entertain in the intimate surroundings of the home.

196th degree

Colour: blue. *Ruler*: Libra. 2nd decan. *Qualities*: Cardinal/ Fixed, Air. *Numerological match*: other 7s.
Positive expression: original views
Negative expression: imprudence

Solar point

The 196th degree gives natives a dignified bearing, keen perception and a love of nature and domestic pets. They are sociable and tend to be popular. There is originality and independence in their views on religious and scientific topics and they show an interest in social welfare. As their ideas can be rather controversial they are liable to bring down the wrath of those in authority upon themselves, but they are usually will able to wriggle out of any problems they get themselves into.

The next very active phase of this degree is in the year 2376 when the age of Aquarius arrives. Those of you with this solar degree are here to prepare the foundations of the future age by the originality of thought you show now. (See also the 198th degree.)

Planetary point

If you have a planet in the 196th degree it indicates in what area you can help to introduce change in society. For example, the Moon would point to some kind of emotional change.

197th degree

Colour: black. *Sign*: Libra. 2nd decan. *Qualities*: Cardinal/ Fixed, Air. *Numerological match*: other 8s.
Positive expression: serious nature
Negative expression: old fashioned outlook

Solar point

The elemental energy of the 197th degree tends to give an affable disposition and a thoughtful, compassionate nature though perhaps a little too serious at times. The natives are deliberate in action and very expressive in speech when interested in the topic of conversation. They tend to be tolerant of the attitudes and lifestyles of others and are thorough in all that they undertake, having the ability to study and apply their knowledge. As a rule they do well financially as they attend to detail and rarely make mistakes through being rash. This carefulness can, however, be a weak point as natives are afraid of all but the tried and tested routes to success and will not speculate or gamble unless it is a certain bet.

People with this degree form long-term friendships or romantic ties and the latter years tend to be far more pleasurable for them than their formative ones. (See also the 198th degree.)

Planetary point

A planet in the 197th degree is an indicator of energy which can be easily summoned up and applied to everyday tasks in natives' lives. If the Moon is in this degree it gives an emotional maturity way beyond that person's years.

198th degree

MAGICAL HOME OF THE ELEMENT AIR
(*Strongest effect*: 5 degrees on either side)

Colour: crimson. *Sign*: Libra. 2nd decan. *Qualities*: Cardinal/Fixed, Air. *Numerological match*: other 9s.
Positive expression: originality of mind and imagination, inventiveness, new ideals
Negative expression: use of mental and creative power for own ends and subjugation of others, deceitfulness

Solar point

The elemental energy of Air is at its strongest in this degree. Those of you born with your Sun in this degree have been selected to prepare mankind for the coming of the age of Aquarius. You are the instigators, inventors and originators in today's society who will help to bring in the new era of technological and social change in our world. You are the new computer wizards, the electronic engineers and inventors, the satellite and space scientists — in other words, the promotors of everything new and forward-looking in our society. It is with your inspiration that the elements of Fire will build upon the new foundations of Earth. You may not feel you are anyone extraordinary or appear any different to your neighbour yet it is your idealism and foresight which will enable mankind to take the next step forward in his future evolution. Have faith in yourselves and act upon your ideals, no matter what adversity you encounter from the dying age of Pisces. Without your idealism to build upon Man will stagnate and become like the dinosaurs — extinct.

Planetary point

Each of the planets listed will have the following effects upon natives and therefore, in the long run, on mankind in this magical degree —

Moon: brings new avenues of emotional expression and makes a person reconsider his or her existing attitude towards home life.

Mercury: creates forward thinkers who will plan and map out new concepts and ideals in a way in which the general massess will understand.

Venus: brings into acceptance new forms of entertainment or artistic expression.

Mars: is connected with the utilisation of manpower and energy, new methods of warfare and the bringing of equality of the sexes.

Jupiter: effects how money is earned and spent and will bring about acceptance of new religious beliefs or help stabilise older ones.

Saturn: helps to stabilise and consolidate new ideas so that they turn into the firmly based institutions of the future, while maintaining balance with the old.

Neptune: by the powers of imagination and intuition, and through the psychic senses, helps the old age of Pisces make way for the new age to come.

Uranus: comes into his own in this degree, as it is the planet of inventors and inventions.

Pluto: affects how the many and varied sexual tastes of mankind will be accepted, and perhaps bring some conformity.

The elemental ruler of Water has had more power for the past few thousand years than any other, and too often people have let their emotions confuse the issues. Soon, in the year 2376 AD, it will be the turn of the element of Air and those who are inventive enough can become the rulers of our destiny as well as their own.

199th degree

Colour: white. *Sign*: Libra. 2nd decan. *Qualities*: Cardinal/Fixed, Air. *Numerological match*: other 1s.
Positive expression: creative mind, leadership qualities
Negative expression: destructive tendencies

Solar point

The 199th degree gives natives a creative mind and leadership qualities. If you were born with this solar point you should ask no-one to do things that you would not undertake yourself. You are fortunate in that you have the ability to lead us all into the dawn of a new era, to conceive and implement new ideas and to lead by the example that you yourself set. You should learn to assert yourself in whatever environment you find yourself in, be that at home with the family or in the world of commerce. If you succeed in this task you will at the same time attain all the material wealth and happiness that you desire. (See also the 198th degree.)

Planetary point

If you have a planet in the 199th degree it indicates what energies you must learn to control and how you should lead others by example. If the Moon is here, you will set new trends in home life and partnerships for the future. With Mercury here, you will become a brilliant communicator and be able to explain complex concepts and ideas in an easy-to-understand manner.

200th degree

Colour: grey. *Sign*: Libra. 3rd decan. *Qualities*: Cardinal/Mutable, Air. *Numerological match*: other 2s.
Positive expression: patience, compassion
Negative expression: emotional instability

Solar point

The elemental energy of the 200th degree blesses the natives with intuitive understanding and the desire to help others with their problems. Therefore the kind of work they will most enjoy is in the welfare services or in the entertainment field. Actors and all kinds of entertainers, barmaids and anyone working in the service industries as well as people in the caring professions, such as nurses, could well fall within the realm of this degree.

If you were born with this solar degree, you have intuition and compassion beyond the normal and you need only find the right environment to put it to work. If you share things with others it is more than likely that they in turn will respond and share with you. The purpose of this degree is to help mankind overcome his selfishness. (See also the 198th degree.)

Planetary point

A planet in the 200th degree is indicative of how natives may learn to share with others (and in so doing teach them also to share). Those with Venus here can find their best expression through the arts, the entertainment world or whatever has feminine connections. Anyone with Mars here would be a great sportsman or protector of the weak.

201st degree

Colour: violet. *Sign*: Libra. 3rd decan. *Qualities*: Cardinal/Mutable, Air. *Numerological match*: other 3s.
Positive expression: stabilising effect
Negative expression: selfishness

Solar point

The elemental energy of the 201st degree gives natives the ability to analyse their problems and those of society in general. This fits them for work dealing with the problems of others, such as in the Citizen's Advice Bureau or various kinds of social work.

Problems come with the ever increasing speed and complexity of modern society, and it is the task of persons born with this degree to help bring healing and balance to a strife-stricken society. Work connected with mental disorders, stress and related fields would suit then ideally, and so too would advisory positions in large companies and corporations. Natives are capable of a special perspicacity which allows them to solve the new kinds of problems which stump others as the next century approaches. (See also the 198th degree.)

Planetary point

The 201st degree gives an intuitive and intellectual understanding of the energy of the planet placed here. Natives can use it to help others understand also. Mars here gives an understanding of physical energies and what motivates people. Natives can therefore draw the best from people and would make good sports trainers or military commanders.

202nd degree

Colour: orange. *Sign*: Libra. 3rd decan. *Qualities*: Cardinal/Mutable, Air. *Numerological match*: other 4s.
Positive expression: protection of established institutions
Negative expression: living in the past

Solar point

The elemental energy of the 202nd degree promotes the secure, stable institutions of society. Those of you born under its influence are to become the guardians of that which is to be saved and cherished for future generations.

There must always be people who maintain the institutions which ensure our society does not revert to the age of chaos and in a small way you are a part of that scheme. The bank employees who protect the wealth of our nation, the government ministers who introduce our laws, museum curators who protects our history and the librarians who guard our knowledge are all types who may be born with this solar degree. If you are blessed with this energy you are one of those citizens who help keep a stable society. (See also the 198th solar degree.)

Planetary point

If you have a planet in the 202nd degree, it is an indicator of the energy or the kind of institution which you will profit from. With the planet Saturn here, you may work to maintain our country codes and to see that our national heritage is not lost. You are also likely to work for a large company. If you have Venus here, you would strive to keep the arts alive. (See also the 198th degree.)

203rd degree

Colour: scarlet. *Sign*: Libra. 3rd decan. *Qualities*: Cardinal/
Mutable, Air. *Numerological match*: other 5s.
Positive expression: sociability, lack of snobbery
Negative expression: frivolity

Solar point

The elemental energy of the 203rd degree gives natives the
communicative powers to transcend cultural and social differ-
ences between peoples and to mix with all.

No matter how roguish persons with this degree may appear,
you just can't help liking them. They were born with the ability
to break down the barriers created by social class and wealth
and reintroduce the children of Eden back into the realms of
sharing. You may find them anywhere. One might be a charitable millionaire, another just the man on the street corner but
whoever they might be they are people who care for other
people and in some way bring them closer together. There is no
class distinction for them and they will be at home wherever
they find themselves, being able to gain the trust of others. (See
also the 198th degree.)

Planetary point

A planet in the 203rd degree is an indicator of how natives may
teach others to share what they have with their fellows. If the
Moon is here a native can bring out the emotional feelings of
people who never usually express them. With Venus a native
would seek to bring the arts to all classes of society. Someone
with Mars may physically fight for what he feels is fair, and so
on.

204th degree

Colour: green. *Sign*: Libra. 3rd decan. *Qualities*: Cardinal/
Mutable, Air. *Numerological match*: other 6s.
Positive expression: artistic flair, physical beauty
Negative expression: vanity, desire for luxury

Solar point

The 204th degree often gives natives the attributes of the
goddess Venus. They may have marked physical beauty and

grace, or a sensitivity to beauty that they express through the arts.

People born with this degree do, however, require reassurance from others that what they are doing is appreciated, otherwise they may give up trying. Their artistic sensitivity may reach to the heights of artistic genius if allowed adequate expression, and if they have more than three points in the Fire elements then they can win public acclaim as well as admiration from their immediate friends and family.

A native of this degree has a lesson of peace to teach, but first that person must find the peace within himself.

Planetary point

If there is a planet here, it points to where natives should direct any artistic abilities they might have. The Moon here would indicate in the home or through feminine activities such as hairdressing or modelling, while Saturn would make someone a better collector of the arts than an originator in this field.

205th degree

Colour: blue. *Sign*: Libra. 3rd decan. *Qualities*: Cardinal/ Mutable, Air. *Numerological match*: other 7s.
Positive expression: artistic inspiration
Negative expression: bad luck in finance

Solar point

As a solar point the elemental energy of the 205th degree gives the native a creative talent in music or drama but perhaps not the confidence of the performer.

If you have this solar degree you could do well in the field of the arts, but not as a performer in the concert hall or on the stage. You would do better as a composer of music or as a playwright. You are very attracted to the opposite sex, and are likely to form a long lasting partnership early in your life as you badly need someone to support you — in the emotional sense rather than in the physical. This is generally a good degree for those who live in contentment with someone they love.

There can be mediumistic or clairvoyant ability, but natives are advised not to become too deeply involved in occult matters as they are too impressionable and could become emotionally disturbed by some of the events which can occur to those who delve deeply into the mysteries of the other world.

Planetary point

A planet in the 205th degree can be an indicator of how natives may find an outlet for their artistic inspiration. Mars here could give them the energy and confidence to be a performer in whatever art form they may have taken up, while Jupiter here would indicate the employment of others to produce artistic works.

206th degree

Colour: black. *Sign*: Libra. 3rd decan. *Qualities*: Cardinal/ Mutable, Air. *Numerological match*: other 8s.
Positive expression: creative builder
Negative expression: stealer of others' creations

Solar point

The elemental energy of the 206th degree gives the native the ability to build, both on the emotional and the physical level. On the one hand energy can be put into building up a sound marriage partnership and happy family relationships. On the other hand, on the physical side, a person with this degree can become involved in the building industry. In other words, this degree has much to do with partnerships, families and the expression of love and the arts, and it can also be concerned with the building contractors, painters and decorators and such like who construct or maintain those very homes we raise our families in.

Original in thought and deed, though always practical, people with this degree are often found in jobs to do with the design and planning of towns or houses, or in local government departments concerned with building or domestic needs.

If you were born with this degree your best outlets are through partnerships and a construction industry or in any form of maintenance work.

Planetary point

A planet in this point is an indicator of how natives may form partnerships or build their future homes. If Uranus is here, natives (who are still quite young at present) will be unpredictable and may choose houses of funny designs, or they may make unusual choices of decor or partner. Those with Venus would require luxury and comfort in the home and a beautiful decor.

207th degree

Colour: crimson. *Sign*: Libra. 3rd decan. *Qualities*: Cardinal/Mutable, Air. *Numerological match*: other 9s.
Positive expression: spiritual energy
Negative expression: religious fanaticism

Solar point

The elemental energy of the 207th degree gives natives a zeal for converting others to their beliefs, be they political, religious or whatever. The best outlet for the energy is through the principal religious faiths of the times. But I am sure that many members of the unusual or way-out cults and evangelical religious sects were born with this solar degree. The working of this energy can be found in all walks of religious life, however, including among those who have religious beliefs while still living a perfectly normal life. An example of the degree's negative manifestation is that of the religious fanatics found in countries like Iran and Israel. Balance in outlook must be learned if these natives are to enter the kingdoms of glory that they so fervently hanker after.

Planetary point

A planet in the 207th degree can tell us something about the religious beliefs of the natives. People with Mars or Neptune here have beliefs which differ from those of the masses. With Venus, the Moon or Jupiter, they tend to hold more orthodox religious beliefs.

208th degree

Colour: white. *Sign*: Libra. 3rd decan. *Qualities*: Cardinal/Mutable, Air. *Numerological match*: other 1s.
Positive expression: wealth, prestige
Negative expression: greed

Solar point

The 208th solar degree has a karmic lesson to teach. Those born under its influence can rise to high positions of power and authority over others. But they can just as easily have that power taken from them by the angelic forces that granted it, if they fail to apply their gifts with compassion. An example might be that of the high court judge who is disgraced in a sex scandal; he is punished because of his sanctimonious and hypocritical treatment of similar cases. Another is that of the wealthy industrialist who takes more from society than he gives and ends up in financial ruin. All such cases might be attributed to the energy of this degree.

People with this degree are given a rise in station because they are owed a karmic debt, but if they show that they are too spiritually immature to handle what they have been given, they will have it stripped from them just as a hord of ants will do to a carcase.

If you were born with this degree, your karma is to accept responsibility. With it can come riches or ruin — the choice is yours.

Planetary point

As a planetary point, the 208th degree is an indicator of the area in which the native should develop his or her responsibilities. With Venus here, vanity must be put aside and the native should strive instead to bring beauty to others. With Mars, the native must learn to control the great physical energy given by this planet for the benefit of others.

209th degree

Colour: grey. *Sign*: Libra. 3rd decan. *Qualities*: Cardinal/Mutable, Air. *Numerological match*: other 2s.
Positive expression: ability to share
Negative expression: disputatiousness

Solar point

This is the last degree of the Scales. Those born under its vibrations are offered a chance to share with others all that they have, including their innermost secrets. Nearly always the natives either marry or becomes involved with those who would be considered by some as socially inferior. There is good reason for this. It is so that the natives share their worldly goods with the less well off rather than in having a partner who helps provide for them. They must also open all their hidden closets and share with someone else their deepest feelings and thoughts. 'Not me,' I hear you say, yet it is only by being completely open that a person can ever hope to make spiritual progress. People born with this degree will have to learn to take care of others in some way if they are to evolve and tread upon the path of enlightenment.

Planetary point

A planet in the 209th degree indicates to natives where they failed in past incarnations to share a part of themselves fully with somebody else. If the Moon is here, it means they have never fully opened up emotionally to anyone in the past, but they should have the ability to do so in this incarnation. When Mercury is here, a native must learn to broaden his or her mind.

210th degree

Colour: violet. *Sign*: Scorpio. 1st decan. *Qualities*: Fixed, Water. *Numerological match*: other 3s.
Positive expression: deep probing
Negative expression: failure to face reality

Solar point

The 210th degree gives natives a philosophic bent and the intuition to delve into the mysteries of life, be that in the fields of religion, science or history. The minds of these natives are inquiring and, if not satisfied with official explanations or answers to any question, they will investigate and try to find the truth of the matter themselves.

Work in any form of research is good for people with this solar degree but their true karma is to seek out and find the solutions to the problems that our race will encounter now that the Aquarian Age is close upon us.

In romance, persons with this degree can have the habit of checking up on their partner if they think anything is amiss.

Planetary point

A planet in the 210th degree determines in what direction the investigative leanings of natives will take. For example, Mars here makes marvellous policemen and detectives who will put great effort into sorting out public disorder or in solving crimes.

211th degree

Colour: orange. *Sign*: Scorpio. 1st decan. *Qualities*: Fixed, Water. *Numerological match*: other 4s.
Positive expression: strong will, determination
Negative expression: proneness to accidents

Solar point

As a solar point the elemental energy of the 211th degree gives such qualities as strength of mind, will-power determination, tenacity and powers of concentration.

If you were born with this solar degree, you should have the strength to carry out social reforms in the environment in which you live. You may suffer persecution from others but in the end, through sheer persistence, your efforts on everyone's behalf will be recognised by all. On a mundane level, you can succeed at whatever you apply yourself to. You have only yourself to blame if a project fails, because that would mean that you gave in instead of fighting to the death. The three hundred Spartans of Greek mythology who gave their lives while holding back the whole Persian army till their country was ready to defend itself are examples of this type.

Planetary point

Any planet in this elemental point is indicative of what powers of determination the native possesses. The young person born with Uranus here will be ambitious and seek self-advancement and personal gain. He or she will have practical ability and is likely to become involved in the occult. Neptune here gives inventiveness and perseverance in the sciences.

212th degree

Colour: scarlet. *Sign*: Scorpio. 1st. decan. *Qualities*: Fixed, Water. *Numerological match*: other 5s.
Positive expression: boldness, positiveness
Negative expression: sarcasm

Solar point

The 212th degree makes natives somewhat obstinate. They are bold, though with a tendency towards recklessness. Also, ingenuity and shrewdness is displayed. There is a desire for knowledge, though not always with any special purpose in mind. They are frequently secretive about what they have learned, being unwilling to share it with others. Also, they tend to be unwilling to lean upon other people in any way.

There can be a great attraction towards the mysteries and occult sciences.

The knowledge gathered in this life will be of great benefit to natives in the next incarnation. It is for this reason that no great use may be made of what has been learned in this lifetime — this is just the gathering time.

Planetary point

For those of you with a planet here, this degree concerns the knowledge you need to gather for your soul's future existence. With Venus here, you need to absorb artistic beauty so that it may flower again in the future. If Mars is here, you need to strengthen the soul through persisting with arduous physical effort.

213th degree

Colour: green. *Sign*: Scorpio. 1st decan. *Qualities*: Fixed, Water. *Numerological match*: other 6s.
Positive expression: carefree nature, generosity
Negative expression: desire for luxury

Solar point

The 213th degree gives a person born with it a carefree and generous nature and an inclination to lavish expenditure on things which bring comfort. This degree is one of the soul's resting points and natives born with their solar energy here will have everything provided for them in this life with the minimum of effort — they only have to learn to reach out and grasp what is being offered. In particular, legacies can leave them well provided for in the middle period of their lives.

With regards employment, anything to do with the watery elements or matters connected with the dead would be suitable.

This location of solar energy increases the passions and emotions and can create a love of sensation, luxury and pleasure. Natives will be ardent in love and demonstrative in their affections.

Planetary point

A planet in the 213th degree indicates the form of assistance natives will receive most in this life, particularly in relation to the Elements. The Moon or Neptune would indicate emotional assistance (Water), while Mars and Jupiter would indicate benefit through Fire and the energy to win. Mercury would give the mental inspiration to succeed (the Element of Air).

214th degree

Colour: blue. *Sign*: Scorpio. 1st decan. *Qualities*: Fixed, Water. *Numerological match*: other 7s.
Positive expression: intensified emotions
Negative expression: emotional instability

Solar point

The 214th degree endows natives with intensified emotional feelings. They experience levels of joy and pleasure beyond that of the average person, but pain can be felt to a much greater degree also. Temper can be very short as well with this heightened sensitivity. These individuals are often innovative or inventive though they are not always successful at realising their ideas on the physical plane. They need a partner with good practical sense and a head for business to complement their talent for producing novel ideas.

People with this degree consume more beverages than is the norm as there is a great need to replenish bodily fluids.

Planetary point

The placement of a planet in this degree shows in what way natives may have a raised sensitivity. For example, with Venus they would have a sensuous nature and be able to both give and receive great love.

215th degree

Colour: black. *Ruler*: Scorpio. 1st decan. *Qualities*: Fixed, Water. *Numerological match*: other 8s.
Positive expression: emotional wisdom
Negative expression: reclusiveness

Solar point

People born with the Sun in the 215th degree are wise beyond their years with regards the emotional side of life. This is because they bring with them the emotional wisdom of the many lives they have lived before. There is less need for these people to become in love with love as they have already learned that lesson in previous lives and have come back to assist others learn that same lesson. They tend to love the natural world — the land, plants and animals — rather than a particular individual.

People born with this solar degree can be most stubborn fighters when it comes to saving that which they love. They are often good at scientific subjects, especially chemistry. Because of their persistance and dogged effort they generally manage to achieve whatever they set their heart on.

Planetary point

A planet in the 215th degree is an indicator of what energies natives have in abundance to share with others and to help elevate them. For example, Jupiter gives natives a philosophic nature to help get to the very root of others' problems.

216th degree

Colour: crimson. *Ruler*: Scorpio. 1st decan. *Qualities*: Fixed, Water. *Numerological match*: other 9s.
Positive expression: firmness, determination
Negative expression: vindictiveness

Solar point

The 216th degree gives the natives leadership qualities and the capacity for hard work, so that they are able to accomplish much if they choose. They are very good at practical things, with a good mechanical sense and inventiveness. Their character shows determination and forcefulness. However, their matter-of-fact attitude and brusque manner can give the impression that they are insensitive to the feelings of others and thus upset people. Actually they tend to hide their thoughts and feelings and would make loyal employees who could be trusted with any work that needs to be kept confidential. They would also make cool diplomats who would never reveal the true intentions of their governments.

This karma is an active one and many varied and stimulating circumstances must be encountered and conquered by natives in the course of this life.

Planetary point

The 216th degree shows, by the planet resident in it, what environments or circumstances must be conquered in this life. Someone with Mars here would travel much and become involved in the quarrels and disputes of others, while at the same time seeking to protect those who cannot help themselves. Whoever has Neptune here has much to learn in the secret or occult arts to further spiritual development.

217th degree

Colour: white. *Sign*: Scorpio. 1st. decan. *Qualities*: Fixed, Water. *Numerological match*: other 1s.
Positive expression: authority and leadership
Negative expression: cold criticism, suspicion

Solar point

The 217th degree creates a strong willed, ambitious native who possesses a shrewd mind and keen judgement.

People born with this degree are openly critical of that with which they disagree. They can be painfully blunt to others, though their intention is not to hurt but rather to bring out into the open whatever offends them. They can be original, daring and enterprising, putting a good deal of energy into anything they decide to do, but they are sceptical of whatever others promise and prefer a bird in the hand rather than two in the bush.

Natives do best when self-employed as they hate to be watched over by others.

Planetary point

If you have a planet in the 217th degree, it represents what you are sceptical of or have reserved feelings about and must test before you are certain about them. With Mars here, you must fight your own wars and win your own battles to assure yourself of your physical capabilities. If Jupiter is in this degree you must have independence in financial matters or control the purse-strings in the home.

Colour: grey. *Sign*: Scorpio. 1st decan. *Qualities*: Fixed, Water.
Numerological match: other 2s.
Positive expression: emotional support
Negative expression: problems with children

Solar point

Everyone born with the Sun in the 218th degree has a karmic debt to pay. Natives must in this life strive to be of emotional comfort and assistance to those in need, but they should not expect to receive thanks for their efforts. They are capable of benefiting others through their advice but are unable to be their own counsel or find what they truly seek this life, having already taken what was not theirs in a previous existence. They can at times be quick-tempered and aggressive, sensing that all is not as it should be and resenting that others should have what they desire while they do not. They will find it extremely difficult to sustain acts of kindness for any length of time and yet would give anything to be the recipients of kind deeds on the part of others.

There will be strife in marriage or loss through business partnerships unless other planets in the birth chart are more favourably placed.

Planetary point

With a planet in the 218th degree you have a karmic lesson to learn in this lifetime. The Moon here is similar to the solar point and indicates an emotional lesson to do with giving to others rather than receiving. Saturn here would indicate a long life of responsibility, and by long life we mean 75 years or more.

219th degree

Colour: violet. *Sign*: Scorpio. 1st decan. *Qualities*: Fixed, Water.
Numerological match: other 3s.
Positive expression: gain by legacy
Negative expression: over-indulgence

Solar point

The 219th degree brings freedom from hardship and generally a restful life to those born under it. More will be earned by their partner than by themselves. While this may allow them to take it easy in this life, it is in fact a lesson to be learned in trusting others by being in some way dependent upon them.

If you were born with this degree, it does not mean that you will never have to work or may just lie back and let others serve you. You will have to work at least at establishing other people's confidence in you and, if you succeed in this, you may reap the rewards of contentment.

Natives of this solar degree have a highly developed curiosity and are generally interested in the sciences. Many delve into the occult in an endeavour to understand why they are here and why they live as they do.

Planetary point

A planet in the 219th degree is an indication of the kind of energy natives have been given to assist them in gaining the assistance of others. People with Venus here can use their beauty or some kind of artistic talent to beguile others into caring for them. Those with Mercury in this degree would develop their minds to attract the kind of partner who is stimulated by mental brilliance.

220th degree

Colour: orange. *Sign*: Scorpio. 2nd decan. *Qualities*: Fixed/Mutable, Water. *Numerological match*: other 4s.
Positive expression: confidence, self-assurance
Negative expression: nervous disposition

Solar point

If you have the Sun in the 220th degree, there are special tasks for you to perform in this life. You may appear confident and self-assured to others and you may attain positions of authority and responsibility whether you seek them or not. But the real task of this life that this degree will thrust upon you is to be able to take care of others as well as yourself. You may acquire wealth, friends and prestige and then suddenly lose it all, having to start again from scratch — because you forgot those who helped you rise in life. If you do move up the social ladder and stay there it is a reward for what you have accomplished; but the load you must now carry, the care of others, may be doubled. Try not to fight your karma as the rewards in the hereafter can be tremendous.

Planetary point

If you have a planet in the 220th degree, it is an indicator of how you may become responsible for others. For example, with Neptune here you may work in the medical field and be responsible for your patients.

221st degree

Colour: scarlet. *Sign*: Scorpio. 2nd decan. *Qualities*: Fixed/Mutable, Water. *Numerological match*: other 5s.
Positive expression: longevity, sharp mental faculties throughout life
Negative expression: nervous disorders

Solar point

The elemental energy of the 221st degree gives natives a keen, inquiring mind and especially a thirst for studying the mysteries of life.

If you were born with this solar degree you should take up occult studies in order to stimulate both your own spiritual development and that of others. The inner understanding which this occult knowledge brings can make you an extraordinary person. You will discover the true feelings and expression of the soul during the course of this life. Learn this lesson well and you will be mentally active till your death, and be able to pass on your wisdom to others. But if you should fail to recognise your duty your old age will be spent in a state of childlike senility as a punishment for not using the occult faculties you were given.

Strong links with brothers and sisters are kept by natives of this degree.

Planetary point

The 221st degree shows by the planet placed in it how natives may find the knowledge they seek in the world of the occult. Venus here would indicate that a Greek soul has been reborn and must make contact with his or her past, while the Moon has more of a relation to the cultures of pagan Britain or ancient Egypt, so studies should be concentrated there.

222nd degree

Colour: green. *Sign*: Scorpio. 2nd decan. *Qualities*: Fixed/Mutable, Water. *Numerological match*: other 6s.
Positive expression: artistic flair, romantic feelings
Negative expression: vanity, egocentricity

Solar point

People born with the Sun in the 222nd degree have to learn to tear themselves away from the past. On the positive side they are always provided with a partner or friend of higher status or social background who will give them financial security. But the lesson of this degree is that they must stop clinging to the safety of their past lives and step forth with confidence into the future.

On a mundane level people with this degree are often vain and egocentric. They need the reassurance of the approval of others to be able to progress upon their chosen path, but this is really a reflection of the soul's uncertainty about where it must go which makes it cling to the known. The beautiful actress, now old, who lives in her memories of her days of fame rather than in the present, or the gambler who dreams of the thousands he has lost but thinks he will win back (but never does) are instances of the working of this degree.

Planetary point

If you have a planet in the 222nd degree, this means something is holding you back in your karmic development, probably by making you cling to the safety of the past. Venus or the Moon here can indicate that you live for a love you once had and refuse to move on to other relationships.

223rd degree

Colour: blue. *Sign*: Scorpio. 2nd decan. *Qualities*: Fixed/Mutable, Water. *Numerological match*: other 7s.
Positive expression: imagination, inspiration
Negative expression: timidity

Solar point

The elemental energy of the 223rd degree has much to offer those brave enough to step into its realms.

You have with this degree the ability to step upon the spirit planes and gain knowledge and insight through your experiences there. Advancement in this life will rarely be by normal means. More likely it will be by peculiar circumstances and, with the aid of others, you will be thrust forth to the success you desire — provided by a little reflection you acquire an understanding of your aspirations and motives and accept things for what they are. Death can bring financial gains into your life; that may be through the demise of a member of your family or through work you do in fields associated with death.

You are certain to have mediumistic, clairvoyant or clairaudient powers and could develop them to such a level that others would seek you out for advice. The astral planes are open to you should you decide to venture into them.

Planetary point

A planet in the 223rd degree indicates that natives will acquire occult knowledge or that peculiar circumstances may affect them in this life. The Moon is linked to the astral planes, and Neptune is connected with imagination and inspiration, and so on.

224th degree

Colour: black. *Sign*: Scorpio. 2nd decan. *Qualities*: Fixed/Mutable, Water. *Numerological match*: other 8s.
Positive expression: spiritual guardianship
Negative expression: depression

Solar point

As a solar point the elemental energy of the 224th degree blesses natives with a level of spiritual maturity beyond their years. The soul is an old and much travelled one which is reborn only when it has a special mission.

If you were born with this degree you may not be aware of why you are here but you will almost certainly have a feeling of being out of place in this world. That is because in fact you are, and your reason for being here is to assist souls who you befriended in past lives or who were of assistance to you in your time of need, and it is to these people you will be drawn in this life to help them achieve their goals. Everything will be provided for this task. If you were born with riches or have earned them, this wealth was provided so that you can assist old friends. Giving financial assistance is not, however, the principal means you have of helping them. They will need your wisdom and experience to help them out of trouble and guide them on spiritual paths.

Planetary point

The 224th degree indicates, according to which planet is in it, how natives may help others in working out their karma and evolving spiritually. Neptune here is indicative of work with the masses rather than with individuals, while the Moon points to a life of emotional support of another.

225th degree

Colour: crimson. *Sign*: Scorpio. 2nd decan. *Qualities*: Fixed/Mutable, Water. *Numerological match*: other 9s.
Positive expression: enthusiasm, ambition
Negative expression: squandering

Solar point

As a solar point the elemental energy of the 225th degree gives natives energy, drive and enthusiasm for success, but they need to learn to tie themselves down to one task at a time. This degree mixes the element Fire with that of Water from the sign of Scorpio. There is thus a tendency to be impulsive, rash and hot-headed but their actions are usually taken with the right motives. Much hard work must be carried out and a good deal of experience gathered in this incarnation, but rewards are likely to follow wherever there is an emphasis on physical endeavour.

This is also a good degree for those who wish to participate in rather than watch sporting activities. Vigorous outdoor sports would suit natives much better than quiet indoor games such as snooker.

People born with this degree will both work hard and play hard as they need to unwind or find outlets for their physical energy.

Planetary point

The 225th degree is an indicator of the area of life in which much effort will be required on the part of the native if he or she wishes to become successful. When the Moon is here a person can have trouble in keeping partners and would need to put a good deal of effort into maintaining relationships. Whoever has

Jupiter here could have trouble in managing their finances and should take care how they spend their money.

226th degree

Colour: white. *Sign*: Scorpio. 2nd decan. *Qualities*: Fixed/ Mutable, Water. *Numerological match*: other 1s.
Positive expression: leadership, compassion
Negative expression: cold, calculating logic

Solar point

People with the Sun in the 226th degree have the ability to calm the emotions of those that they come into contact with. They are gifted with both compassion for others and the balanced expression of their own feelings. They are able to take command when those around them panic. Because they are strong willed and determined, people tend to look to them as some form of authority. However, natives do not actively seek authority or try to dominate or compel others in any way; their influence is mainly through the emotions. On a wider front natives become the conscience prickers of society, those who make the governments of the day recognise the plight of the needy. Or they may draw the public's attention to the needs of the Third World, working for famine relief, and so on.

Planetary point

If you have a planet in the 226th degree, this shows what funds of energy you have at your disposal for promoting the emotional wellbeing of others.

If Venus is here, you will like to entertain people and help them forget their worries and problems for a time. If the planet Jupiter is here, you would make a great counsellor or financial consultant.

227th degree

Colour: grey. *Sign*: Scorpio. 2nd decan. *Qualities*: Fixed/ Mutable, Water. *Numerological match*: other 2s.
Positive expression: inventiveness, imagination
Negative expression: delusion

Solar point

The elemental energy of the 227th degree gives natives the imagination and inventive powers to take old or worn out things from the past and reform them for use in the present. These people waste very little in their lives, be that time, effort or resources. Give them a pile of junk and they will give you back recycled products for a price. Give them a failing business and, if it is possible to rebuild it, then they will succeed. Their efforts are unstinting in whatever they do in all areas of life, and they can become very peeved if others do not apply themselves with the same dedication. They may be called all the names under the sun by those who fail to live up to their standards but they are respected by their peers for their industriousness.

Planetary point

A planet in the 227th degree shows how natives are most likely to find success through their effort and industriousness. If any of the beneficent planets are here (the Moon, Jupiter or Venus), natives would do best working for the welfare of others. If Mars, Saturn or Neptune reside in this degree, natives would be better off working for themselves.

228th degree

Colour: violet. *Sign*: Scorpio. 2nd decan. *Qualities*: Fixed/ Mutable, Water. *Numerological match*: other 3s.
Positive expression: spirituality, philosophic interests
Negative expression: roguish behaviour, money-grubbing

Solar point

The 228th solar degree gives a mild, pleasant and thoroughly likeable disposition to those born under its influence. They may have serious views in respect of religious or philosophic matters. But on the whole they are hard working and always ready to take part in social activities and are therefore popular with their fellows. This in fact is their principal gift: that others tend to like them enormously. They can enlist the help of anyone they have ever befriended whenever the need arises. And they really do appreciate friends. There's no living in a cave like a hermit for them, for they demand social interaction and the joy that the company of other people brings.

The best kind of work for natives of this degree would be an extension of a hobby, e.g. the amateur astrologer who becomes a writer for a newspaper or book publisher.

Planetary point

A planet in the 228th degree shows how natives may put a hobby to good use and even earn money from it. An example is the person with Venus here who draws for friends. Another example is someone with Jupiter, who likes a gamble, or with Mercury, whose poetic verses are published. There are literally thousands of ways to enjoy your employment, but the answer lies in the energy of the planet placed here.

229th degree

Colour: orange. *Sign*: Scorpio. 2nd decan. *Qualities*: Fixed/ Mutable, Water. *Numerological match*: other 4s.
Positive expression: building on the emotional plane
Negative expression: social and political agitation

Solar point

The elemental energy of the 229th degree enables natives to earn the trust and respect of those they come into contact with, in the long term. If they should try to rush anything, however, then they usually fail in that task for there is a lesson in patience and the sooner they learn to develop this quality the sooner they will find themselves on the path to success. Lessons as always appear only to be learnt the hard way and it appears that those born under this degree must experience a good deal of disappointment and upheaval before they settle down and raise a family, a goal that they ultimately desire.

As mature adults these people make fine counsellors, having learned by their own mistakes and having acquired the patience and wisdom to advise others. They are found in all walks of life. They have their heart in the right place — if only they could learn patience sooner rather than later.

Planetary point

As a planetary point, the 229th degree is an indicator of what mistakes natives are likely to make on their way to achieving maturity both in the emotional and spiritual sense. When someone has Venus or the Moon here, they must lose a love before they can understand what it really means to love, while whoever has Mars here might have to be burned before he or she understands the Element of Fire.

230th degree

Colour: scarlet. *Sign*: Scorpio. 3rd decan. *Qualities*: Fixed/Cardinal, Water. *Numerological match*: other 5s.
Positive expression: reforming zeal
Negative expression: rebelliousness

Solar point

Natives of the 230th degree have a difficult task to perform. They were born to be the instigators of social reform and this is never an easy task. They must learn to use the sharp mind and wits they have been given to both introduce and bring about the changes which are necessary in our society.

Considered as rebels by the extreme right and too radical by the extreme left, they must learn to mediate between extremes and bring a balance into society. For example, AIDS is one of the principal fears of this century, and it is people like these who will quell the terrors of those who over-react, yet they will also communicate the need for caution in those who hitherto had taken no notice. Thus the two extremes are brought into balance and the new rules which we must all learn to abide by are heeded.

This energy will find its outlet through whatever is out of balance, be it physical, emotional or anything else.

Planetary point

If you have a planet in this degree, it points to how you could most easily influence others by expressing your opinions, and what these are likely to be about. Mercury would indicate influence through the media or the education system. Saturn would reflect opinions about the distribution of land and wealth, and so on.

231st degree

Colour: green. *Sign*: Scorpio. 3rd decan. *Qualities*: Fixed/Cardinal, Water. *Numerological match*: other 6s.
Positive expression: adoring parenthood
Negative expression: emotional trauma

Solar point

The elemental energy of the 231st degree gives a person a loving personality with a tendency to look for the best in people, and there will be a soft spot for the underdog.

There is a strong sexual drive in this degree. Those born under it will have many children, to whom they will be devoted. Natives generally suffer some form of emotional trauma in their early years which leads them to overprotecting their children in their desire to help them cope with the stresses of life.

Very close ties are formed between the native and his or her children, which last throughout their lives.

The karma of those of you born under the 231st degree is to build and sustain happy relationships in the family unit. No matter how many times you marry (though once is best) the important thing is to keep on good terms with your offspring and to maintain ties.

Planetary point

As a planetary point the 231st degree is an indicator of the kind of qualities natives have that will help maintain the family unit. Mars here gives physical strength to work with, while the Moon imparts compassion and understanding. Those with Neptune will have intuition and imagination.

232nd degree

Colour: blue. *Sign*: Scorpio. 3rd decan. *Qualities*: Fixed/Cardinal, Water. *Numerological match*: other 7s.
Positive expression: creative imagination
Negative expression: fears and phobias

Solar point

Natives of the 232nd degree have been blessed with the creative imagination and intuition to bring about some form of spiritual rebirth within themselves and society at large.

If you were born under the sway of this degree you may find yourself questioning the orthodox religious beliefs of your day, sensing that all is not as it should be. You may become involved in some new spiritual group or society or just find yourself entering a new state of spiritual consciousness. This does not mean that you will become a monk, hermit or priest, but rather that you are a part of the larger movement which is searching for new answers to the age-old questions about creation and our reasons for existing.

This degree creates deep-thinking individuals from all walks of life who will help to bring about spiritual reform.

Planetary point

The 232nd degree indicates, through the planet resident in it, in what manner natives' spiritual beliefs may be expressed. With Mars here they will hold strong views and practically force them on both family and friends. Those with Neptune will be more subtle and imaginative in their manner of persuasion in such a sensitive area of life.

233rd degree

Colour: black. *Sign*: Scorpio. 3rd decan. *Qualities*: Fixed/Cardinal, Water. *Numerological match*: other 8s.
Positive expression: industriousness
Negative expression: parsimony, niggardliness

Solar point

As a solar point the elemental energy of the 233rd degree creates a serious personality with a reliable nature and a capacity for hard work in stressful or inhospitable environments. Such a person is prepared to undergo periods of self-denial in order to achieve long term aims, but he or she should be careful not to expect others to do the same as they may not be so strongly motivated.

This degree can produce solemn, serious and austere types who are well suited to work in politics, local government, the law, or any kind of bureaucratic environment.

In romance people with this degree can be quite old-fashioned and would much prefer to have one partner for life, though this does not always turn out to be the case. Karmic responsibility and moderation are the lessons to be learned but this does not mean a dull life, merely a moderate use of available resources.

Planetary point

A planet in the 233rd degree reflects the kind of beliefs natives may hold in serious aspects of life. Someone with the Moon here can be old-fashioned when it comes to romantic relationships and will not be openly demonstrative. With Jupiter, the native can have firm religious beliefs or have strong views about the way we earn and spend money.

234th degree

Colour: crimson. *Sign*: Scorpio. 3rd decan. *Qualities*: Fixed/ Cardinal, Water. *Numerological match*: other 9s.
Positive expression: great ambition
Negative expression: ruthlessness

Solar point

The elemental energy of the 234th degree gives natives a strong and forceful character in order that they may achieve their aims. There is a great deal of ambition and capacity for hard work under arduous conditions, but they need to be inspired with the right sort of motives.

If you were born with this degree you have in this life to learn to stand upon your own two feet and accept both the rewards for worthy endeavours and the punishments for failure. To this end, this elemental degree has provided you with the strength, tenacity and will power to achieve your goals. You may question yourself occasionally, feeling guilty about your ruthless ability to achieve your own ends. But rest assured, just as it is your lesson to achieve, so have the people who allow themselves to be exploited by you a lesson to learn. The elemental ruler demands in this case that you share a part of your gains with those who are less well off.

Planetary point

If you have a planet in the 234th degree, it indicates in what way you failed in a past existence and are being given the energy to try again. The Moon or Venus in this point would indicate that you must strive to achieve stability in the home. Jupiter or Mars would be indicative of a desire for financial gain.

235th degree

Colour: white. *Sign*: Scorpio. 3rd decan. *Qualities*: Fixed/ Cardinal, Water. *Numerological match*: other 1s.
Positive expression: authority over others
Negative expression: abuse of trust

Solar point

As a solar point the elemental energy of the 235th degree gives the native a strong pessonality with the ability to use it to attain authority over others. He will readily walk over anything or anyone if they hinder him from achieving his desired ends, which he usually attains through the strength of his will as much as anything. He will fight strenuously for what he believes in and feels invigorated by confrontation and conflict.

If you have this solar degree your strength of will is too overpowering for most people. The karmic lesson you have to learn, however, is to resist temptation. You have the necessary strength of mind for leadership, but you are prone to misuse it for your own selfish ends. This is an almost irresistible temptation in our society, yet resist it you must and direct that energy into good causes.

Planetary point

A planet in this point has been supercharged by the effects of this degree, and if you have a planet here you must learn to control its energy. If Mars is here you may have violent tendencies and tremendous physical energy which you must learn to curb and use in a controlled, constructive way. If you have Venus here, you may have great beauty and grace, so try not to be vain.

236th degree

Colour: grey. *Sign*: Scorpio. 3rd decan. *Qualities*: Fixed/Cardinal, Water. *Numerological match*: other 2s.
Positive expression: resilience to change
Negative expression: over-sensitivity

Solar point

The 236th degree blesses natives with resilience to change. They have also a calming effect upon others in such circumstances.

If you were born with this solar degree you are able to make the best out of most circumstances and can exert a subtle influence on others. If ever you dreamed of saving the world, the whales of anything else, you were, without realising it, in contact with this elemental angel who has granted you the ability to emotionally respond to and assist those in trouble.

You should learn to listen to your inner self for it is in contact with the higher forces that direct the lives of many, and the angel has chosen you as one of his tools in bringing back into balance that in nature which men have unstabilised and abused.

Planetary point

This degree indicates, by the planet in residence, how natives may best serve themselves and others in protecting our planet and its plants and animals. With Mars here, the native could become actively involved in the defence of those natural habitats that some would destroy out of greed.

237th degree

Colour: violet. *Sign*: Scorpio. 3rd decan. *Qualities*: Fixed/Cardinal, Water. *Numerological match*: other 3s.
Positive expression: benevolence
Negative expression: lack of realism

Solar point

The elemental energy of the 237th degree blesses the native with an optimistic and positive personality as well as natural leadership ability and a caring, generous disposition.

If you were born with this degree you can affect or influence others in subtle ways for your own benefit, but you rarely misuse this gift. You can see beyond the superficial and get to the core of problems quickly, and thus respond to them speedily. 'Great,' I hear you say, 'but why have I been given these attributes?' The ability to earn a high income and influence the behaviour of others is given so that you can promote the spiritual growth and understanding of those you come into contact with. If you fail in this task all that was given can be quickly taken away. For example, a person may be a multi-millionaire and donate millions to worthy causes, the arts, and so on. You too must give back something to society.

Planetary point

If you have a planet in the 237th degree, it indicates the area of life in which you have something you should protect or promote.

With Venus here you should protect the arts, the theatre or any similar fields, while if Jupiter is the planet in question you will be religiously inclined and stick up for your faith.

238th degree

Colour: orange. *Sign*: Scorpio. 3rd decan. *Qualities*: Fixed/Cardinal, Water. *Numerological match*: other 4s.
Positive expression: originality
Negative expression: logic ruling the heart

Solar point

People born with the 238th solar degree possess an original mind, intuition and inventiveness. These assets help them solve most of the problems that lie in their path.

This degree favours those who wish to study the sciences or metaphysics. Being so extremely inventive, natives are often able to find practical uses for other people's rubbish or discover new applications for old or outdated equipment. But they can be too cool and calculating in their personal lives. They are apt to make the mistake of treating another person, including their partner, as a machine — machines give them much pleasure, but human beings are not so predictable and not so easily manipulated.

Planetary point

If there is a planet in the 238th degree, the nature of it will indicate in which area of life natives may utilise a logical approach or apply scientific methods. If Neptune is the planet, they are able to conceive original ideas and then see that they become realities.

239th degree

Colour: scarlet. *Sign*: Scorpio. 3rd decan. *Qualities*: Fixed/Cardinal, Water. *Numerological match*: other 5s.
Positive expression: mental flexibility
Negative expression: snap judgements

Solar point

The elemental energy of the 239th degree endows those individuals born under it with a flexible mind which allows them to size up new situations and change their tactics to meet the circumstances. They are also able to persuade by argument or browbeat others in order to get their own way.

If you have this solar degree, your talents were given you so that you can crystallise the ideas for social reform that you and others have in such a manner that they become clear and acceptable to the larger masses of society. You must, however, fight off the urge to use your mental talents to manoeuvre other people into fulfilling your own desires, for, if you do so, the angelic ruler of the degree will exact his revenge.

Planetary point

A planet in the 239th degree shows that the native has great adaptability. If the Moon is here, the native is emotionally adaptable and able to conform with the needs of his or her chosen mate. A person with Mars in this degree is very adaptable to any terrain, climate or physical conditions he or she may encounter.

240th degree

Colour: green. *Sign*: Sagittarius. 1st decan. *Qualities*: Mutable, Fire. *Numerological match*: other 6s.
Positive expression: sociability, good nature, sense of humour
Negative expression: frivolity

Solar point

People born with the Sun in the 240th degree are blessed with artistic flair and the talent for expressing themselves well and entertainingly. This gives them the ability to lighten the hearts of those with whom they associate. Their disposition is mild, kindly and obliging. They have a love of peace and quiet, and there is a danger of them allowing people to take advantage of them as rather than argue they will agree with others.

The keynote of the degree is that of social interaction and social acceptance. It is the responsibility of those of you born with it to learn to mix and share with others in all levels of society, and to try to close the gap which at present exists between class groups. You are also responsible for entertaining others and in so doing helping them to forget their worries and problems for a time.

Planetary point

If there is a planet in the 240th degree, the nature of it indicates how natives will go about mixing with others socially, or entertaining them. Someone with the Moon here will do a lot of entertaining at home, and always has a shoulder for a friend to lean upon. The person with Venus always does things artistically when entertaining and enjoys parties and social gatherings.

241st degree

Colour: blue. *Sign*: Sagittarius. 1st decan. *Qualities*: Mutable, Fire. *Numerological match*: other 7s.
Positive expression: psychic ability, philosophic studies
Negative expression: impressionability

Solar point

The 241st solar degree give natives clairvoyance or at least an intuitive sense.

If you were born with this solar degree you will find yourself drawn towards the studies of spiritualism, psychic phenomena and philosophy. The knowledge that you gain will be useful to you on this plane of existence and it will also lead to advantages for you in the next. On a mundane level, you are likely to have a fondness for travel and a love of change. These characteristics will cause you to investigate new places and seek out new experiences. You may dream of places before you visit them or see your partner before you actually meet him or her, such is your precognitive ability. You will also have intuitive foresight when it comes to business matters or politics. You should direct your talents into some form of psychic study to maximise your hidden potential.

Planetary point

A planet in the 241st degree will show, according to its nature, how natives are likely become psychically aware. Young people with Neptune here are likely to have a vivid imagination, and dreams will frequently have some form of message or lesson to be learned. Anyone having Jupiter or Mercury here would be inclined to take up psychic studies.

242nd degree

Colour: black. *Sign*: Sagittarius. 1st decan. *Qualities*: Mutable, Fire. *Numerological match*: other 8s.
Positive expression: frankness, courage
Negative expression: nervous troubles

Solar point

The elemental energy of the 242nd degree gives persons born with it a frankness and fearlessness. They are likely to achieve positions of authority and power through personal merit, though there is a tendency to resent those with power over themselves when instead they should be trying to win their favour.

It is common for a native of this degree to have more than one occupation, or he or she may work in two separate places at the same time. They generally have an intuitive understanding which should enable them to deal with the majority of problems that they will encounter. Marriage can be late in life and the children more than likely to be spoiled. There can be a danger of a nervous breakdown in the latter part of the life unless the native has made an effort to safeguard the health throughout.

Planetary point

The 242nd degree shows by the planet in it what way the fearless courage of the native may be applied. With Venus here someone could open up new fields of artistic endeavour, or bring new meaning to old arts. Whoever has the Moon in this point would readily be stirred into sticking up for the rights of others.

243rd degree

Colour: crimson. *Sign*: Sagittarius. 1st decan. *Qualities*: Mutable, Fire. *Numerological match*: other 9s.
Positive expression: plain speaking, ambition
Negative expression: odd ideas and beliefs

Solar point

Being born with the Sun in the 243rd degree makes people frank, generous and ambitious. At times they may be too impetuous in speech and action if they feel restrained in any way. The mind is active and they are fond of debate, but they hate to lose an argument. Plain speaking to the point of bluntness, they have no fear of what others think about them. There is often a good mechanical sense. They are also fond of sports and go in for the more adventurous hobbies — people with this degree must play hard as well as work hard.

Natives make excellent soldiers or policemen. Financial gain may well be made through marriage to someone higher up the social scale (there may be more than one union).

There can be difficulty coming to terms with religion as the natives are sceptical of anything that cannot be proven to them.

Care should be taken with fires.

Planetary point

As a planetary point, the 243rd degree is an indicator of how natives may develop through debate and discussion with others. For example, those with Jupiter here will want to examine and discuss the ideas of leading philosophers.

244th degree

Colour: white. *Sign*: Sagittarius. 1st decan. *Qualities*: Mutable, Fire. *Numerological match*: other 1s.
Positive expression: joviality, generosity
Negative expression: self-indulgance

Solar point

Being born with the 244th solar degree makes natives bright, jovial and generous in their disposition. They are also self-reliant, enterprising and persevering — they are not discouraged easily. There can also be an interest in science or philosophy.

Another notable characteristic is their love of freedom. They therefore like to be their own master — they hate to be driven or harrassed by others. In fact their mission in life is, metaphorically speaking, the throwing off of the chains and encumbrances of society, whenever these are too burdensome.

More important than becoming self-employed, natives need to be master of their own personal lives, to hold to their beliefs and make their own decisions.

Importantly, it is the amount of enthusiasm mustered by the

native which will determine the level of success he or she can achieve in this life.

Planetary point

If you have a planet in the 244th degree, it points to what you have to learn to master in this present incarnation. If you have Jupiter here, you must study philosophy and seek to understand what lies behind the various religions, orthodox or otherwise. With Mars, you will be adventurous, always wanting to see what is over the next horizon.

245th degree

Colour: grey. *Sign*: Sagittarius. 1st decan. *Qualities*: Mutable, Fire. *Numerological match*: other 2s.
Positive expression: charitableness
Negative expression: vacillating opinion

Solar point

People born with the Sun in the 245th degree have a karmic debt to pay to the rest of humanity. They are natural teachers, philosophically minded and have good overall judgement. In some way or other they will be drawn to work connected with the public, probably in matters to do with religious, political or educational reform. It could be that the karmic debt will bring them into some form of welfare work or service to the public, for example as a teacher in a classroom, or simply as the shoulder for friends to cry on.

Benefits can come from females and from legacies in the latter years; these could be considered as rewards for a karma fulfilled (if the responsibility is shirked the rewards never materialise).

Natives tend to have a love of the countryside, children, pets and various sports.

Planetary point

The 245th degree shows, by the planet resident, where the native's karmic debt may lie. If Saturn is here, that person will become responsible for the natural resources from the land and the uses they are put to. If Jupiter is the planet, there will be responsibility in the field of education of the young or in religious movements.

Colour: violet. *Sign*: Sagittarius. 1st decan. *Qualities*: Mutable, Fire. *Numerological match*: other 3s.
Positive expression: courtesy, tolerance
Negative expression: quarrelsome nature

Solar point

People with this solar degree always find someone they can trust who will build with them the material base they require for a harmonious existence together. They are never happy acting alone and need to find a kindred soul with whom to share their joys and sorrows. Another trait is their strong urge to leave behind something by which they can be remembered, be that an institution, child or ideal. They often have high morals or strong religious views but these are never so extreme that natives forget how to let their hair down and enjoy themselves.

The finding of a marriage partner and the building up of a family is what preoccupies the native most. He or she will usually be polite, courteous and generous, all these qualities being conducive to forming a stable relationship with the kindred soul.

Planetary point

If there is a planet in 246th degree, by its nature natives shuld be able to perceive where they could find their soul mate. Someone with Venus here could well marry a person connected with the arts or the theatre. The Moon represents the motherly type or the sensitive, stay-at-home partner. Someone with Mars here would seek an adventurous mate with a dominant personality.

247th degree

Colour: orange. *Sign*: Sagittarius. 1st decan. *Qualities*: Mutable, Fire. *Numerological match*: other 4s.
Positive expression: broad-mindedness, originality
Negative expression: conflict with nature

Solar point

A person who has the Sun in the 247th degree is fortunate

indeed, because he or she should be successful in almost anything they undertake. Natives with this degree display a broad scope of mind with originality of thought. Sometimes there is a kind of quirkiness in their manner of reasoning. Because of their wide interests they frequently study a great deal and join groups and societies promoting their special interest. Foreign travel, all forms of exploration or anything to do with communications or invention could be of benefit to the native.

The degree creates an individual whose nature is refined, sociable, humanitarian and progressive. Furthermore he or she is likely to be intuitive and to have good judgement and foresight. Those of you born with this solar degree are allowed all these great rewards because of selflessness in your previous lives. Your service to others in this life can bring rich rewards indeed.

Planetary point

If you have a planet in the 247th degree, it will show you how rewards may come to you in this life. For example, Mercury can brings an understanding of something unusual which could be turned to your advantage.

248th degree

Colour: scarlet. *Sign*: Sagittarius. 1st decan. *Qualities*: Mutable, Fire. *Numerological match*: other 5s.
Positive expression: idealism
Negative expression: impressionability

Solar point

The elemental energy of the 248th degree gives natives a versatile creative mind. They are cheerful and conscientious, generous and kind, but also somewhat candid.

If you were born with this solar degree you have very high ideals and think lofty thoughts. It is your responsibility to communicate your thoughts and ideals to those less gifted or capable. Success is best achieved through literature, the sciences and professional occupations. If supported by other planets in the chart, there can be achievement in governmental, legal or church affairs.

If you study the occult, this solar degree inclines towards

visions, psychic experiences and success when experimenting with automatic writing.

Planetary point

With a planet in the 248th degree the native has much wisdom and many good ideas to impart to others. If Mars, is here, for example, he or she would show others how to apply their energy constructively to the task in hand rather than wasting it.

249th degree

Colour: green. *Sign*: Sagittarius. 1st decan. *Qualities*: Mutable, Fire. *Numerological match*: other 6s.
Positive expression: strong imagination
Negative expression: extravagance, amorousness

Solar point

The elemental energy of the 249th degree strengthens the imagination and poetical side of the nature and endows natives with a keen appreciation of beauty in the realm of colour, form, touch and sound. The degree bestows popularity and esteem upon those who earn it. It inclines natives to act in a charitable and sympathetic manner. People born under this degree are often good humoured and optimistic. They also tend to be fond of pleasure and like elegant clothes and sumptuous surroundings. Gains are principally made through social contacts and natives are generally fortunate in matters of love and romance. General good fortune will descend on those who learn the karmic lesson of this degree, which is the refinement of expression in speech and manners.

Planetary point

The 249th degree shows, by the planet resident here, what area of the native's life needs refinement. If Mercury is here the person may seek refinement through knowledge and higher education and will take care how he or she verbally communicates his thoughts and emotions. Someone with the Moon here learns to be feeling in personal relationships and so becomes more patient, caring and considerate.

Colour: blue. *Sign*: Sagittarius. 2nd decan. *Qualities*: Mutable/Cardinal, Fire. *Numerological match*: other 7s.
Positive expression: artistic refinement
Negative expression: peculiar beliefs

Solar point

The elemental energy of the 250th degree gives an artistic nature and a sense of poetry to most natives. Their imagination is developed and they show a desire for social interaction. The degree also inspires a benevolent and courteous disposition, so that making friends is easy for people born with the Sun here.

The psychic faculties can be developed through dream interpretation. There is also intuitive insight, which means that natives' hunches about people tend to be correct.

Work with people, either in the entertainment field or the welfare services, would suit — at clubs and pleasure resorts on the one side and hospitals and sanitariums on the other.

Natives of this degree do not cope well with stress and are more likely to give in to the demands of others or run away than face open conflict. This does not mean to say that they are psychologically or physically weak but rather that they prefer the peaceful path in finding solutions to their problems.

Planetary point

As a planetary point, the 250th degree is an indicator of how natives may find an outlet for their refined artistic tastes. Venus here would point to a love for the arts and social activity outside the home, while Saturn would point to activities including gardening, natural history or anything to do with the countryside.

Colour: black. *Sign*: Sagittarius. 2nd decan. *Qualities*: Mutable/Cardinal, Fire. *Numerological match*: other 8s.
Positive expression: capacity for acquiring much knowledge
Negative expression: mishandled finances

Solar point

The 251st is a fortunate solar degree for those who follow academic pursuits. The mental faculties are excellent, with a good memory and capacity for deep concentration. The will-power is strong, which gives natives the determination required to overcome any obstacles they may encounter. They are best suited to studies in the philosophical or scientific fields.

This elemental degree also favours those born under it with help from their elders or those in positions of authority. This should result in their attaining some form of executive position eventually.

If you were born with this solar degree, the knowledge that you are capable of retaining was meant to be put to good use. There are rich rewards for you if you follow the path of service to others.

Planetary point

If you have a planet in the 251st degree, it will indicate to you, according to its nature, where knowledge may be of most benefit to you in this life. For example, if you have Jupiter here you would need to know a good deal about banking, finance and economics.

252nd degree

Colour: crimson. *Sign*: Sagittarius. 2nd decan. *Qualities*: Mutable/Cardinal, Fire. *Numerological match*: other 9s.
Positive expression: industriousness, frankness
Negative expression: overbearing manner

Solar point

The 252nd degree gives the native a frank and generous disposition. It also allows those born under it to stick at arduous tasks for periods of time which others would balk at. Natives can, however, show a lack of patience with bureaucracy and with those who fail to apply themselves with the same zeal as they do to given tasks. No matter how wealthy or independent the native may become, he or she always needs to carry on working to the end and many an aged company director who refuses to retire would have this degree active.

The karma of the degree is to achieve through strenuous

effort and adverse circumstances, and accordingly natives are provided with great physical energy and considerable mental aptitude. So if you were born under this degree and you fail to achieve anything worthwhile, you have only yourself to blame because of neglect of your capabilities.

Planetary point

As a planetary point, the 252nd degree is an indicator of mental and physical energies and, according to the nature of the planet here, where or how natives should ideally channel their efforts. For example, natives with Mars here must have independence at work to make the best of themselves and are better off self-employed, while those with Saturn here are happier when employed by others.

253rd degree

Colour: white. *Sign*: Sagittarius. 2nd decan. *Qualities*: Mutable/Cardinal, Fire. *Numerological match*: other 1s.
Positive expression: spiritual leadership
Negative expression: dogmatism

Solar point

People born with the Sun is the 253rd degree must set others an example by the way they live their life. Their friends and associates are likely to adopt the same moral and spiritual values, so this is quite a responsibility. Success and a rise to a position of authority is almost a certainty for those born with this degree, but care should be taken that limits are not exceeded with regard to adopting the fashions, morals or customs of whatever society they find themselves within.

If you have this solar degree, your karma is to lead others by your own personal example. In particular children should be set an example in good manners. Values learned in adolescence will serve as a foundation for the rest of their lives.

Planetary point

A planet in the 253rd degree is an indicator, for anyone born with it here, of the area in which he or she must learn to set an example to others. If Mercury is here, a native could set examples in the fields of education or communications. The person with Mars here could demonstrate the constructive rather than destructive application of physical energy.

254th degree

Colour: grey. *Sign*: Sagittarius. 2nd decan. *Qualities*: Mutable/Cardinal, Fire. *Numerological match*: other 2s.
Positive expression: appreciation of beauty
Negative expression: fear of change

Solar point

The 254th degree gives natives a lively imagination, intuition and an appreciation of things of beauty together with the ability to communicate all this to others. There is also great vitality, resourcefulness and good reasoning power with the ability to judge things for their true worth.

The best kind of occupation for people with this degree would be anything to do with communications or involving the arts or things of beauty, such as doing hairdressing or working as a beautician or fashion designer. Another possibility is any work to do with preserving the past, such as in museums, libraries or archives. Also money can be made in the publishng field, writing on subjects to do with art or history.

If you were born with this degree and ever thought of writing a book, have a go. Remember that you have been blessed with heightened sensitivity to beauty and ought to communicate it to others.

Planetary point

If you have a planet in the 254th degree, it shows what gifts you are likely to have and these will be increased through your powers of imagination and intuition. If you have Mercury here, the intuitive mind can be developed to a high degree.

255th degree

Colour: violet. *Sign*: Sagittarius. 2nd decan. *Qualities*: Mutable/Cardinal, Fire. *Numerological match*: other 3s.
Positive expression: pleasing nature, amicableness
Negative expression: eccentricity

Solar point

The elemental energy of the 255th degree gives natives benevolence and compassion. They are also prudent, knowing when to speak out and when to keep their peace. This degree also strengthens the constitution and increases the physical vitality for those who wish to become involved in the more adventurous types of activity. Natives tend to go for physical rather than intellectual pursuits though their minds are by no means slow.

If you have this degree, you earn plenty of money fairly easily but just as quickly spend it, and it would appear to some that your life was just one big merry-go-round. This, however, is not the case. The karma of the degree says, 'Work hard and play hard.' But others only seem to see you when you are playing rather than when you are working. Your occupations are those where you can mix work with pleasure.

Planetary point

A planet in the 255th degree is an indicator of how natives could find a means of livelihood that they would thoroughly enjoy. For example, someone with Venus here might love singing songs at home for family and friends but also make a living by singing. Or he or she could enjoy model making, and turn this hobby into a profit-making concern by opening a model-makers' shop. Those natives who have Saturn here are likely to revel in the responsibility that local government or financial institutions would create for them.

256th degree

Colour: orange. *Sign*: Sagittarius. 2nd decan. *Qualities*: Mutable/Cardinal, Fire. *Numerological match*: other 4s.
Positive expression: broad-minded outlook
Negative expression: imaginary problems

Solar point

The elemental energy of the 256th degree gives natives a broad-minded, philosophic outlook upon life. Not only can they take the established for granted and act upon it, they also readily accept new ideas and concepts and apply them with equal gusto. Their powers of reason and logic are such that they are able to assimilate the given facts and make sound judgements based on concepts both new and old. Natives' karmic task is to get society to accept new social ideas while still maintaining a balance with the old. Jobs as town planners, scientists, lawyers or in local government would all suit natives of this degree down to the ground. Foreseeing future trends is one of their strong points.

Planetary point

If you have a planet in the 256th degree, according to its nature it will show you how you may apply your gift of foresight. For example, if Mars is here, you have both the adventurous spirit and the energy to lead others on new paths.

257th degree

Colour: scarlet. *Sign*: Sagittarius. 2nd decan. *Qualities*: Mutable/Cardinal, Fire. *Numerological match*: other 5s.
Positive expression: progressive ideas
Negative expression: impatience with fools

Solar point

The elemental energy of the 257th degree concerns advanced ideas, or so you might think. It is in fact an energy which enables natives to convert old ideas and concepts to new and updated forms. An example is the progressive church minister who introduces rock music into the church choir. This is more acceptable to modern youth than traditional church music, so it helps bring in young people to the church who would not otherwise have attended. New ideas like this can be brought into any area of life by natives, who are able to communicate what seems a new concept but is really an old one restyled so as to become more acceptable. Their flair for communicating with others has been given to them from higher sources, so they really should make an effort to develop it to the maximum.

Planetary point

The 257th degree indicates, by the planet in residence, how or where natives should apply its forward-looking energy. Someone with Jupiter here might update the philosophies and religious ideas of the past so that they have relevance for the present day. With Venus here, a native might find fresh modes of artistic expression.

Colour: green. *Sign*: Sagittarius. 2nd decan. *Qualities*:
Mutable/Cardinal, Fire. *Numerological match*: other 6s.
Positive expression: grace, refinement
Negative expression: fussiness

Solar point

People with the Sun in the 258th degree are fond of pleasures of
the senses, adventure and the opposite sex. They are also
ambitious and very demonstrative in both love and hate. In this
incarnation their karma is to satisfy their material needs and
then, having experienced them, move on to form purer and
more spiritual types of relationship. Pleasure for the sake of
pleasure is not a pleasure at all, in fact it is a hell, but it is only
through a life of indulgence in pleasure that we can learn the
truth of this. If you were born with this solar degree, enjoy what
pleasures life has to offer you, but remember, there is generally
a price to pay.

Planetary point

A planet in the 258th degree is an indicator of what area of the
native's life will bring pleasure and amusement. Venus here
shows involvement with the opposite sex and activities in the
artistic fields. It also emphasises places of entertainment and
shows that the native will require plenty of social activity.
Natives with Jupiter here will derive pleasure from philosophical concepts, or in the attainment of wealth.

259th degree

Colour: blue. *Sign*: Sagittarius. 2nd decan. *Qualities*: Mutable/
Cardinal, Fire. *Numerological match*: other 7s.
Positive expression: compassion, caring
Negative expression: egocentricity

Solar point

This is the degree of imagination and inspiration. Natives are
also endowed with a compassionate and caring disposition.
However, because of their brusqueness they are often mis-

understood. No matter how hard. forceful or bombastic these people may appear, the fact is that they have a heart of gold. They simply do not express their inner feelings adequately. They can, however, express themselves well on paper and have a good imagination for creative writing. The prolific author George MacDonald (1824–1905) wrote many fairytales and fantasies while Emily Dickenson (1830–86) rarely stirred from the family home but her poetry ranged over and beyond the realms of this world. Both of these people found outlets for their compassionate feelings which brought them fame though they rarely appeared in public life. Both were born with the Sun in this point.

Planetary point

If you have a planet in the 259th degree, it will show you where you may find outlets for your imagination and hidden talents. For example, if Mercury is here, the mental faculties are emphasised. In particular you should develop your powers of communication or any literary ability that you may possess.

260th degree

Colour: black. *Sign*: Sagittarius. 3rd decan. *Qualities*: Mutable/ Fixed, Fire. *Numerological match*: other 8s.
Positive expression: responsibility with wealth
Negative expression: greed

Solar point

People with the Sun in the 260th degree have the responsibility to maintain equilibrium in financial matters, whether it be in the home or in a wider context. Christina Onassis, heiress of a vast family fortune, was born with the Sun in this degree. It is not so much the wealth itself but the use that she puts it to which typifies the degree's energy.

If you were born with this solar point, the less wealth you were born with, the easier will be the karmic lesson. Conversely, the more you have, the greater the responsibility becomes, for wealth signifies nothing without wisdom. Think carefully whenever you covet material wealth about the responsibility that comes with a large fortune, as it can be more detrimental to one's happiness than having no money at all.

Above all, you must learn prudence when dealing with financial matters.

Planetary point

A planet in the 260th degree is indicative of how natives may handle finances. With Saturn here, a person would only use safe and conventional ways of investing money.

261st degree

Colour: crimson. *Sign*: Sagittarius. 3rd decan. *Qualities*: Mutable/Fixed, Fire. *Numerological match*: other 9s.
Positive expression: coming before the public
Negative expression: egotism, brashness

Solar point

As a solar point the elemental energy of the 261st degree gives natives artistic ability and communicative skills which can hold the masses in sway. Dion Warwick and Connie Francis are popular singers who use their voices to communicate a feeling of love and tenderness. The late Frank Sinatra is another example of a native of this solar degree.

If you are a native of this point, you may not become a famous singer or stage performer. However, your own home can be your stage and your friends and family your public. With a little practice you will find you have a way with words and a charismatic charm that can melt the hardest of hearts. So write that poem to the person you love, sing that ballad to the one you desire, and the dreams of your youth can become the realities of your adulthood. Forget the restrictions of your upbringing and environment, have faith in your inner feelings and you will find that others will put their trust in you.

Planetary point

If you have a planet in the 261st degree, according to its nature it will indicate to you how you will find the most rewarding means of emotional expression. For example, if Venus is here you are a true romantic. With the planet Jupiter here, you are likely to have a career on the stage or be in front of the public in one way or another.

Colour: white. *Sign*: Sagittarius. 3rd decan. *Qualities*: Mutable/Cardinal, Fire. *Numerological match*: other 1s.
Positive expression: social conscience
Negative expression: subversiveness

Solar point

As a solar point the 262nd degree gives natives a concern about social problems. They may become actively involved in peace movements, try to solve neighbourhood tensions or stick up for the underdogs.

There is a karmic need to put right that which is out of balance, which can find its best expression through political parties, trade unions or welfare groups and clubs which defend the needy. Some natives merely have strong views on these topics and will vote for the political parties which best represent them. Many become vegetarian because they disagree with the way animals are farmed and slaughtered. No matter what outlet the energy finds, natives will be concerned in general about the welfare of others.

Planetary point

A planet in the 262nd degree indicates by its nature how natives give support to good causes and strive to help those in need. Someone with the Moon here will be soft-hearted and supportive of those in emotional distress, especially in relation to the home itself. With Jupiter here, natives may become fund raisers or contributors to charities or organisations which support their beliefs.

263rd degree

Colour: grey. *Sign*: Sagittarius. 3rd decan. *Qualities*: Mutable/Cardinal, Fire. *Numerological match*: other 2s.
Positive expression: laughter and good cheer
Negative expression: inability to be serious

Solar point

People born with the Sun in the 263rd degree have the ability to bring joy into the lives of everyone they meet. Their disposition is bright, cheerful and generous and they are always optimistic. For them every cloud must have a silver lining.

If you were born with this degree, your karma is to bring joy where there is sorrow and laughter where there is gloom. At the same time you should not shirk the normal responsibilities which society demands of you. In fact you are capable of achieving anything that you set your heart on and can even win round your worst enemies if you so wish. Your life can be as rich and fulfilling as you desire, for even in poverty you can find comfort in the simplest of surroundings.

Planetary point

If you have a planet in the 263rd degree, it will point to where you should direct your infectious sense of fun to help relieve people's tensions. With Mars here you can entertain by the use of slapstick. If Mercury is the planet here, you might be more successful as the script-writer of a comedy rather than trying to be a comedy actor.

264th degree

Colour: violet. *Sign*: Sagittarius. 3rd decan. *Qualities*: Mutable/Fixed, Fire. *Numerological match*: other 3s.
Positive expression: business sense
Negative expression: woolly mind

Solar point

The elemental energy of the 264th degree brings to mind the life of Paul Getty. He was one of the richest men the world has ever seen yet he had a task to perform that none of us would desire if we knew what it really entailed. People born with this solar degree will, whatever their status in life, be called upon to distribute and share with others what they possess. Paul Getty may have been a rich man but was he truly happy when constantly bombarded with requests for financial assistance from the needy and the greedy? The sharing of personal wealth is not an easy task for anyone and brings criticism as well as praise.

You may not be a Paul Getty but you will be called upon to help preserve the society which you live in. Perform that task with devotion and the rewards can be tremendous but so also can be the stress caused by your heavy responsibilities.

Planetary point

If you have a planet in the 264th degree, it is an indicator of what burden you must learn to bear in relation to the society you live in. Saturn here gives a responsibility connected with elderly people and you may have to support an older member of your family. If Mars is here, you may have to learn to work for others or become involved in the defence of the land and property or the general well-being of others.

265th degree

Colour: orange: *Sign*: Sagittarius. 3rd decan. *Qualities*: Mutable/Fixed, Fire. *Numerological match*: other 4s.

See the 270th degree for effects.

266th degree

Colour: scarlet: *Sign*: Sagittarius. 3rd decan. *Qualities*: Mutable/Fixed, Fire. *Numerological match*: other 5s.

See the 270th degree for effects.

267th degree

Colour: green: *Sign*: Sagittarius. 3rd decan. *Qualities*: Mutable/Fixed, Fire. *Numerological match*: other 6s.

See the 270th degree for effects.

268th degree

Colour: blue: *Sign*: Sagittarius. 3rd decan. *Qualities*: Mutable/Fixed, Fire. *Numerological match*: other 7s.

See the 270th degree for effects.

Colour: black: *Sign*: Sagittarius. 3rd decan. *Qualities*: Mutable/
Fixed, Fire. *Numerological match*: other 8s.

See the 270th degree for effects.

Any of the five degrees on either side of the pinnacle point of
the pentagram (see p. 15) come under the collective rulership of
the element Ether, and it is his home degree you should read if
your solar point or any planetary point falls here. He has a
special task for you in this incarnation.

MAGICAL HOME DEGREE OF THE ELEMENT
ETHER
(Strongest effects: 5 degrees on either side)

Colour: crimson. *Sign*: Capricorn. 1st decan. *Qualities*: Cardi-
nal, Earth. *Numerological match*: other 9s.
Positive expression: spiritual regeneration, humanitarianism
Negative expression: destruction of good, greed for power

Solar point

The elemental ruler of the 270th degree is that of the ether,
which is a balanced combination of the qualities of the elements
of Earth, Air, Fire and Water.

His rule is absolute. He can be a creator or destroyer. He
inspires creation through the forces of good or brings destruction through the elements of evil. However, he is in essence
neither good nor evil, being only a reflection of how natives use
his creations. He may be the greatest benefactor man could
desire or a terrible, nightmarish demon.

If you were born with this solar degree or with any of the five
degrees on either side of this one, you have contact with the
source of creation itself and have been selected as one of the
tools of his energy. Be you saint or sinner, your life is controlled by forces beyond your ken and your tasks are universal.
You may think you are merely Joe Bloggs, slogging away at
your daily task, yet in some way your very existence is essential

for the well being of mankind — or you may be instrumental in our destruction.

It could be that you will be one of the progenitors of the future race who will travel space and contact other intelligences. Or you might be the man who presses the button to unleash nuclear war.

People born with this degree of solar energy (and five degrees either side) will in some way, no matter how trivial, become those who are responsible for the management of the human race, the future direction that we take and our physical and moral welfare.

Planetary point

A planet in the 270th degree affects natives in the following way—

Moon: gives intense emotions; also responsibility for the emotional well-being of others and for the upbringing of children.
Venus: gives the ability to bring art, joy and entertainment to others, and an appreciation of nature and things of beauty.
Mars: gives physical energy and courage to fight for human rights.
Jupiter: creates a philosophic outlook and the ability to probe deeply the mysteries of existence and explain difficult concepts. Brings about religious stability and rebirth, as well as competent financial management and use of resources.
Saturn: brings maturity and shouldering of responsibility as well as hard lessons learned through personal experience, self-denial and arduous work. (This planet is much misunderstood by astrologers because of the severity of his way of teaching, but without him mankind would stagnate and die for he is also the symbol of rebirth.)

271st degree

Colour: white. *Sign*: Capricorn. 1st decan. *Qualities*: Cardinal, Earth. *Numerological match*: other 1s.

See the 270th degree for effects.

272nd degree

Colour: grey. *Sign*: Capricorn. 1st decan. *Qualities*: Cardinal, Earth. *Numerological match*: other 2s.

See the 270th degree for effects.

273rd degree

Colour: violet. *Sign*: Capricorn. 1st decan. *Qualities*: Cardinal, Earth. *Numerological match*: other 3s.

See the 270th degree for effects.

274th degree

Colour: orange. *Sign*: Capricorn. 1st decan. *Qualities*: Cardinal, Earth. *Numerological match*: other 4s.

See the 270th degree for effects.

275th degree

Colour: scarlet. *Sign*: Capricorn. 1st decan. *Qualities*: Cardinal, Earth. *Numerological match*: other 5s.

See the 270th degree for effects.

The five degrees above fall under the orb of power of the element Ether (see page 220).

276th degree

Colour: green: *Sign*: Capricorn. 1st decan. *Qualities*: Cardinal, Earth. *Numerological match*: other 6s.
Positive expression: refined tastes
Negative expression: over-indulgence

Solar point

The elemental energy of the 276th usually lifts those born under it into positions of trust and responsibility. Natives are endowed with refinement of taste, which often brings them into higher social circles than would have been the case otherwise. Many natives of this solar degree marry people older, maturer or socially better placed than themselves and through whom they benefit. They are likely to have friends in high places and get help or advancement from them.

In matters of love they are ambitious and they may well marry someone merely for status reasons. Marriages of convenience have also been known.

If other factors in the chart agree, then the native can achieve fame or public recognition in the second half of the life, but only if the ambitions of the first half are adhered to.

Planetary point

A planet in the 276th degree is an indicator of how a native may be able to refine the qualities of the energy of the planets placed in it. Someone with Mars here, for instance, can put physical energy to constructive use and may show marked physical beauty well into old age.

277th degree

Colour: blue. *Sign*: Capricorn. 1st decan. *Qualities*: Cardinal, Earth. *Numerological match*: other 7s.
Positive expression: psychic insight
Negative expression: emotional excess

Solar point

The 277th degree produces a person with strong faith and intuitive powers. There is marked psychic ability which can be turned to profit. Actually, this is one of only a few degrees which actually encourages natives to seek material gain and financial wealth by tuning in psychically and following their hunches. Natives tend to be cautious about initiating projects yet they are courageous once committed to them.

These individuals are almost certain to achieve financial security or even wealth by their mid-thirties. Work should be sought in areas involving the arts or music, or with large business corporations; those who follow these career paths will receive increasing rewards as they grow older.

Planetary point

If you have a planet in the 277th degree, it indicates that your use of psychic powers or intuition will bring you a rise in station or some form of success. If Venus is here, you are likely to work in the field of the arts while Saturn would make you a good company employee or civil servant.

278th degree

Colour: black. *Sign*: Capricorn. 1st decan. *Qualities*: Cardinal, Earth. *Numerological match*: other 8s.
Positive expression: profound thought
Negative expression: despondency

Solar point

As a solar point the elemental energy of the 278th degree gives good reasoning capacity to those born under it. They are best suited to an academic career. They tend to be extremely ambitious and very anxious to rise in life, though this will only come about through tact, diplomacy and long-term commitment. Although they may be slow starters, once set upon a course of action they are very hard to stop, having already thought out the problems they may encounter and are prepared for them.

Some people may scoff at the native's cautiousness, yet they are the ones who will eventually be left behind because of the superior abilities of the native.

A word of warning to those of you born under this degree. Make sure you get the facts right when researching for any project, because once you have reasoned out your path it is hard for you to change course.

Planetary point

A planet in the 278th degree, according to its nature, is an indicator of how the native's logical thought may be applied to achieve success in this life. For instance, the person with Saturn here is a loner, relying upon himself and no one else.

Colour: crimson. *Sign*: Capricorn. 1st decan. *Qualities*: Cardinal, Earth. *Numerological match*: other 9s.
Positive expression: courage, reliability
Negative expression: hostility, confrontation

Solar point

The 299th degree makes natives brave, bold and adventurous. They will tread where others fear to go and succeed where others have failed. Ambitious, enterprising and industrious, they are certain to be in authority over others at some point in their lives. Academically they do not excel, because they neglect their early education through impatience with book learning. That does not mean they are necessarily illiterate. However, they do particularly well when it comes to learning by actually doing things. Natives have a love of duty and responsibility, and many enter the armed forces in order to travel and find adventure. Any occupation with a degree of risk would suit them in fact. Great gains and a settling down period can be attained through marriage.

Planetary point

A planet in the 279th degree indicates where natives may find adventure and stimulation. The person with Mars here enjoys risk occupations and many become self-employed. If Saturn is here, the native is most likely to find his or her risk factor through big business deals.

280th degree

Colour: white. *Sign*: Capricorn. 2nd decan. *Qualities*: Cardinal/Fixed, Earth. *Numerological match*: other 1s.
Positive expression: maturity, responsibility,
Negative expression: sanctimoniousness

Solar point

Only old souls, who have maturity and can handle responsibility, are born with this solar degree. If you are one of these, in some way you will be called upon in this life to sacrifice your own personal interest for the good of others.

Typical of this degree are the dedicated nurse, honest politician, social reformer and selfless charity worker, as they sacrifice their own desires for the needs of the masses. This does not, however, mean that they cannot live normal family lives. They are called upon to sacrifice just one facet of their lives for the sake of others. In so doing they learn the final lesson of their long string of incarnations. If this lesson is learned, this soul will never again return to this world unless it chooses to do so in order to help souls it befriended in other lives.

Planetary point

When there is a planet in this degree it indicates how natives must be of service to others. If Jupiter is here, the native must take care of people's religious or financial needs, etc.

281st degree

Colour: grey. *Sign*: Capricorn. 2nd decan. *Qualities*: Cardinal/Fixed, Earth. *Numerological match*: other 2s.
Positive expression: prudence, reliability, diligence
Negative expression: jealousy, pessimism

Solar point

The elemental energy of the 281st degree creates a prudent, reliable and trustworthy individual who will give a sympathetic ear to those in trouble.

Careers best suited to natives are those with a fair amount of responsibility and accountability to others. They are best employed by others rather than working for themselves. Excess is not one of their faults. They can be relied upon to obey orders and carry out routine jobs without making a fuss. That does not mean they are mindless zombies, however. They just want a peaceful existence, and have the ability to work diligently for long periods.

If you were born with this solar degree, you will reach the higher positions of your chosen career through hard work and long service to one employer.

Planetary point

If you have a planet in the 281st degree, it will determine how best you can concentrate your efforts. A native with Mars here will have a competitive spirit and excel in a sales career. If Saturn is the planet, the native will have to work his way up in his job from the bottom to the top.

282nd degree

Colour: violet. *Sign*: Capricorn. 2nd decan. *Qualities*: Cardinal/ Fixed, Earth. *Numerological match*: other 3s.
Positive expression: devotion to duty
Negative expression: adoption of wrong causes

Solar point

People born with the Sun in the 282nd degree tend to devote themselves throughout their lives to one partner, career or objective. They often hold deep spiritual beliefs and uphold the moral values of society. Clergymen, monks, nuns and any persons who dedicate themselves to one particular occupation, including loyal and loving marriage partners, are the kind of people who are likely to be natives of this solar degree. If you were born with it, you may not obtain great material rewards in this incarnation but the spiritual progress you can make is far more rewarding.

Natives of this solar degree often have to care for aged parents or relatives in the course of their lives. Many marry foreigners.

Planetary point

If you have a planet in the 282nd degree, it indicates in what area you may show great devotion. With Jupiter here, you would make a great religious worker or a fund raiser for charities or worthy causes. If you have Mars here, you would very likely wish to serve your country in some way, probably in the armed services.

283rd degree

Colour: orange. *Sign*: Capricorn. 2nd decan. *Qualities*: Cardinal/ Fixed, Earth. *Numerological match*: other 4s.
Positive expression: strength of mind
Negative expression: violent outbursts

Solar point

The elemental energy of the 283rd degree strengthens the minds of natives, giving them the ability to concentrate, organise and bring to fruition any plans they may make. Their perseverance coupled with a belief in themselves generally results in high achievement. However, they should be very careful in how they lay the foundations for their projects as they are inclined to try to bring changes where they are not wanted by others and thus they bring about their own downfall. Although an idea may be a good one in itself, if it is implemented at the wrong time or place it is ultimately doomed to failure. People born with this degree frequently ignore advice from others. Sometimes it would be to their benefit to act upon it. Many of those people who make a fortune and then squander it display both the positive and the negative effects of this degree.

Planetary point

Whoever has a planet in this degree acquires the qualities associated with that particular planet, but stronger than usual. Someone with Mars here, for instance, can be even more materialistic and ambitious, while with Jupiter the native can both earn and spend a huge amount of money.

284th degree

Colour: scarlet. *Sign*: Capricorn. 2nd decan. *Qualities*: Cardinal/ Fixed, Earth. *Numerological match*: other 5s.
Positive expression: good intellect
Negative expression: acerbity

Solar point

The elemental energy of the 284th degree endows people born under it with a sharp mind, retentive memory and good intellect. Positions of authority and respect can be acquired and there can be a taste for literature. There is also an ability to spot a bargain or make a good deal. Natives have a competitive nature and this together with resourcefulness and adaptability gives them a good chance to succeed in the world of commerce.

The tongue can be sharp at times and the outer nature may appear cold and uncaring. This, however, is not the case. The native tends to concentrate all his or her energies on achieving what he or she has set out to do and this intenseness can be interpreted as indifference. There is sensitivity but the native does not often show it.

Planetary point

When there is a planet in the 284th degree, it shows what kind of mind or intellect the native has. A person with Uranus here would now be very elderly, but in the course of his or her life would have been unconventional and inconsistent. He or she would have worked well in stressful, changing situations rather than being stuck in one office with a dull routine. This is a position that produces successful inventors. The Moon here inclines the native to public work.

285th degree

Colour: green. *Sign*: Capricorn. 2nd decan. *Qualities*: Cardinal/ Fixed, Earth. *Numerological match*: other 6s.
Positive expression: popularity, friendliness
Negative expression: over-indulgence

Solar point

As a solar point the 285th is a degree which favours honours, popularity and friendships. The natives are very able and also have a pleasant and agreeable manner. They will enjoy much success in this lifetime. Another characteristic of people born with this degree is a dislike for trouble of any sort — they will go out of their way to avoid it. Gains or honours often come through the parents or elders. With regards choice of occupation, preference is shown for those which involve beautifying or harmonising the surroundings.

Unusually for Capricornians, natives can be great entertainers, as Jan Leeming and Pamela Sue Martin (Fallon) of Dynasty have shown. If well aspected by the Sun, Moon or Jupiter, natives are certain to obtain social distinction, honours and financial success as well as the favour and good will of those in positions of authority.

Planetary point

The placement of a planet in the 285th degree concerns social contacts and friendships and how they may come about. A person who has Venus here would make friends with artistically inclined people. If Jupiter is here, the native would be more likely to make firm friends with business contacts.

286th degree

Colour: blue. *Sign*: Capricorn. 2nd decan. *Qualities*: Cardinal/Fixed, Earth. *Numerological match*: other 7s.
Positive expression: inspiration
Negative expression: impressionability

Solar point

People born with the Sun in the 286th degree are capable of attaining respect and honour through some form of peculiar or unique achievement. Work in any occupation involving sanitation, hygiene, health or hospital boards or in the artistic or scientific fields could bring high honours. There is often a great liking for mysteries, and many a detective has this solar degree. In fact the degree favours all activities involving mystery, secrecy and inspiration. Success is never planned; it comes in a flash, by accident or by being in the right place at the right time. Natives of this degree have a gift for simplifying that which others have made complicated, which makes them good arbitrators in the disputes of others. They are, however, impressionable and should keep away from psychic research if they find it scary.

Planetary point

If you have a planet in the 286th this shows that you often get flashes of inspiration. The nature of that planet shows in which area of life that inspiration may originate and is a clue to how you may follow it up. If you have Mercury here, you can understand the most complex concepts without having studied them to any great extent. If the planet is Venus, you have a feel for the arts and are a natural entertainer.

287th degree

Colour: black. *Sign*: Capricorn. 2nd decan. *Qualities*: Cardinal/Fixed, Earth. *Numerological match*: other 8s.

Positive expression: persistent endeavour
Negative expression: lack of humour

Solar point

The 287th degree gives those born under it a mental maturity way beyond their physical years. They are capable of achieving a good deal quite early in life because of their ability to stick at things. Although deprived of opportunity early on, by perseverance they should be able to convince others of their suitability for taking on responsible jobs. They may think in early life that they suffer too much. But they must learn to cope with hardship in order to develop their metal, for those born under this degree are destined to become the guardians of our social structure in the mid-term of their lives. Success after 40 is indicated and this will be far superior to anything achieved before then.

Planetary point

A planet in the 287th degree indicates what is the best direction the native should take in life to develop maturity of outlook. For example, a native with Mercury here tends to work through the system, starting at the bottom and eventually reaching the top, and is ideally employed in a government body or large corporation.

288th degree

Colour: crimson. *Sign*: Capricorn. 2nd decan. *Qualities*: Cardinal/ Fixed, Earth. *Numerological match*: other 9s.
Positive expression: freedom of spirit
Negative expression: impulsiveness

Solar point

People born with the Sun in the 288th degree have a spirit of freedom and a desire for conquest, which is sometimes to their detriment. Impulse and force of feeling may override the reason and common sense.

Natives are courageous and enterprising and are therefore capable of conducting their own business. However, they accomplish more when they are mature enough to allow the head to control their passions.

If you have this solar degree, remember, once this control is achieved the world is your oyster and you can be whatever you desire. Approach one task at a time and you'll find success.

Planetary point

A planet in the 288th degree denotes the area of the native's life in which he or she most desires freedom of expression. If Venus or the Moon is here, the person requires free love or emotional expression. If the planet is Mercury, the native desires free speech and the ability to follow his or her own interests without outside interference.

289th degree

Colour: white. *Sign*: Capricorn. 2nd decan. *Qualities*: Cardinal/Fixed, Earth. *Numerological match*: other 1s.
Positive expression: good birth, plentiful opportunities
Negative expression: haughtiness

Solar point

The key feature of the 289th degree is that of karmic reward. Those who have their solar energy in this degree, so long as it is unafflicted by ill-aspected planets, are born into families of good social standing and influence from which they have their springboard to general success. This success is usually steady no matter what business or occupation they choose. This is partly because they readily obtain the favour of those in high places who are in a position to be of assistance to them. They have vitality and a high code of moral conduct.

All the right opportunities arise for those born with this degree. They only have to reach out and take them.

Planetary point

If you have a planet in the 289th degree, it is an indicator of what assistance you can expect from others in this life, Saturn here brings the advice, protection and help of elders and those in authority, while the Moon would ensure the emotional support of others in your times of need. Venus here can indicate good, reliable social contacts.

Colour: grey. *Sign*: Capricorn. 3rd decan. *Qualities*: Cardinal/Fixed, Earth. *Numerological match*: other 2s.
Positive expression: sensitivity to others' needs
Negative expression: public scandal, notoriety

Solar point

The elemental energy of the 290th degree gives natives an understanding and sensitivity which would find its best outlet through involvement in public life. Femininity and sensitivity are keynotes of this degree. Many of those born with it have been shaped by their mothers.

If you were born with your Sun at this point, women can play an important role in your life be you male or female. You like to feel wanted and useful, and a career in any of the welfare organisations would prove fulfilling. Alternatively, you could use your aptitudes in something like beauty therapy, cosmetics or any related feminine-orientated industry. Marriage tends to take place later in life but it should be a long-lasting one. The children are likely to be spoilt.

Planetary point

With a planet here, the 290th degree is an indicator of where your sensitivity to others' needs will come into play. The Moon or Venus here points to your being emotionally supportive to others and incidentally you will thereby find your own stability. If Jupiter is the planet, you will be inclined to support others when they need financial help.

291st degree

Colour: violet. *Sign*: Capricorn. 3rd decan. *Qualities*: Cardinal/Fixed, Earth. *Numerological match*: other 3s.
Positive expression: luck, good fortune, good mentality
Negative expression: failure to grasp opportunities

Solar point

If you were born with the Sun in the 291st degree, you are lucky indeed. Jump in front of a bus and it will swerve and miss you;

fill out the pools for a friend and hit the jackpot. No matter what area of the life this degree affects, its outcome is fortunate. People born under this degree will find themselves in the right places at the right times and whatever their chosen career, progress should be quicker than most. There is marked ability in practical and financial matters. Gains are likely to be made through the father or, for a woman, from marriage to an older man. The degree favours the accumulation of money and possession. Benefits will come especially through legacies or lawsuits.

Planetary point

A planet in the 291st degree shows on what particular area of the native's life fortune may shine. Someone with the Moon here can have gifted children, or receive the aid of females. Those who have Mars here will find the law of the land in their favour in any disputes. This planet attracts a strong guardian angel as well as increasing physical energy.

292nd degree

Colour: orange. *Sign*: Capricorn. 3rd decan. *Qualities*: Cardinal/ Mutable, Earth. *Numerological match*: other 4s.
Positive expression: adaptability to change
Negative expression: enforcement of change

Solar point

Natives of the 292nd degree can expect strange and eventful circumstances in this incarnation. Originality is a gift possessed by them, but they have been blessed with it in order that they may be able to adapt to the many and sudden changes in fortune they will experience.

Natives are always seeking to be different in everything they do, and follow uncommon lines of thought and philosophy. They make much effort to break away from the accepted codes of conduct of whatever kind of society they are born into, desiring to bring into being new modes of behaviour for the future. Bringers of necessary change as they may be, they do not always choose the right times or methods. As a result they can stir up much bad feeling in other people.

Planetary point

A planet in the 292nd degree is an indicator of the way in which natives may become involved in some form of social reform or change in society. For example, with Pluto here they can become involved in sexual reform or the law, while if Saturn is the planet they would be interested in the land and the earth's resources.

293rd degree

Colour: scarlet. *Sign*: Capricorn. 3rd decan. *Qualities*: Cardinal/ Mutable, Earth. *Numerological match*: other 5s.
Positive expression: probing for facts, truth-seeking
Negative expression: cold calculation

Solar point

The elemental energy of the 293rd degree gives natives a logical mind. Therefore academic occupations tend to suit them best. You will find them as writers, publishers, lecturers, teachers, solicitors and the like. They do not like other people having secrets and will go to extremes to uncover what they feel may be an injustice. While not emotionally demonstrative they do, however, have, deep down, very passionate feelings. They can give the impression of being somewhat prudish.

Great researchers and fact-finders, you would be wise never to lie or hide something from natives of this degree as they will eventually find you out.

Planetary point

If you have a planet in the 293rd degree, it indicates the area of life you most readily understand. With Jupiter here you can be a great financier, understanding all the intricacies of the money markets, while with Venus you would have an eye for beauty and a feeling for the arts.

294th degree

Colour: green. *Sign*: Capricorn. 3rd decan. *Qualities*: Cardinal/ Mutable, Earth. *Numerological match*: other 6s.

Positive expression: sympathy, modesty
Negative expression: parsimony

Solar point

People born with the Sun in the 294th degree are sympathetic, modest and sincere. Success is likely to come through marriage or partnerships. There is a tendency to be thrifty which some might interpret as meanness though I would just say that more often natives merely show good management of money.

Natives tend to be fairly well liked and respected and have the ability to make the most out of any opportunity that arises. Friendships formed are more likely to last for a considerable period, even a lifetime. There will be loyalty and honesty in these relationships through thick and thin.

Sexuality and physical expression are generally heightened and care will have to be taken to avoid excess.

Planetary point

The 295th degree indicates, by the planet in it, how friendships and relationships may be formed from common interests. Venus here would suggest that the native prefers artistic and gentle people, while someone with Mars here would prefer the more adventurous outdoor types.

295th degree

Colour: blue. *Sign*: Capricorn. 3rd decan. *Qualities*: Cardinal/Mutable, Earth. *Numerological match*: other 7s.
Positive expression: depth of thought
Negative expression: inquisitiveness

Solar point

A person born with the Sun in the 295th degree is prone to thinking deeply about philosophical and spiritual matters. This shows that he or she is an old and much travelled soul.

Natives of this degree are generally thought to be dreamers by those who do not really know them well. But who can tell what is going on in these individuals' minds? Clairaudience, clairvoyance and other psychic faculties are often developed by them yet they never openly speak about them. Flashes of intuition give natives the key to solving personal problems.

They also have special insight that enables them to accomplish tasks which others would find too perplexing.

This degree favours advanced studies or any type of investigation into matters concerning history or metaphysics. Deep thinkers are rarely understood in their own day. The passage of time will prove their true value to society.

Planetary point

Whoever has a planet in the 295th degree has the capacity for deep thought and concentrated study. If the planet is Jupiter, for instance, that individual would become a philosopher, seeking out the answers to such questions as why we are here and so on.

296th degree

Colour: black. *Sign*: Capricorn. 3rd decan. *Qualities*: Cardinal/Mutable, Earth. *Numerological match*: other 8s.
Positive expression: business acumen
Negative expression: oppressive tendencies

Solar point

As a solar point the elemental energy of the 286th degree gives the natives the tenacity and stubborness of a bull terrier in achieving their ambitions. But they will need to be careful how they go achieving them if they want to avoid incurring the wrath of others. Al Capone was born with the Sun in this degree and he was ruthless in the way he achieved his aims and ambitions. He was a wily businessman who greased many palms. But eventually he had to face up to the way he had acquired his wealth and died a lonely, sick man in jail.

Natives of this degree are capable of abandoning all morality wheo it suits their plans, yet, on the other hand, they may still desire to be loved and respected for their charitable nature. They can take with one hand and give with the other, and need to find a balance if they are ever to find the joy they seek.

If you were born with this solar energy you can be either ruthless or kind, it is up to you alone which it is to be.

Planetary point

If you have a planet in the 296th degree, it points to the area of your life where you will stop at nothing to achieve security. For example, if the Moon is here, you will allow no hindrance to your emotional expression and will seek to remove any obstacles that prevent your winning the partner you seek.

297th degree

Colour: crimson. *Sign*: Capricorn. 3rd decan. *Qualities*: Cardinal/ Mutable, Earth. *Numerological match*: other 9s.
Positive expression: bold, pioneering nature
Negative expression: proneness to accidents

Solar point

The elemental energy of the 297th degree creates a risk-taking pioneer. People born under its sway are typified by the adventurous business man or woman, prepared to take risks and gambles that others would avoid. They accordingly reap the rewards or accept the failures as they come. Some may think that natives of the sign of Capricorn are incapable of taking risks, but that is not so with this degree. They are gifted with a good deal of energy and staying power and are drawn into an adventurous stream of society without necessarily wanting it. What they ultimately seek is a quiet, tranquil place to rest their bones.

   Those of you born under this degree can both earn and lose fortunes. One thing that can be said about having this degree is that it will make this incarnation eventful!

Planetary point

A planet in the 297th degree is an indicator of where natives may find adventure and relief from the tedium of their everyday lives. Those with Mars here will be competitive and combative on the sports field, while these with Venus would get out and about on the social scene.

298th degree

Colour: white. *Sign*: Capricorn. 3rd decan. *Qualities*: Cardinal/ Mutable, Earth. *Numerological match*: other 1s.
Positive expression: self-reliance
Negative expression: pedantry

Solar point

The elemental energy of the 298th degree creates a loner, who can be self-reliant to an extreme. Even when married, natives of this degree never fully commit themselves to the partnership. Inwardly they lack something, but do not know what it is; they can search for it for a lifetime. Their karma is to relearn all that their soul has achieved and to lay the foundations for their future incarnation by seeking new ideals and aspirations and thereby find completeness.

On a more mundane level, natives are able to look at a situation objectively and can distinguish the rights or the wrongs of it. They are then able to express their viewpoint clearly to others. Hence they make great leaders. They often have good business sense and managerial ability, but they do not like to be in the public eye, preferring to work behind the scenes. Many people born with this solar energy become advisers to others in authority, making them the real decision makers.

Planetary point

A planet in the 298th degree reveals the chief lesson the soul must learn in this life. Mercury here, for instance, shows that the native must develop his or her mental powers.

299th degree

Colour: grey. *Sign*: Capricorn. 3rd decan. *Qualities*: Cardinal/Mutable, Earth. *Numerological match*: other 2s.
Positive expression: responsibility
Negative expression: inconsistency

Solar point

People born with the Sun in the 299th degree have a lesson in responsibility to learn in this incarnation. In previous lives they paid too much attention to their own desires, regardless of the consequences for others, and now they must pay the price.

If you were born with your solar energy here you will find that others thrust responsibility upon you, whether you want it or not, and it is your diligence when taking it upon your shoulders that will determine the level of material success you will achieve in this life. You may be just old Joe Bloggs from down the street with a wife and five kids to support on your meagre salary, but nevertheless this is a lesson which must be learned if you are to rest in your latter years. Think about it. Children rarely desert those who have sacrificed so much for them; they return the deeds in later life. No matter what your task, be sure you do it well.

Planetary point

A planet in the 299th degree shows that accepting heavy responsibilities is your lot in this life. If Mars is here, you must be self-supporting and learn to use the physical strengths given you by this planet to help others. With Jupiter you may well have to take on heavy financial responsibilities.

300th degree

Colour: violet. *Sign*: Aquarius. 1st decan. *Qualities*: Fixed, Air.
Numerological match: other 3s.
Positive expression: original thinking
Negative expression: eccentricity

Solar point

People born with this solar degree seek to develop the higher mind and are the originators of the ideas of today which will give rise to the realities of tomorrow. Friends, partnerships, clubs and associations will play an important role in the life of the natives, especially in view of their ability to persuade others to follow their ideas. One of their biggest failings, however, is that they can allow pride to get in the way of their ambitions. Sometimes they disassociate themselves from anyone critical of their point of view instead of trying to use their persuasive powers to bring them around to their way of thinking.

Original thinkers never find easy acceptance and need to demonstrate at least a belief in themselves if they are to convince others.

Planetary point

If you have a planet in the 300th degree, it will indicate to you in what way you can be original. With Jupiter here, you may introduce new philosophical concepts, or find a new way of earning money. If Mercury is here you might try to teach others how to expand their mental horizons.

Colour: orange. *Sign*: Aquarius. 1st decan. *Qualities*: Fixed, Air. *Numerological match*: other 4s.
Positive expression: extraordinary abilities
Negative expression: peculiar hopes

Solar point

People with the Sun in the 301st degree have an air of unconventionality about them. For a start, they have extraordinary abilities, but these depend upon what other planets aspect the Sun. Then their views and ideals can be so peculiar that others nod their heads and declare them fit for the funny farm.

Well aspected, the degree brings friends from the occult fraternities. It also gives tremendous talent to those who want to become inventors, writers or government officials. If ill-aspected, then eccentric or unreliable friendships can be formed which end in estrangement. Or there may be impulsive attachments to individuals who are likely to bring conflict into their lives. Either way, the native of this degree is born out of his or her time and will have to work hard to adjust to the present day which is perhaps 100 years ahead or behind them.

Planetary point

If you have a planet in the 301st degree, it indicates that you have great ability or that you are born out of your time. Those old folk with Uranus here will have been extremely inventive on the one hand but highly unconventional and unpredictable on the other.

302nd degree

Colour: scarlet. *Sign*: Aquarius. 1st decan. *Qualities*: Fixed, Air. *Numerological match*: other 5s.
Positive expression: charisma, persuasive speech
Negative expression: falsehood, charlatanry

Solar point

Natives of the 302nd degree have the gift of being able to hold the attention of crowds with brilliant oratory. The mind is imaginative and inventive and natives can express themselves with great feeling.

There is no such thing as a shy native of this degree, merely an unawakened ability to use what he or she has been given. The best use of this energy is in helping others to help themselves, examples being agony aunts Peggy Makins and Claire Raynor. If you have this solar degree, you may never receive such public acclaim for your efforts in assisting others. Nevertheless, you have a karma which impels you to lend a sympathetic ear to those in trouble.

Receptionists, telephonists, barmaids and all those who communicate with the public at large are the kind of people most likely to have this degree's energy at work.

Planetary point

A planet in the 302nd degree indicates how natives may use their communicative ability for the good of others as well as themselves.

Those with Mars here will be outspoken challengers and fighters for human rights. Those with Venus may be specially concerned with work for children, and so on.

303rd degree

Colour: green. *Sign*: Aquarius. 1st decan. *Qualities*: Fixed, Air.
Numerological match: other 6s.
Positive expression: happiness through friends
Negative expression: inability to trust others

Solar point

Natives of the 303rd degree have a knack for making friends and will benefit greatly through social activity and through the arts.

If you were born with the Sun here, your marriage partner may be so well heeled that you do not need to continue at work, though you may choose to carry on for the love of it. By and large your life will be one continual round of social events, possibly in high society. You will find much enjoyment through the arts in general, whether you are a participant or a spectator. Your mind is refined and you have good taste. In some way or other you will want to impart an appreciation for the finer things in life to the masses.

Beauticians, hairdressers, fashion designers and all who create things of beauty, are the kind of people who would have this solar degree working for them.

Planetary point

A planet in the 303rd degree is an indicator of how natives may unlock their artistic talent. An individual with Mars here is energetic and forceful and will persevere until people come to appreciate what he or she has to offer. There is a tendency to over-indulge, however. A person with Venus is very refined and a highly talented artist.

304th degree

Colour: blue. *Sign*: Aquarius. 1st decan. *Qualities*: Fixed, Air.
Numerological match: other 7s.
Positive expression: spirituality, psychic faculties
Negative expression: unsuitable attachments

Solar point

Natives of the 304th degree have an intuitional insight which they should learn to develop. They can also have marked literary talent. They frequently work in the field of healing or medicine, researching and developing new treatments. In particular natives become interested in alternative medicine and therapies such as acupuncture, osteopathy, aromatherapy, herbalism and other forms of nature cure.

At some time in the life there will be a desire for overseas travel and the exploration of foreign cultures. This will greatly broaden the mind and perhaps the general outlook on life.

If you were born with this degree, you are likely to be quite tranquil and desire a peaceful existence. A negative effect of the degree, however, is to worry about imaginary problems.

Planetary point

The 304th degree shows, by the planet placed in it, how the natives' psychic faculties or intuition can be helpful to them. Mars here does not make a person particularly aggressive; he or she will know when to fight and when to run. Mercury here strengthens the imagination and opens a channel for the subconscious feelings.

305th degree

Colour: black. *Sign*: Aquarius. 1st decan. *Qualities*: Fixed, Air. *Numerological match*: other 8s.
Positive expression: courtesy
Negative expression: vindictiveness

Solar point

The elemental energy of the 305th degree gives natives an affable and courteous disposition. By nature serious and reserved, they open up when they feel really comfortable in any particular environment or social situation. They have good reasoning ability, are decisive in action and don't mince their words. They take great pains over anything that they undertake, feeling they have a duty or responsibility to accomplish successfully tasks which they have set themselves. Furthermore, they need to be able to justify their words and deeds, to themselves at least. And you will not find them doing other people's dirty work for them.

Marriages and partnerships are long lasting though natives are not generally emotionally demonstrative; they tend to hide their emotional intensity from others.

Planetary point

A planet in the 305th degree adds a degree of seriousness to the energy placed there. Natives will tend to be conformists in those areas of their lives governed by that planet. For example, a person with Venus here will have serious views on art and relationships in general. Someone with Jupiter will have a serious philosophic outlook.

306th degree

Colour: crimson. *Sign*: Aquarius. 1st decan. *Qualities*: Fixed, Air. *Numerological match*: other 9s.
Positive expression: reasoning ability
Negative expression: brusqueness

Solar point

As a solar point the elemental energy of the 306th degree gives natives good reasoning power and the capacity to look at things from an unusual or original angle. They are competent speakers and are ever willing to engage others in debate on almost any topic — it is mainly the debate that they enjoy. They tend to make friends easily. However, there can be brusqueness of manner and speech if they feel others do not understand what they are trying to do and they should lose this habit if they really wish to succeed in life. Opinions tend to be fixed and not readily changed by others, but if changes are made they are decisive and complete turn-arounds.

This is a good degree for those who wish to lead by personal example in, for instance, public companies or governmental departments, though many with this degree will become self-employed in some way.

Planetary point

If you have a planet in the 306th degree, it indicates which areas of your life you would like to be brought out into the open and discussed in order to settle problems. If you have the Moon here, you have a deep desire for others to understand your emotional needs. If you have Mercury in this point, you will always be airing your ideas verbally or in writing.

307th degree

Colour: white. *Sign*: Aquarius. 1st decan. *Qualities*: Fixed, Air.
Numerological match: other 1s.
Positive expression: quiet determination
Negative expression: strong likes and dislikes

Solar point

People born with the Sun in the 307th degree have a quiet, patient and determined nature which is faithful to others and expects the same in return. They are rather slow to anger but when their anger is let loose it is very hard to quell. There is a fondness for art, music, philosophy and the occult sciences. Natives tend to be forward-looking, and prefer New Age concepts to old ideas.

Work in electronics, computers, laser technology or any of the new technological fields would suit natives of this degree. They like to be ahead of anyone else, either by creating new inventions or by operating them.

If you were born with this solar degree, you should have great leadership qualities provided the Sun is well aspected in the horoscope chart.

Planetary point

The placement of a planet in the 307th degree shows how natives may find help in their greatest times of need. With Jupiter here they can bring the law onto their side if they keep within it, or perhaps obtain assistance from their church. Mars brings strength of character.

308th degree

Colour: grey. *Sign*: Aquarius. 1st decan. *Qualities*: Fixed, Air.
Numerological match: other 2s.
Positive expression: agreeable nature, intuition
Negative expression: rebellious streak

Solar point

The elemental energy of the 308th degree gives natives an active mind, intuitive powers and quite an agreeable disposition. To a point they are sociable and sympathetic by nature but they are rather independent in outlook and their behaviour tends to be unconventional (and sometimes downright eccentric!). For example, they have a liking for anything which is curious or bizarre and take an interest in new inventions. Strange new fashions can be accepted with open arms, as can New Age philosophy and ideals.

The degree leads all natives towards some form of political activity, educational work or occult investigation and many born with the Sun here are what society sees as extremists, though with the passing of time their ideals may become generally accepted. The natives' karma is to stand alone for their beliefs in spite of fierce opposition.

If you were born with this solar degree, you feel a need to stand out in a crowd, to be seen and appreciated as an individual, not just one of a mass.

Planetary point

The 308th degree, by the planet placed in it, shows in what way natives must learn the lesson of taking on responsibility. Those

246

with Mars here will be responsible for their own physical safety
and well-being. If Jupiter is here, natives must learn to sort out
their spiritual beliefs.

309th degree

Colour: violet. *Sign*: Aquarius. 1st decan. *Qualities*: Fixed, Air.
Numerological match: other 3s.
Positive expression: cheerfulness, compassion
Negative expression: self-indulgence

Solar point

The 309th degree creates cheerful, good humoured and obliging
individuals. Their karmic lesson is to share with others and
show compassion to those who are in need of spiritual, emotional or moral guidance.

If you were born with this degree, remember that your first
concern should be with the foundation of our society — the
family unit itself. Some changes in the way we raise children
that have happened in the last 50 years are for the worse and
must be put right. You are one of those chosen to set the right
example which others may then follow. You will be provided
with all the requirements to accomplish your task but how you
do it is your choice alone. Muggings, violent crime against the
elderly and all that is distasteful in our society stems from the
way we raise our children, especially in their early years. You
may be a parent to many children, and are also partly responsible for those of your neighbours.

Planetary point

If you have a planet in the 309th degree, the nature of it will
indicate the area in your life in which you will be called upon to
be of assistance to others. The person with Mars here may
become a street bobby or perhaps a probation officer, social
worker or some kind of reformer. Anyone with Jupiter in this
point would find their best expression through the schools or
anything to do with education.

Colour: orange. *Sign*: Aquarius. 2nd decan. *Qualities*: Fixed/
Mutable, Air. *Numerological match*: other 4s.
Positive expression: reforming zeal
Negative expression: rebelliousness, conflict with authority

Solar point

The elemental energy of the 310th degree creates a somewhat
awkward disposition in the natives. Though caring, sensitive
and compassionate, they are often discontented with the way
things have been done in the past and try to bring in changes
that they think desirable but may be, as yet, not really acceptable to the masses. This can bring them into conflict with those
in authority and power which can lead them down a path
fraught with dangers.

If you were born with this solar degree, learn to express
yourself from within the system and thereby seek to change it,
for if you attempt rebellion you will end up in a mess. You have
a karmic responsibility in this existence to implement necessary
social changes, but you must do it with the consent of your
fellows rather than by force, which can appear the easier way at
times.

Planetary point

The 310th degree shows, by the nature of the planet placed in it,
how natives may become involved in bringing about changes in
our social structures. Those with Saturn here will either have
great personal power or be in some way associated with those in
power and through them achieve their aims.

311th degree

Colour: scarlet. *Sign*: Aquarius. 2nd decan. *Qualities*: Fixed/
Mutable, Air. *Numerological match*: other 5s.
Positive expression: acquisition of knowledge
Negative expression: one-sided views

Solar point

The elemental energy of the 311th degree gives natives the

capacity to learn easily and acquire much knowledge. The mind is astute and quick to spot errors that others make, and also quick to point them out.

Natives might be thought nosy, but they do have good motives for probing into the affairs of other people. They are seeking answers to life's problems. They also need the stimulus of friends and social activities and really hate to be alone.

With regard to choosing a career, people with this degree would make great welfare workers, social reformers, ecologists or medical scientists who research into killer diseases.

This degree favours women over men, and those with Venus well placed in the horoscope chart can attain great advancement through the arts or in the field of social entertainment.

Planetary point

A planet in the 311th degree shows which side of the personality needs to be developed for the benefit of both the native and other people. For example, whoever has Mercury here will have oratory or literary abilities to develop.

312th degree

Colour: green. *Sign*: Aquarius. 2nd decan. *Qualities*: Fixed/Mutable, Air. *Numerological match*: other 6s.
Positive expression: trendiness
Negative expression: failure to conform or adapt

Solar point

The elemental energy of the 312th degree will refine the taste and widen the forms of artistic expression of those born under it. They should therefore be able to create new art forms and help to make them popular in society at present. People born under this degree may be trend setters, *avant garde* artists or musicians, designers of new fashions or the creators of new synthetic fabrics.

Those of you born with your Sun on this point may become actively involved in any of these fields or similar ones. You may be the first to try new fashions or the first to explore new avenues of social activity but, no matter how you may go about it, you are the ones chosen to refine the New Age concepts and make them acceptable in society.

Planetary point

A planet in the 312th degree shows in what way natives will be involved in social reform or artistic activity. For example, if Jupiter is here, natives would travel about a great deal demonstrating new fashions or airing ideas regarding social change.

313th degree

Colour: blue. *Sign*: Aquarius. 2nd decan. *Qualities*: Fixed/Mutable, Air. *Numerological match*: other 7s.
Positive expression: spiritual awareness
Negative expression: imaginary fears

Solar point

Persons born with the Sun in the 313th degree are highly creative but also highly strung. Great spiritual healers and artists are born under this degree. But the energy can be so intense that it is beyond the control of many natives who then become mentally unstable.

Those of you born under this degree need a strong Mercury or Saturn degree in the chart if the task of this life is ever to be fully accomplished. You have a great need to understand and to be understood, and try to deepen your insight by the study of philosophy or religion. Your intense emotions could find an outlet in one of the arts, such as poetry, drama or music. This energy will be better understood by those born in the next millennium.

Planetary point

A planet here is an indicator of how natives may express their spiritual awareness. With Venus this is usually expressed by example. Those with Mars can become involved in work for the handicapped or socially deprived.

314th degree

Colour: black. *Sign*: Aquarius. 2nd decan. *Qualities*: Fixed/Mutable, Air. *Numerological match*: other 8s.
Positive expression: faithfulness
Negative expression: putting self before others

Solar point

People born under the 314th solar degree are independent and fully able to break away from their origins to find a new base for themselves within the more successful social strata. Although slow to make friends, when they do the friendships tend to last for a lifetime. They excel in conducting long-term projects which require patience and staying power to achieve success. It is in the second half of the life that most rewards come.

Natives of this degree have a karmic responsibility to build upon firm foundations in ever-changing and uncertain circumstances. Great rewards can be had by those who persevere, but great sorrow and a sense of unfulfilment is the lot of those who don't.

Much will be demanded of those born with the Sun in this degree, but if they learn from the wisdom of their elders, they shall receive rewards both here and in heaven.

Planetary point

As a planetary point the 314th is an indicator of how natives may become involved with older people. If Mercury is here, the native will find reward in his or her communicative ability, especially with regard to the elderly. Someone with Venus in this degree may well become involved with caring for the aged.

315th degree

Colour: crimson. *Sign*: Aquarius. 2nd decan. *Qualities*: Fixed/Mutable, Air. *Numerological match*: other 9s.
Positive expression: seeking adventures
Negative expression: unnecessary risk-taking

Solar point

The elemental energy of the 315th degree gives natives the desire for taking risks and all forms of adventure. They tackle tasks that others would shirk from and experiment with the new technologies that herald the Age of Aquarius. They should take care, however, not to act precipitately, but to think carefully first; if Mercury is badly aspected in the chart they could end up with nought but broken dreams and broken friendships. Patience is not one of the virtues of natives of this degree and they do better when they link up with a partner who has this virtue.

The energy of this degree is of the type that can be utilised for finding practical uses for atomic energy. But it should be remembered that haste and mistakes could bring disaster.

Planetary point

The effects of a planet in this degree are more direct and forceful than in most other degrees. Someone with Mercury here could be a great orator and communicator — or a sarcastic, sharp-tonged oaf. The native with Venus in this point could be either artistically gifted or terribly vain, etc.

316th degree

Colour: white. *Sign*: Aquarius. 2nd decan. *Qualities*: Fixed/Mutable, Air. *Numerological match*: other 1s.
Positive expression: leadership ability
Negative expression: reclusiveness

Solar point

The elemental energy of the 316th degree gives the native many talents and fine qualities, including perception, independence, originality and enterprise. On the negative side, the native can be self-seeking and unsociable.

If you were born with this solar degree you have been given all the necessary attributes for leadership as well as good health. You should therefore be able to achieve your ambitions, but you must realise that in the process you must avoid treading over the toes of others. A leader must have followers who are willingly led by him and it is important that you do not force your will or views upon them. If you do you will stir up rebellion as all dictators do eventually.

Those born with the Sun in this degree have a special role to play in leading mankind through these difficult times towards a better one.

Planetary point

If you have a planet in the 316th degree its nature indicates how you may be called upon to exert your authority or stick to your beliefs in certain areas of your life. If you have Saturn here you will have responsibilities in land management and the use of natural resources. With Mercury, you will make your presence felt by your skills in verbal persuasion.

317th degree

Colour: grey. *Sign*: Aquarius. 2nd decan. *Qualities*: Fixed/
Mutable, Air. *Numerological match*: other 2s.
Positive expression: compassion, responsibility
Negative expression: vanity, conceit

Solar point

The role of any person born with the Sun in the 317th degree is
that of a teacher who can impart to others a love of the natural
world and a desire to care for the planet we live upon.

Those of you born with this solar degree will in some way
play a part in shaping young people by making them aware and
mature enough to handle their future tasks. School teachers,
social workers and parents with this solar point have more to do
than they might think, for it is their collective energy which
moulds the children of today into the responsible adults of
tomorrow and thus play a great part in determining the future
of our world. Compassion and understanding are a part of this
process, but do not forget that sometimes some severity is
necessary as some learn not from kindness but through discipline.

Planetary point

People with a planet in the 317th degree become involved with
the care of our young people. If the Moon or Venus is in this
point, natives make great parents or guardians. Natives with
Mars here use his or her physical prowess through sports, etc.

318th degree

Colour: violet. *Sign*: Aquarius. 2nd decan. *Qualities*: Fixed/
Mutable, Air. *Numerological match*: other 3s.
Positive expression: professionalism
Negative expression: overweening pride

Solar point

Anyone born with the Sun in the 318th degree will be blessed
with true friends and association with prominent people, or at
least those with the power to assist in their personal advancement.

Natives are upright in character and they have a good intellect. The most suitable type of career for them is in the professions — as doctors, lawyers, accountants, and so on — or in top management in large companies such as banks.

The karma of those born under this degree is to be responsible for the setting up and running of new social orders. They are people who will help to bring in the social, political and economic structures that will herald the New Age. Man has been given once more the chance to discover his higher self and it is how these people introduce these changes that will determine our future success.

Planetary point

The 318th degree indicates that the person who has a planet in it will become involved in bringing about social changes. If Mercury is here, he or she will be concerned with the way we travel and communicate. With Saturn here the native will be responsible for the management of natural resources.

319th degree

Colour: orange. *Sign*: Aquarius. 2nd decan. *Qualities*: Fixed/Mutable, Air. *Numerological match*: other 4s.
Positive expression: stability, conservative nature
Negative expression: slowness to accept change

Solar point

As a solar point the elemental energy of the 319th degree produces in the native a conservative nature, though one that accepts change when it is due.

Natives of this degree are found in all walks of life. It is their karmic duty to be watchdogs of the changes that are on the way, seeing that fools don't rush in where angels fear to tread.

Those of you born with this degree of solar energy will, as you go about your lives, constantly keep your fingers upon the pulse of change lest you need to react. If you feel some facet of your life is being too radically changed, you are ready to fight to maintain things as they were. You have a duty to use our democractic institutions to make sure that the world of the future is fit for our children to live in.

Planetary point

If you have a planet in the 319th degree it is an indicator of how you will endeavour to prevent negative developments in our world. If Venus is in this point you will try to safeguard moral values, especially in connection with the arts and entertainment and sexuality. If Saturn is here, you will exert your influence through patience and perseverance.

320th degree

Colour: scarlet. *Sign*: Aquarius. 3rd decan. *Qualities*: Fixed/Cardinal, Air. *Numerological match*: other 5s.
Positive expression: clear exposition
Negative expression: impatience, stubbornness

Solar point

The 320th degree gives natives good mental powers, especially in communicating. They can turn their minds to almost anything they choose. They are amicable and well liked and, as they find it easy to communicate with others, they make friends very easily no matter whom they mix with.

They are given these capacities for a special reason: they are to be the communicators to the general public of the changes which will take place prior to the coming Age of Aquarius. Work in communications, computer technology, advertising, the press or any place of learning would be most suitable for them, though they are found in all kinds of jobs. Their principal talent is for imparting information in a way that can be understood even by dunderheads.

You can always recognise a person with this solar degree in any group as he or she is the chatty, knowledgeable extrovert.

Planetary point

Whoever has a planet in the 320th degree has exceptional communicative ability. If that planet is Venus that individual would find his or her best expression through art, music or on the stage.

Colour: green. *Sign*: Aquarius. 3rd decan. *Qualities*: Fixed/Cardinal, Air. *Numerological match*: other 6s.
Positive expression: ability to soothe others
Negative expression: hedonism

Solar point

The elemental energy of the 321st degree blesses those born under it with the ability to soothe away the anxieties and sorrows of others. Many people connected with the entertainment industry or in social or welfare work have this solar degree. They are the people who lend a shoulder for others to cry on.

If you were born with the energy of this degree, it does not matter whether you make a career in song and dance or in welfare work, or whether you just happen to be a friendly neighbour to those in need, so long as you put this energy to use.

Though they never like to admit it, people with this degree have their own fears and inhibitions, which can, however, be released when they counsel others.

Planetary point

If you have a planet in the 321st degree, it indicates, by its nature, how you can alleviate the cares of others and make them happy. For example, with Venus here you could work in fashion and please people by making them look good. If Saturn is in this position, you might work with the elderly and infirm.

322nd degree

Colour: blue. *Sign*: Aquarius. 3rd decan. *Qualities*: Fixed/Cardinal, Air. *Numerological match*: other 7s.
Positive expression: New Age conceptions
Negative expression: mistaken notions

Solar point

People born with the 322nd solar degree have a hard task indeed to perform. They must stand up for their beliefs and ideals, and perhaps be persecuted for doing what is right. But they will be revered after their deaths. Two examples are

Abraham Lincoln, who delivered the famous Gettesburg address and soon after was assassinated, and Charles Darwin, who wrote the book on evolution *The Origin of Species* and was denounced by the church. Yet both are now commonly used as examples of progressive thinkers of their time.

If you have this solar degree, you too will have to communicate to others your personal beliefs and convictions and hope that they will understand what it is you are really trying to say and do.

Planetary point

If you have a planet in the 322nd degree, it indicates an intuitive ability when looking ahead to the future. For example, with Venus here you may foresee what the new trends in fashion will be and wear them before anyone else.

323rd degree

Colour: black. *Sign*: Aquarius. 3rd decan. *Qualities*: Fixed/Cardinal, Air. *Numerological match*: other 8s.
Positive expression: analytical mind
Negative expression: living in a world of one's own

Solar point

The 323rd degree is a profoundly serious one and relates to those who have great responsibility to shoulder, be that for the home and family or in a larger context. People with this degree are rebels, rejecting the customs and social conditioning they were born with. Oliver Reed, Sir Winston Churchill and Georges Simenon were all born with this solar point yet for all their fame they appear to have rejected the very foundations upon which they built their fame.

You as an ordinary individual may find yourself discontented with some aspects of the society we live in which you feel are wrong. It is your karmic task to set about changing them by whatever means you possess, so that as we move into the next century we will be rid of many harmful restrictions.

Planetary point

A planet in the 323rd degree reflects the kind of philosophy the native has. If Saturn is the planet here, the native will be quite a loner, and his or her beliefs, views and ideals will rarely conform to those of the masses. A person with Mars in this point is forceful in debate and discussion, and active in bringing about change.

324th degree

Colour: crimson. *Sign*: Aquarius. 3rd decan. *Qualities*: Fixed/Cardinal, Air. *Numerological match*: other 9s.
Positive expression: positive action, strength of will
Negative expression: impatience with fools

Solar point

As a solar point the elemental energy of the 324th degree creates individuals who know exactly what they want and how they are going to get it. The mind and will are strong and assertive. They need to be on their guard, however, against thinking they know what is right for everyone else and consequently stepping on others' toes. The positive application of the mental energy can, however, bring great benefits.

Natives of this solar degree can have very persuasive tongues, with a bit of practice. They may even become exceptional orators and public speakers. But first and foremost they are doers, and many will be found in the forefront of the new technologies and other adventurous work environments.

If you have this solar point, the world is your oyster if you so choose.

Planetary point

The nature of any planet placed in the 324th degree gives an idea of how the native could best compete in today's world. Someone with Mars here would have determination and pure physical strength to win through. With Venus here, the native would do well in sales-orientated fields.

325th degree

Colour: white. *Sign*: Aquarius. 3rd decan. *Qualities*: Fixed/Cardinal, Air. *Numerological match*: other 1s.
Positive expression: individualism
Negative expression: dictatorial manner

Solar point

The elemental energy of the 325th degree gives natives leadership qualities so that they can build the empires that others only dream of. People born with this solar point, if they are to feel fulfilled, must work either for themselves or where they are not closely supervised (they do not like taking orders as they always feel the boss is less capable than themselves). Charles Tiffany, who founded Tiffany & Co., and Henry Steinway, who founded Steinway and Sons, were both born with this solar point.

Natives of this degree have that killer's touch which can give them the edge over their business competitors. They are single-minded and rather ruthless without the disadvantage of feeling guilty about it. Empires, however, are made up of many people, not just the man at the top, and the karmic task of the native of this degree is to give support to others.

Planetary point

If you have a planet in this point it is an indicator of how you may be competitive and survive in today's world. For example, if Saturn is the planet, you will invest in long-term securities.

326th degree

Colour: grey. *Sign*: Aquarius. 3rd decan. *Qualities*: Fixed/ Cardinal, Air. *Numerological match*: other 2s.
Positive expression: shared thoughts
Negative expression: neurosis

Solar point

The elemental energy of the 326th degree is that of the people who will bring comfort and reassurance to others in our changing world.

If you have this solar degree, you may never be famous, covet wealth or aspire to great things, but if there is anyone in your life who is successful in any way, they would not have been without your support in the background. You and your fellow natives are the support regiments, the shoulders on which to cry, the friends whose doors are always open. You are deep thinkers, emotionally responsive to the needs of others and stable enough to give support to them even when you yourself feel in need of some support. You are the parents of the New

Age children, or the office and factory workers upon whom industry depends. You may never receive your just rewards in this life, but be sure that it is recorded for the hereafter. You are neither ordinary nor extraordinary, yet without your compassion or care of others, society would collapse.

Planetary point

Whoever has a planet in the 326th degree may, without realising it, be an essential cog in the wheel of society. If Saturn is here, the native may work and save and pay his way without being a strain on the welfare state. Someone with the Moon in this point may work with those less able to care for themselves.

327th degree

Colour: violet. *Sign*: Aquarius. 3rd decan. *Qualities*: Fixed/ Cardinal, Air. *Numerological match*: other 3s.
Positive expression: order, an eye for detail
Negative expression: nit-picking

Solar point

The 327th degree gives the native the ability to attend to the order and details of everyday routine and then to be able to relax when work is done. 'Dame Edna' has this solar point and, although outwardly flirtatious and frivolous, she pays great attention to the detailed aspects of her work and dress. 'Edna', alias Barry Humphries, rarely appears in public as his real self. I'm sure he is a very sensitive and responsive person who is just dying to break out of his own self-imposed prison. There is a duality about this degree, as if the individuals want to be someone else but usually cannot. Barry Humphries finds a constructive and entertaining outlet for this energy.

If you have this degree, learn to be the real you.

Planetary point

If you have a planet in the 327th degree, it shows there is a real you that is trying to get out. If that planet is Venus, you would like to be more sensitive and you also desire more luxury than you at present enjoy. With Mars in this place, you would like to be more active, especially in the more adventurous pursuits.

328th degree

Colour: orange. *Sign*: Aquarius. 3rd decan. *Qualities*: Fixed/
Cardinal, Air. *Numerological match*: other 4s.
Positive expression: building on new ideas
Negative expression: peculiar tastes

Solar point

The elemental energy of the 328th degree is indeed a handful.
On the positive side, people born with the Sun here will be the
New Age builders, those who implement and consolidate the
new ideas and concepts of today so that they may become fully
accepted by the next century. They are extremely inventive and
original in their ideas though not yet in tune with the general
majority.

Alexandro Volta, the discoverer of electricity, was born with
this solar point and all can now see the results of his pioneering
research and inventiveness. Yoko Ono was also born with this
degree and her kind of artistic expression is to say the least
extraordinary. Neither of these people could be said to have
been appreciated by the masses.

Natives of this degree are never fully understood by their
contemporaries. Whether their ideas have any permanent value
will only be decided by the passage of time, but without these
people the world would be a duller place.

Planetary point

Anyone who has a planet in the 328th degree is in some way
unconventional. For example, someone who has Venus here
can use unusual art forms to express the inner self.

329th degree

Colour: scarlet. *Sign*: Aquarius. 3rd decan. *Qualities*: Fixed/
Cardinal, Air. *Numerological match*: other 5s.
Positive expression: clear exposition, persuasiveness
Negative expression: selfishness

Solar point

People born with the Sun in the 329th degree have the ability to explain new ideas and concepts in such a way that ordinary people can understand them. They have a desire to meet all kinds of people to share ideas, and there is a fondness for debate, which helps them clarify their minds on contentious issues. This is one of the degrees whose natives are responsible for spreading the idealistic ideas of the New Age. It is their vocation in life to impart to others optimism and general confidence that these dreams can be realised in a practical manner.

Careers in politics, advertising, the media or telecommunications would fit the special abilities that natives of this degree possess.

Planetary point

Any person who has a planet in the 329th degree has the ability to expound new ideas to others. With Mercury here, the native would use his or her literary skills to do this. If Jupiter is the planet here, the native will gather news from far and near and spread it widely.

330th degree

Colour: green. *Sign*: Pisces. 1st decan. *Qualities*: Mutable, Water. *Numerological match*: other 6s.
Positive expression: charitableness, sympathy
Negative expression: self-deception

Solar point

The 330th degree gives natives a benevolent, charitable and sympathetic disposition. They have a great urge to help relieve suffering and to assist the weak or needy.

People born with this solar point are also fond of things of beauty, such as poetry, music and painting. They may not actually participate in any of the arts, but their homes are certain to contain the artistic works of others.

Romantically, they are often attracted to a social inferior. This is because of their sympathy for the underdog. Amiable and cheerful, and desirous of peace and comfort, natives do not operate well under stress (though they can be excellent nurses). Pisces is a sign under which man has developed into what he is now and many born with this solar point can yearn for this past glory. However, they need to learn to live for the future and not to dwell too much in the past.

Planetary point

A placement in the 330th degree is an indication that there is something that the native must learn to refine and then let go of because it is outdated. Persons who have Venus here must learn to care for others rather than themselves, and those with Saturn must learn some hard lesson.

331st degree

Colour: blue. *Sign*: Pisces. 1st decan. *Qualities*: Mutable, Water. *Numerological match*: other 7s.
Positive expression: dignity, inquiring mind
Negative expression: impressionability

Solar point

The 331st degree imparts an air of dignity to the native and an ability for serious study or profound contemplation. The degree's energy is also good for the development of the inspirational side of the nature and it can intensify mediumistic qualities. Many with this degree become involved in some form of metaphysical research or study.

Many women with this degree will marry more than once. They are very likely to do domestic work or work in industries connected in some way with homes. Men will have to learn to find an outlet for their emotions which have for too long been suppressed. For both men and women, work connected with liquids, the sea or shipping could bring financial security.

Natives of this solar degree have a karmic development to make in this life which can no longer be put off or avoided.

Planetary point

If you have a planet in the 331st degree, it is an indicator of what lessons you must learn in this life. If the planet is Jupiter, you must evolve your own philosophy and test its worth. If you have Mars here, you must do your own dirty work and seek the wisdom of this lesson.

332nd degree

Colour: black. *Ruler*: Pisces. 1st decan. *Qualities*: Mutable,

Water. *Numerological match*: other 8s.
Positive expression: persistent effort
Negative expression: bad choice of friends

Solar point

The elemental energy of the 332nd degree creates a persevering nature in those born under it. They make gains through prolonged hard work, slowly and steadily, never overnight. There can be a degree of intrigue or even notoriety in the lives of these people, examples being Edward Kennedy (the car incident) or Christina Keeler (the Profumo affair). Both these individuals had long-standing, successful careers but seemed bent upon self-destruction. You could also say that Niki Lauda risks everything, namely his life, every time he races.

Persistence in following chosen paths can bring great rewards but the path down is always shorter than the one up so, if you were born with this degree, take care. You may not become one of the famous, but you can still make great progress in your life or totally change your environment. Just be sure that you do not also become the talk of your neighbourhood.

Planetary point

If you have a planet in the 332nd degree, it indicates what area of your life will demand persistent effort on your part, or how intrigue and scandal can be avoided. If the planet Venus is here you would have to be careful about whom you hob-nob with as any careless words you speak could be repeated and used against you by others, and so on.

333rd degree

Colour: crimson. *Sign*: Pisces. 1st decan. *Qualities*: Mutable, Water. *Numerological match*: other 9s.
Positive expression: adaptability
Negative expression: too much diversification

Solar point

The 333rd degree gives natives adaptability and versatility to the extent that they can turn their hands to anything that catches their interest. The problem is that they become interested in so many things that they can dissipate their energies.

They therefore tend to be good at lots of things but excel at nothing. Actors and entertainers could, however, have no better solar degree for the energy at play lets them switch from role to role and set to set with ease.

If you were born with the Sun in this degree, you are likely to be the joker in your home and an actor (or actress) in your relationships with other people.

Planetary point

A planet in the 333rd degree is an indicator of adaptability. Anyone with Mars here can accomplish more than one task at a time or be good at both sports and academic work. If Venus is the planet, the native may play several musical instruments or be good at more than one kind of artistic pursuit.

334th degree

Colour: white. *Sign*: Pisces. 1st decan. *Qualities*: Mutable, Water. *Numerological match*: other 1s.
Positive expression: leadership ability, compassion
Negative expression: eccentricity

Solar point

People born with the Sun in the 334th degree have the ability to lead others. This is because the kindness and sympathy which they show to their fellow man inspires people to trust and respect them and thus also the decisions they make. Although kind and generous by nature natives can be firm and authoritative when necessary.

Many people with this solar point choose careers to do with the emotional and physical well-being of others, in nursing for example, or in the welfare services. Many others take up concerns to do with ecology, such as the fight for endangered species of plants and animals. They are nearly always keepers of pets and there can in some extreme cases be a substitution of pets for human relationships.

Planetary point

A planet in the 334th degree gives some indication of how natives display leadership qualities. If this planet is Mars, you may well find the native at some time on a picket line. At any rate, he or she likes to be in the thick of any turbulent activity. On the other hand, whoever has Mercury here is a talker, not a doer.

335th degree

Colour: grey. *Sign*: Pisces. 1st decan. *Qualities*: Mutable, Water. *Numerological match*: other 2s.
Positive expression: generosity, openness
Negative expression: lacking in confidence

Solar point

The 335th degree inclines people born under it to share a great deal with others. That does not necessarily mean in the material sense; more often they share their feelings or pass on their knowledge and skills. Teachers, who patiently pass on what they know to their pupils, parents, who take the time to listen to what their children have to say, and shop workers, who go out of their way to show you the best products rather than the ones with the biggest profits, could well have this solar degree. The personal achievements of natives of this degree are rarely outstanding but their children or pupils can be. Renoir never became famous in his lifetime yet inspired many later artists through his artistic genius.

If you were born with the Sun at this point, you have mature understanding and compassion which you must learn to put to good use if you are to fulfil your karma.

Planetary point

If you have a planet in this degree, it is an indicator of how you may inspire others to do great things in their lives. If Venus is the planet here, you can help to make other people beautiful in some way, or teach appreciation of beautiful things to others. With the Moon in this degree you can bring out the emotional side of people's natures.

336th degree

Colour: violet. *Sign*: Pisces. 1st decan. *Qualities*: Mutable, Water. *Numerological match*: other 3s.

Positive expression: deep thought
Negative expression: high-falutin' notions

Solar point

People born with the Sun in the 336th degree throw themselves into the deepest forms of study, such as philosophy, and attain a level of understanding of spiritual and religious matters beyond that of natives of most other degrees. This tends to make them inward-looking and reserved and others may take that as a sign of insecurity or a lack of confidence. Another characteristic of these people is that they totally commit themselves to the partnerships they form and the tasks they undertake. They may be slow to act at times, but you can be sure that when they do every possible eventuality has been weighed up and assessed and it is with the confidence of certain success that they act. In marriage they are loyal and devoted partners; though not demonstrative in public, they are in private.

If you have this solar degree, you will often ponder about the meaning of life and why you are here. The energy of the degree will help you find some answers.

Planetary point

A planet in the 336th degree is always connected with natives' spiritual understanding. The native with Mercury here could become a student of theology, or of the occult. If the planet Mars is here, the native could become a doctor or surgeon, or he or she could be the peace-maker whenever there is a dispute.

337th degree

Colour: orange. *Sign*: Pisces. 1st decan. *Qualities*: Mutable, Water. *Numerological match*: other 4s.
Positive expression: home building
Negative expression: partnership problems

Solar point

Those of you born with this solar degree must learn to work towards fulfilling your dreams and achieving your ambitions without the help or assistance of a partner, either marital or business. If you should marry, remember that you must be the stronger partner, otherwise you will have the person you lean upon taken from you.

Elizabeth Taylor is a prime example of the elemental energy of this degree at work. On the one hand she is the successful actress; on the other she has had many failed marriages. So, too, has the ballerina Antoinette Sibley who also has this degree.

Natives of this degree make great entertainers, but personal happiness is only found when they shoulder responsibility for the welfare of others rather than just look after themselves. Marriage after the age of 30 is always better for these people. (See also the 362nd degree.)

Planetary point

A planet in the 337th degree shows how natives must learn to become self-reliant rather than depend upon others. The person with Saturn here matures at a relatively early age, having to take charge of younger members of the family or care for elderly people. If Mercury is in this point, the native learns to think for himself rather than relying on being told what to do by others.

338th degree

Colour: scarlet. *Ruler*: Pisces. 1st decan. *Qualities*: Mutable, Water. *Numerological match*: other 5s.
Positive expression: investigative ability
Negative expression: lack of staying power

Solar point

The elemental energy of the 338th degree gives natives the desire to investigate and solve the mysteries that they come across in their lives.

People born with this solar point may appear nosy to some, though in fact they don't really want to poke into other people's business. They merely have a desire to know and to expand their personal horizons, especially in things which particularly interest them. Be sure, however, that if you try to hide anything from a native of this degree, and leave any clue at all, you will set him or her upon a path of discovery that you may later regret.

Anything to do with adventure, the sciences, medicine or the occult could all appeal to the native, though this is not usual for Pisceans.

If you were born with this solar degree, learn to tackle one task at a time as there can be a tendency to be drawn into other projects which appear to hold more mystery than the present occupation, partnership or whatever it is you do. (See also the 342nd degree.)

Planetary point

A planet in the 338th degree is an indicator of the investigative abilities natives possess. Someone with Mars here will knock down castles and climb mountains to satisfy his or her curiosity, while a person with Venus in this degree would use guile and charm to do this.

339th degree

Colour: green. *Sign*: Pisces. 1st decan. *Qualities*: Mutable, Water. *Numerological match*: other 6s.
Positive expression: romantic or artistic nature
Negative expression: unfaithfulness in love

Solar point

People born with the Sun in the 339th degree are romantic at heart, no matter how much they may deny it. This point when expressed through the Sun also gives artistic ability and a desire for comfort, peace and security.

Natives are quite capable of finding what they seek whatever their background, be it among the stars at Hollywood or in the terraced rows of the East End of London. They are affectionate and sensitive, sometimes excessively so. When in love (which is most of the time), they desire to be loved as much in return. If they feel unappreciated, they will soon seek company elsewhere.

Being liked, respected and loved by all who get to know them, natives of this degree rarely have a hard time in life. But they should learn to trust people as they expect to be trusted themselves. (See also the 342nd degree.)

Planetary point

If you have a planet in the 339th degree, by its nature it will tell you how your romantic inclinations may find expression. If you have the planet Mars here, you would brave any danger to win your loved one. With the Moon, you can easily achieve an emotional rapport with persons you find attractive.

340th degree

Colour: blue. *Ruler*: Pisces. 2nd decan. *Qualities*: Mutable/Cardinal, Water. *Numerological match*: other 7s.
Positive expression: intuition
Negative expression: self-doubt

Solar point

As a solar point this degree blesses natives with a highly developed intuition, which helps them with decision making. There is frequently mediumistic ability with clairvoyance and clairaudience. Not all people born with this degree realise they have strong psychic powers; when their hunches seem to pay off, they may put it down to good judgement of character or to luck. If they should ever realise that they have a gift among gifts and develop these latent faculties, there is little in their lives which could go seriously wrong. With the foresight it provides they could lead a life of peace and prosperity.

The best careers for them are those which afford a quiet, peaceful work environment. Recommended too is working for a large institution. It should also be reiterated that a native of this degree would make an excellent medium, provided that the planetary configurations of the chart support the Sun. (See also the 342nd degree.)

Planetary point

A planet in the 340th degree shows how a native's intuition may be very useful to him or her. If a person has the Moon here, it is an indication that he or she should use this gift to help others with their emotional problems. Anyone with Mercury here would make a great astrologer, writer or communicator of any type.

341st degree

Colour: black. *Sign*: Pisces. 2nd decan. *Qualities*: Mutable/Cardinal, Water. *Numerological match*: other 8s.
Positive expression: success in seclusion
Negative expression: despondency, sorrow

Solar point

As a solar point the elemental energy of the 341st degree gives natives a will and determination to achieve the most arduous tasks, provided they are left to work alone and in their way. Trust is not one of their strong points, which is why they prefer to work alone and in their own manner. At the end of the day when work is over they find relaxation difficult unless they are content with what they have done. For this reason they often bring their work home, but this can create domestic problems.

On the brighter side, natives of this solar point are loyal and faithful in love. Families tend to be small, but they are devoted to them. Pets are often a part of their lives and their sorrow at the loss of one of them can be very intense, for they feel they have lost part of themselves. (See also the 342nd degree.)

Planetary point

If you have a planet in the 341st degree it is an indicator of how you will look for seclusion in your life. If you have Mars here, you will fight for your own piece of land to which you can retreat. If the Moon is in this point, you will find seclusion in your imagination, living in a world of your own.

342nd degree

MAGICAL HOME OF THE ELEMENT WATER

(*Strongest effects*: 5 degrees on either side)

Colour: crimson. *Sign*: Pisces. 2nd decan. *Qualities*: Mutable/Cardinal, Water. *Numerological match*: other 9s.
Positive expression: making do with what is available
Negative expression: unfortunate adventures, mistaken trust

Solar point

The angelic ruler Gabriel controls the energy of the 342nd degree which is the home base of the element of Water, which concerns feelings and emotions. All degrees within 5 degrees of this point fall under his immediate influence and the reading for this degree therefore applies to you if your solar point falls in any one of them.

Water carries our emotions along on its tide and if you were born with the Sun in this degree then your life of feeling will be well and truly tested. You will be tossed on emotional tides in order that you may learn by these experiences and grow in maturity. You will feel the most intense pleasure as well as the greatest sadnesses in the course of this life. You may be called upon to sacrifice your own happiness for that of others or you may be sent to bring joy to those who have none. The age of Pisces and approximately 2000 years of rule by the element of Water comes to an end in by the year 2376 AD. This is Man's last chance to learn his emotional lessons before the new era of Aquarius takes over and the scientific age prevails. If your solar energy is in Pisces, in this degree, the lessons are personal ones for you to learn.

Planetary point

The planets placed within this degree are the indicators of lessons, particularly those connected with the feelings and emotions, that must be learned by those who are born under them. These lessons are as follows —

Moon: emotional control
Mercury: sharing of feelings or being able to communicate them
Mars: responsible action, self control
Venus: shedding vanity and all self-seeking
Jupiter: broadening of the mind and outlook, achieving material security
Saturn: perceiving the disadvantages of too much solitude
Uranus: adaptability to change

343rd degree

Colour: white. *Sign*: Pisces. 2nd decan. *Qualities*: Mutable/Cardinal, Water. *Numerological match*: other 1s
Positive expression: mediumship
Negative expression: inflamed emotions

Solar point

People born with the Sun in the 343rd degree are old souls who have returned to Earth to remind themselves for perhaps the last time what it is like to live in the material world.!In childhood, they are markedly mature for their age and unusual in that they never seem to fit into any particular category or type. It may be that they have returned to help an old friend through a testing incarnation, or perhaps merely to refresh their memories of mortal life.

Their intuition can be highly developed, and many become involved with charities and worthy causes — they are drawn to them because, being purified souls, they cannot allow the needy to go unassisted. (See also the 342nd degree.)

Planetary point

The 343rd degree shows, by the nature of the planet placed in it, what final conflict may exist within the soul of the native or how best he or she may fulfil his or her karma. If Mercury is in this degree, the native has an investigative task to carry out. The person with Saturn here has returned to taste the fruits of a previous life well spent in ensuring the well-being of other living creatures on this Earth, either humans or animals.

344th degree

Colour: grey. *Sign*: Pisces. 2nd decan. *Qualities*: Mutable/Cardinal, Water. *Numerological match*: other 2s.
Positive expression: love of life
Negative expression: lacking trust

Solar point

The elemental energy of the 344th degree gives those born under it a desire for love and completeness. Only a very special partner will do for a native of this degree, someone who can satisfy his or her every need and desire. Partners should therefore be chosen very carefully. There is always great personal pain for natives of this degree should anything go wrong. Besides being passionate, they are very caring people who love the company of others. Children are doted on and thoroughly spoilt — they are nearly always in some way unusual or gifted.

The lives of these people are consolidated through hard work and they are best employed where they can feel sure that what they are doing is really useful. If their work doesn't seem worthwhile they feel very unhappy. (See also the 342nd degree.)

Planetary point

The 344th degree shows, by the planet placed in it, what natives desire most to share with friends and associates. People with

Mercury here tend to chatter on endlessly and want to share their knowledge, ideas and thoughts. Those with Venus in this point are caring and supportive of others.

345th degree

Colour: violet. *Sign*: Pisces. 2nd decan. *Qualities*: Mutable/ Cardinal, Water. *Numerological match*: other 3s.
Positive expression: benevolence
Negative expression: peculiar attachments

Solar point

The 345th degree gives natives the ability to succeed in chemistry or occult studies, and in any work to do with asylums, hospitals or public institutions. Frequently they find employment in places remote and far removed from their place of birth. They are amicable and make friends easily. Enmities, when they occur, are never long lasting as the angelic ruler of this degree has the power to turn aggression into love.

The political or religious beliefs of these natives tend to be rather singular, though no-one seems to be offended in the way that they express them. Family life is always maintained, but many with this solar point will build new homes in far off places as they both desire to experience the wonders of the world and to imbibe different cultures. Being philosophically minded, they can take life's knocks without rancour. Not surprisingly, therefore, they generally succeed in whatever they set out to do. (See also 342nd degree.)

Planetary point

A planet in the 346th degree points to how natives may broaden their outlook by travel and personal experience. Those with Mars here never like to stay in one place for too long, always wanting to be on the move to seek out new cultures, ventures and partners. Those with Saturn, on the other hand, stop long enough to really absorb all they can from a place.

346th degree

Colour: orange. *Sign*: Pisces. 2nd decan. *Qualities*: Mutable/ Cardinal, Water. *Numerological match*: other 4s.

Positive expression: creativity
Negative expression: zany behaviour

Solar point

The elemental energy of the 346th degree gives its natives intuitive understanding, originality and creativity. They tend to be attracted to anything that is unusual or peculiar, which is highlighted in the way they use their creative ability. Frankie Howard was born with this solar point and though lovable and funny you could hardly say his sort of comedy was ordinary or banal.

People born with this solar point have the ability to create new things out of old or to find novel ways of interpreting other people's creations. A mechanic could modify an engine, making it more efficient, while a playwright could rewrite a Shakespeare tragedy and turn it into a comedy. Whatever they do is original, inventive and clever.

If you have this solar point, look around you and see what you would like to alter or modify. (See also the 342nd degree.)

Planetary point

A planet in the 346th degree indicates that natives have inventive powers and creativity of an unusual kind. Those with Mars here will try and try again until their achievements are recognised while those with the Moon will always be seeking new ways of self-expression.

347th degree

Colour: scarlet. *Sign*: Pisces. 2nd decan. *Qualities*: Mutable/ Cardinal, Water. *Numerological match*: other 5s.
Positive expression: practical sense, resourcefulness, artistic ability
Negative expression: unreliability

Solar point

The elemental energy of the 347th degree gives natives a fertile imagination coupled with practical ability. They tend to be receptive to new ideas and methods and able to apply them in everyday life. The degree favours those who work with pharmaceuticals, canned goods, oils, beverages — in fact any kind of liquid, including the sea itself. There may either be an affinity for or a fear of water. Natives often have a marked musical ability or a gift with words. Any literary ability is enhanced if they also have a well placed Mercury in the chart.

In romance natives require a stimulating, lively partnership if they are to remain loyal.

Natives of this degree can be found in most areas of society. An example of someone who shows its effects is Lord Snowden who is of course very artistic. (See also the 342nd degree.)

Planetary point

If you have a planet in the 347th degree it shows that you can be practical as well as artistic. If the planet is Mercury and it is conjunct the Sun, you could be a literary genius. With Venus, you could make use of your artistic flair when entertaining.

348th degree

Colour: green. *Sign*: Pisces. 2nd decan. *Qualities*: Mutable/ Cardinal, Water. *Numerological match*: other 6s.
Positive expression: fondness of the arts
Negative expression: misplaced confidence

Solar point

The elemental energy of the 348th degree inclines natives towards a fondness for art, music, singing and drama. Many become successful actors or stage performers. An example is Lynn Redgrave who was born with this solar degree. However, the degree's usual effect upon individuals is to introduce just a touch of theatrical expression into their everyday lives. The feelings and emotions of these natives are intensified, and while love, sympathy and artistic appreciation can be highlighted, so too can adverse tendencies which include self-satisfaction and vanity.

It is a fortunate degree for those who wish to work with large numbers of people, such as trusts or institutions, as the capacity to satisfy the needs of many is present. The desires of natives can at times be beyond their reach and most suffer disappointment when they try to attain what deep down they know to be impossible.

Planetary point

Whoever has a planet in the 348th degree has some way of

reaching out to a crowd or large audience and of influencing them. If the planet is Mercury, the native can be a great speaker or orator, being able to sense the mood of the listeners and to adapt his or her speech accordingly. Someone with Mars can make himself appear stronger than he really is by bluffing.

349th degree

Colour: blue. *Sign*: Pisces. 2nd decan. *Qualities*: Mutable/ Cardinal, Water. *Numerological match*: other 7s.
Positive expression: philosophic outlook
Negative expression: idle dreaming

Solar point

The 349th degree is that of those who work to turn the dreams of their youth into realities. Those of you born under this angelic force will tend to find yourselves always striving to attain some goal in life which you have long aspired to, be it material or spiritual. It matters not what circumstances you were born into, whether you be rich or poor, you will feel impelled to follow a course in life which will lead to fulfilment of your childhood dreams. If you have always wanted to climb Everest, you will at some point try. If you have always wanted that dream car, at some time you will buy it even if you have to wait for many years.

Natives of this degree must realise their dreams by holding to them and never giving up if they are ever to progress on their karmic path.

Planetary point

Those of you who have a planet in the 349th degree should know that it is an indicator of the dreams that you can make come true in this life. If you have Saturn here, you can be an empire builder. With Venus, you may find the means of artistic expression you seek and receive wide acclaim for your achievements.

350th degree

Colour: black. *Sign*: Pisces. 3rd decan. *Qualities*: Mutable/ Fixed, Water. *Numerological match*: other 8s.

Positive expression: good mental concentration
Negative expression: narrow mindedness

Solar point

People born under the 350th solar degree may have the mental concentration and application to succeed in anything they wish to try (within reason). Or their own shortsightedness and narrow minded stupidity can destroy any hope of their achieving their ambition. There are no half measures for natives of this degree: they are either their own best friends or their own worst enemies who will always try to blame others for their own shortcomings. If you have this solar degree, success will come from keeping your mind on the job and sticking at it. For this you will have to learn patience, which is a virtue natives often lack. The world is your oyster, but you have to be patient enough to allow the pearl to form before you crack it open.

Prince Edward is a prime example of this degree's effects. He has to cultivate the patience to discover himself and find what he truly wants to do in life, while living in the shadow of senior members of the Royal Family.

Planetary point

A planet in the 350th degree is an indicator of where natives could succeed if they only learn to be patient. If Mars is the planet in this point, the native learns that only fools rush in where angels fear to tread. Those with Uranus here should have learned to modify their iconoclastic ideas so that they have become acceptable.

351st degree

Colour: crimson. *Sign*: Pisces. 3rd decan. *Qualities*: Mutable/Fixed, Water. *Numerological match*: other 9s.
Positive expression: dynamism
Negative expression: bombastic manner

Solar point

The 351st degree has indeed great energy for those who wish to use it constructively, but it can be the cause of self-destruction for those who cannot control it. This is a very fiery degree and especially so for the sign of Pisces. If you were to chat casually with one of them you would never guess what energies are at play under the surface.

Rupert Murdoch is a prime example of a native of this degree with a rags-to-riches tale; by aggressive application of the energy of his solar point he has built a huge news empire. Now his energy spurs him on ever further, into the realms of television and international airlines. Here is a lesson for every native: with this degree's energy you will never be able to reach a point when you reckon you have done enough. You will remain active to the bitter end.

Planetary point

If you have a planet in the 351st degree, it will spur you on in your search for fulfilment. If you have Mars in this degree you will be virtually unstoppable once you have set your heart on something. With Mercury here, you should be able to inveigle others into giving their support in whatever you decide to do.

352nd degree

Colour: white. *Sign*: Pisces. 3rd decan. *Qualities*: Mutable/Fixed, Water. *Numerological match*: other 1s.
Positive expression: refinement, authority by example, easygoing nature
Negative expression: constant criticism

Solar point

When the Sun is in the 352nd degree natives will be able to command the respect of others and are automatically looked up to as leaders. These individuals, by the very example they set and the charismatic charm which they possess, inspire others to have confidence in them (even if they sometimes lack it in themselves). However, a problem that can occur is that they can become carried along upon a tide rather than taking control of the tiller, so to speak. Jim Slater, who founded a banking empire worth 300 million, but over-reached himself, is an example of what natives of this degree can do but also of what can happen if they lose their control.

They have the ability to take the ideas of their colleagues and refine them and make them workable. However, they should guard against falling for extravagant promises.

In romance natives of this degree are capable of finding love where few could.

Planetary point

As a planetary point, the 352nd degree concerns anything that must be refined, processed, developed or opened up to make it useful. People who have Saturn here, for example, might develop an unpopulated, isolated place and turn it into a tourists' resort. A native with Jupiter might make money out of almost nothing, and so on.

353rd degree

Colour: grey. *Sign*: Pisces. 3rd decan. *Qualities*: Mutable/Fixed, Water. *Numerological match*: other 2s.
Positive expression: inspiration, mediumship
Negative expression: lack of confidence

Solar point

The elemental energy of the 353rd degree makes those born under it very imaginative. When feeling inspired, they can succeed in any field of endeavour they wish. Too often, however, they suffer from doubts.

Partnerships and associations always play an important part in the life of these people, and it is through groups and societies that they achieve most success. In particular they need a partner who will give them moral support and also press them to continue when they have their periods of self-doubt and despondency. If this partner is selected correctly there is nothing which the native cannot face and conquer.

If you were born with this solar point, stop trying to do everything yourself. Learn to work in groups or partnerships and you will find rewards soon follow.

Planetary point

If you have a planet in the 353rd degree, you will need a partner you can talk things over with in your frequent periods of uncertainty and self-doubt. If you have Jupiter in this point, you are likely to challenge generally held religious beliefs or philosophical or economic concepts. With Mars here you will need someone to calm and direct your physical energy.

Colour: violet. *Sign*: Pisces. 3rd decan. *Qualities*: Mutable/ Fixed, Water. *Numerological match*: other 3s.
Positive expression: firm beliefs
Negative expression: secret sorrows

Solar point

The elemental energy of the 354th degree helps natives to have faith in themselves and gives them the courage to stand by their principles and beliefs. It also gives artistic flair and poetical gifts and the emotional side of the nature is strengthened.

People born with this degree will have some form of honour bestowed upon them by the community they live in or the people they work with, in recognition of their hard work and dedication. They may never be rich in a material sense, but they certainly will be rewarded in the spiritual hereafter.

Those of you born with your solar energy here are in a karmic layby, recharging your batteries for future lives to come. You should therefore experience a life of joy and contentment, unless there are planetary points in the chart indicating the contrary.

Planetary point

If you have a planet in the 354th degree, it is indicative of the vast quantities of reserve energy you can call upon should you require it, or of the karmic debts owed to you that may be paid off. If you have Saturn here, you can gain the assistance of other people or those in authority. If Mercury is the planet, you will always have someone to speak for you.

355th degree

Colour: orange. *Sign*: Pisces. 3rd decan. *Qualities*: Mutable/ Fixed, Water. *Numerological match*: other 4s.
Positive expression: intuitive understanding
Negative expression: impressionability

Solar point

When the Sun is in the 355th degree, natives acquire an intuitive understanding of the problems of people they come into contact with. People with this solar point are good listeners and always sympathetic. They are really able to identify themselves with the person in trouble. They would make excellent personnel officers, arbitrators or social workers. Even if they do not take up any of these occupations, in some way they will find themselves in the middle of other people's problems.

If you were born with this solar point, the energy of the degree says you have yourself been in difficult situations in former lives and have had help, so now you should use the experience gained to assist others. Your life can be much enhanced by the emotional support you can give to those who seek you out. Fail not or you may not receive any help yourself next time you need it.

Planetary point

The 355th degree is particularly concerned with giving assistance to others, and the planets in that degree indicate how that may be done. People with the Moon here can give emotional support to those who need it, for example. If Mercury is the planet here, natives can help others fill out those awkward forms which bureaucracy concocts.

356th degree

Colour: scarlet. *Sign*: Pisces. 3rd decan. *Qualities*: Mutable/Fixed, Water. *Numerological match*: other 5s.
Positive expression: fertile imagination
Negative expression: restlessness, excitability

Solar point

The elemental energy of the 356th degree creates natives with a fertile imagination and an alert, practical mind. There is also sensitiwity, versatility and, if planetary positions in the chart are supportive, even literary brilliance.

Natives are receptive to new ideas and concepts and many with this degree are the first to adopt new fashions or go in for the latest in technological advancement. The intuition can also be well developed and the sympathy is such that they feel what others feel and rarely need to be told that they are acting out of place.

The only negative effect is a tendency to excitability owing to the intensified emotions. This can sometimes lead to a lack of tact, yet even so natives are rarely offensive.

If you have this solar point you have all you need for happiness.

Planetary point

Those of you with a planet in this point have a fertile imagination, adaptability and versatility that you can put to your advantage. If you have Mars here, you are able to adjust quickly to changes in your physical environment. If Saturn is here, you can maintain the old moral codes and at the same time adapt to new ones.

357th degree

Colour: green. *Sign*: Pisces. 3rd decan. *Qualities*: Mutable/ Fixed, Water *Numerological match*: other 6s.
Positive expression: likeableness
Negative expression: stifled self-expression

Solar point

The elemental energy of the 357th degree gives natives a fondness for art, music, singing, drama aod beauty in all shapes and forms. Many people born with this solar degree will show signs of this beauty and grace in their own personal appearance or in the way they carry and express themselves. They quickly make friends and soon warm to any show of kindness, sympathy, love or appreciation on the part of others. They are attractive to the opposite sex and, with other good aspects in the birth chart, may pursue mystical interests.

If you were born with this solar point, you should bear in mind that this is a fortunate degree for making money out of large institutions and amusement resorts (especially if they are in places by, in or around water).

Planetary point

The 357th degree indicates, according to the planet placed in it, how natives may utilise their ability to entertain others. Someone with Venus in this degree could become a professional entertainer, such as an actor or dancer, tapping the boards of the stage. Whoever has Mars here is capable of breaking down social barriers.

Colour: blue. *Sign*: Pisces. 3rd decan. *Qualities*: Mutable/Fixed, Water. *Numerological match*: other 7s.
Positive expression: investigative ability
Negative expression: reclusiveness

Solar point

The elemental energy of the 358th degree gives the native benefits through mediumship, psychical research and occult investigations, or through quiet, secluded or secret work, such as that of a detective or laboratory research scientist. People born with this degree often prefer to work alone, away from distractions, and do not like to be closely supervised. They tend to be impressionable and even gullible. Too soft for their own good at times, they are prepared to give up almost anything for peace and tranquillity. Quiet, kind and amiable types, they are prone to stress and nervous disorders if constantly harrassed.

If this is your solar degree, don't allow others to put their worries on your shoulders.

Planetary point

If you have a planet in the 358th degree, it points to the areas of research and investigation that may hold rewards for you. For example, if you were born with Uranus here, you may have had a career as a research scientist. If you have Jupiter here you could become a notable historian.

359th degree

Colour: black. *Sign*: Pisces. 3rd decan. *Qualities*: Mutable/Fixed, Water. *Numerological match*: other 8s.
Positive expression: industriousness
Negative expression: melancholia

Solar point

The 359th degree creates natives who are private persons, closely secretive about their feelings and emotions. Nevertheless, they have a natural desire to help others which in some cases can result in their giving themselves utterly to the service of mankind. This service to others can have a therapeutic role in aiding the native to find himself or herself through the experiences thus gained. On the other hand, the native sometimes requires more help than he or she can give.

There is also a tendency natives have to let others take advantage of their sympathic nature which can leave them with insufficient time for themselves, and that in turn can lead to periods of self-pity.

If you were born with this solar point, you must try not to become too involved in the problems of other people. Your karma is to find yourself through others, but don't overdo it.

Planetary point

With a planet in the 359th degree, there is an area of conflict within yourself that you must find and face up to. For example, if you have the Moon here, you must find some way of giving vent to your emotions without becoming unstable, and in this you could learn a lot from others.

360th degree

Colour: crimson. *Sign*: Pisces/Aries. *Numerological match*: other 9s.

Solar point

The elemental energy of the 360th degree is a mixture of the elements of Fire and Water which can simmer nicely along or evaporate through too much heat or dowse the ambitions through too much Water. This degree makes for too much unpredictability to enable its effects to be judged in detail. Only you who possess its power can deduce its real effects.

Planetary point

The same unpredicability as for the solar degree goes for the effects of any planet here.

CHART ASSESSMENT SHEET

Name _____   D.O.B. ___/___/___   Strongest number _____

Planet	Degree	Numerological/Match	Ruling/Colour	Element				Qualities		
				E	A	F	W	Card	Fixed	Mut
Sun										
Moon										
Mercury										
Venus										

Mars	Jupiter	Saturn	Uranus	Neptune	Pluto